Happy Traveling

Daria Salamun

DON'T TRY THIS
AT HOME

DON'T TRY THIS AT HOME

ONE FAMILY'S (MIS)ADVENTURES AROUND THE WORLD

DARIA SALAMON
&
ROB KRAUSE

TURNSTONE PRESS

Turnstone Press
Artspace Building
206-100 Arthur Street
Winnipeg, MB
R3B 1H3 Canada
www.TurnstonePress.com

Turnstone Press gratefully acknowledges the assistance of the Canada Council for the Arts, the Manitoba Arts Council, the Government of Canada through the Canada Book Fund, and the Province of Manitoba through the Book Publishing Tax Credit and the Book Publisher Marketing Assistance Program.

This book is a memoir and reflects the authors' experiences as they have recalled them. Names, events, dialogue and characterizations may have been changed, compressed or recreated for the purposes of telling their story.

Cover photograph courtesy of Daria Salamon and Rob Krause

Printed and bound in Canada.

Library and Archives Canada Cataloguing in Publication

Title: Don't try this at home : one family's (mis)adventures around the world / Daria
    Salamon, Rob Krause.
Names: Salamon, Daria, author. | Krause, Rob, 1968- author.
Identifiers: Canadiana (print) 20189067675 | Canadiana (ebook) 20189067683 |
    ISBN 9780888016539 (softcover) | ISBN 9780888016546 (EPUB) |
    ISBN 9780888016553 (Kindle) | ISBN 9780888016560 (PDF)
Subjects: LCSH: Salamon, Daria—Travel. | LCSH: Krause, Rob, 1968-—Travel. |
    LCSH: Voyages around the world. | LCSH: Voyages and travels—Anecdotes.
Classification: LCC G440.S25 S25 2019 | DDC 910.4/1—dc23

MANITOBA ARTS COUNCIL
CONSEIL DES ARTS DU MANITOBA

Canada Council   Conseil des arts
for the Arts   du Canada

Funded by the Government of Canada
Financé par le gouvernement du Canada | Canadä   Manitoba

DON'T TRY THIS
AT HOME

WHOSE IDEA
WAS THIS ANYWAY?

"I think I left a pair of dirty underwear in the hamper," I tell Rob.

"What are you talking about?"

"At the house. I showered. And I'm pretty sure I threw my underwear into the hamper."

"So?" he shrugs.

"They weren't just any underwear. They were that ratty, nasty, stains-that-never-come-out pair. You know, the ones I wear when I think I might be getting my period?"

"Except you never know when you're getting your period, so you're always wearing them. Those ones?"

"Yeah, I meant to throw them in the garbage, but I tossed them in the hamper by mistake. I worked so hard to make the house pristine and ready for this family. But when they look in that hamper ..."

Taking a year-long break from our lives to travel the world was my version of a mid-life crisis. This was an expensive and elaborate way for me to avoid the fact that I was moving into my forties. What better method of distraction from this whole "mid-life business" than dragging my family halfway around the world to fifteen different countries, where we don't speak the languages or understand the cultures? Let's take a five-year-old, who needs structure and routine, stick her on all-night bus rides at dizzying altitudes, and feed her semi-cooked pork skewers bought in the street, late at night, from strange men with barbeques attached to their bicycles. And, for good measure, temporarily misplace her in Thailand for an hour. Let's take a seemingly normal eight-year-old boy on an adventure that will turn him into an explosives expert and activate a passion for kleptomania. Let's test the limits of my marriage by ditching the comforts of home that we'd spent a decade forging, cram our entire lives into backpacks, and navigate ourselves around the globe with very loose plans and limited funds. In retrospect, maybe I should have just renovated the bathroom, or gone with a breast lift.

Extensive travel adventures are often reserved for the young, who travel before or after university, before getting so rooted into a career they can't leave for fear of missing out on a promotion or raise. Or, these trips are a carrot for the retired. Punch in thirty years at your job, retire, cash in on your pension, and then you may spin the globe and hop on a plane.

When I started talking about the idea of taking a year off to travel abroad, no one in my family took me seriously until the *Lonely Planet* and *National Geographic* books started arriving in the mail, and I started monopolizing dinner conversations with tales of places no one had heard of. *Did you know you can swim with jellyfish in Palau? There's this hotel in Japan that's run almost entirely by robots! There's a place in Asia where you can get your teeth cleaned by monkeys!*

I started to wonder why you can't bust up mid-life with some serious travel and adventure. There's a certain sensibility that comes with middle age that you don't necessarily have when you're young, but health and mobility still allow you to do most things—so it seems like the perfect time to embark on a trip.

But once you have kids or an established career, it becomes much harder to extract yourself from life, and harder still to pack up your family and take off. In several European countries, it's illegal to pull your kids out of school for any reason—even short trips. Sister's getting married? Too bad. Uncle Fred passed away? Send flowers. Won a trip for four? Head to Goa with the in-laws because the kids can't go. Government officials will not grant permission for students to miss school, and parents in some countries, such as Sweden, are fined or sued for neglecting their children's education. We met a Swedish family in Samoa who actually had to hire lawyers in order to do a world trip. They lost the case, so the father fudged some sort of illness that required him to recuperate in various tropical locations. I often feel a bout of this coming on myself.

As kids get older, they start playing AA hockey. Or AAA hockey. Or A-to-the-power-of-infinity hockey, on top of soccer, swimming, and skiing practices seventy-five times a week. It's awkward explaining to a competitive coach that you're going to have to miss the next one hundred and fifty practices and forty-seven games. In a workplace where you're needed and valued (not really an issue for Rob or me), applying for a year off so you can watch turtles hatch in the South Pacific is a tough sell and not a regular work request.

I wanted to experience the world *with* my children when they had no choice in the matter, before they reached that age when they would pretend not to know us when we bumped into them at the mall with their friends. Let me be clear: long-term, extensive travel on a tight budget with young children is a probable lapse in judgment, an exercise in chaos, and a direct attack on one's sanity. But it was an idea I wanted to pursue. I thought it would be remarkable if, as a family, we could sink ourselves into new experiences together. Whether the experiences were good or bad—and I knew we would encounter both—the memories would become the glue, or maybe duct tape, that binds us. And so, just around my fortieth birthday, we decided we would embark on a year-long trip around the world.

I swing the door open. A woman with dark hair and a warm smile stands there, flanked by her teenage son and daughter. I have been touring families through our home and as they try to get a sense of the place, I try to get a sense of them.

Isla Blue and Oskar trail behind me as we walk through the rooms and I explain the particulars of parking and laundry to the family.

"The washer and dryer are brand new," I say.

"That's not true, Mom. We got those things like three months ago," Isla pipes in, hands parked on her tiny waist.

"My LEGO Republic Gunship doesn't come with the house," Oskar announces. "It took me two weeks to build!"

"I'm taking my stuffies *with* me," Isla adds, eying the teenaged girl as we pause at a trunk full of pandas and kittens that stare back at us with glassy pupilless eyes. "This tour is kinda boring, huh?"

Forget the Republic Gunship and the stuffed animals—would they be careful dusting the light fixture in the kitchen? We built it using the wooden hiking sticks from our West Coast Trail trek. Our home has become a gallery of relics from past holidays. In the living room, we pass a framed photo that I took at Versailles. *Need to take that down,* I think. It is from one of my first trips.

Even though my parents had never gone to Europe, they saw the value in sending both their kids overseas. For me, at seventeen, seeing Paris emerge out of the night fog as the plane descended was a wondrous experience. To this day, I can still see the glowing red and white bulbs on the windmill at Moulin Rouge with my mind's eye; I can still taste chocolate wrapped in flaky, buttery pastry; and I can still hear the melancholic songs of the buskers' violins echoing through the subway.

Two important things came out of that trip to France: exposure to the exhilarating possibilities of travel, and the literal exposure of a weird French guy.

My girlfriend Natasha and I decided to explore the hills overlooking the Mediterranean Sea. We asked a gentleman if he would mind taking our photo. This was before the era of phone cameras and selfie sticks. We handed my camera to the man and posed along the stone wall overlooking the sea on that sunny afternoon. Goofy smiles exploded across our faces, and a warm breeze swept through our hair. But as we stood smiling and posing, the man we had enlisted to take our picture was fumbling around with his pants. We waited, thinking maybe he was just doing up his fly. He was, it turns out, undoing his fly. Instead of taking our picture, the man unzipped his pants, pulled down his underwear, and flashed his dick at us.

And that's how I learned that while the world is filled with salty oceans and chocolate for breakfast, it is also full of weirdos with dubious intentions.

The process of whittling down our lives started off pretty methodically, but by the end, I was shoving things wherever I could find room and making many runs to the Thrift Store donation bin. Who knew the kids still played with half the stuff I gave away? They hadn't touched that pull toy with the peeling paint or the partially decapitated doll with the bulging eyes for years, but suddenly their "toy radar" started blaring the second their evil mother banished these prized possessions to a bin at the Salvation Army. I found myself living in a scene from *Toy Story*—all of a sudden, every cast-off toy had a personal identity and huge stake in shaping

Oskar's and Isla Blue's characters. Those toys would probably find their way back home and exact their revenge on me, if there was anything left after the children were through with me.

I was enveloped in the mammoth task of emptying the house and readying it for long-term rental. Departure Day was drawing near. Our house had been a revolving door of Kijiji vultures buying off our things, from old coffee makers to unused furniture. The anticipation of our journey was already making us less attached to our belongings. We were purging our conventional life and preparing for a year abroad.

Should we sell this George Foreman Grill? YES!
Should we get rid of that ugly vase my uncle willed us? HELL, YEAH.

But, as the departure date and reality of actually leaving drew closer and our belongings slowly disappeared, my purging started to get interrupted with a lot of moments when I wondered, *What the hell are we doing?* As I was stacking photo albums into boxes, one caught my eye: *Europe 1991.*

By nineteen, I was back in Europe, travelling by train with my best friend, Jill, establishing a pattern for the kind of wanderer I would be for the rest of my life. We saw some sights: the Eiffel Tower, the Acropolis, and what was left of the Berlin Wall that had been knocked down a few years before. Some pieces of the concrete wall, courtesy of Jill, are still on display in an ashtray on her dad's coffee table. We represented Team Canada in an ouzo-drinking competition at a place called the Pink Palace on the island of Corfu. We wore pink shirts and had pink plates smashed over our heads as we downed our last pink shots, narrowly beating Team USA. *Opa!* Beyond that, I'm drawing a blank.

That trip with Jill was about much more than the destinations. It was about the experiences. It was about branching off on our own and figuring out who we were as adults away from the comforts of home and our parents. That trip established a sense of independence, of being out in the world by ourselves and not screwing up too badly. There were many lessons I learned that would set me up for the rest of my life, lessons I didn't even realize I was learning. Like how your parents won't be there to bail you out when you blow your budget on gondola rides and striped T-shirts in Venice. You have to get creative, which means finding free places to sleep. Mr. Booth, a math teacher from our high school, was on sabbatical in a villa in Spain, and although neither of us had actually been taught by him, or even knew him well, that didn't stop us from showing up at his door. When we explained that we were former students at the high school where he taught, he was flummoxed, but he took us in anyway. We lay around on the sandy beach in front of his villa, ate dinner with him and his daughter, and helped ourselves to the free food and bath products. After about a week, bellies full, skin exfoliated, we left. I should track down Mr. Booth, send him a thank-you card and a basket of wine and chutney on behalf of my impolite, nineteen-year-old self. Or maybe I'll just pay it forward. If there are any broke nineteen-year-olds travelling across Canada right now who need a place to stay, I will happily take you in. I get you and I applaud your journey. Unless you have scabies or lice. In that case, I recommend the hostel up the road.

During that trip, Jill and I forged new friendships (Jill woke up one morning at Bob's Hostel in Amsterdam to find a skinhead she'd never met in her bed; turns out the hostel had a tendency to overbook the beds), learned about new cultures (who knew Germany had so many beer festivals?), and established our independence (though a note to self that paying for public transportation in Europe is not dependent on whether you have the money, and trying to outrun the police through narrow, cobbled streets in Athens will land you in a holding cell).

We were constantly throwing ourselves into new situations.

Those experiences, for better or worse, played a role in establishing the kind of people we would become. Freeloading thieves. Who knew some of these lessons in resourcefulness would come in handy when I would travel with my children twenty years later?

I closed the album and tucked it into a cardboard box. It was another reminder of why we were packing up and selling off our lives to go on this trip. But, of course, I still had lines I was not ready to cross.

"What do you mean, you sold the car?" I stare at Rob in disbelief.

"You said to put it on Kijiji," he replies.

"I didn't think someone would actually buy it!"

"Well, that's kind of how Kijiji works."

I'm probably one of only a handful of people who would have serious attachment issues to a thirteen-year-old, scratched-up Honda Civic. But the memory of standing in the dealership parking lot with my baba overwhelms me. Until that point in 2001, I'd been driving a 1965 Plymouth Fury that I'd found in the shed on her farm. It was black with a red vinyl interior and had a push-button AM radio and no power steering. The muscle required to make a right turn justified a gym membership. It took half an hour to heat up in the winter so I could always see my breath while driving, and in the summer it got so hot that it was basically a crematorium on wheels. The car had lap belts that didn't tighten, so in the event of a collision you'd definitely smack your head on the windshield, but you'd be prevented from going right through it.

It made my grandmother crazy that I was driving on the highway out to her farm in this car. "It's not safe," she said. Are you kidding? I was the only person driving a small tank. I loved the Fury, mainly because it was cool and different and didn't look like every other car. I even briefly lived in it during a bad patch of a dysfunctional relationship. When that relationship was over and I no longer required the car for housing, I went to the dealership with my grandmother and picked out a brand-new Honda Civic.

Now I was on the verge of selling the car, and betraying these memories and this generous gift. This purging wasn't just about getting rid of unwanted things; it was also about letting go of past memories, to make way for new ones.

"Tell her we drove to the West Coast on our honeymoon in that car," I call after Rob as he heads outside to meet the Kijiji vulture. "We drove to the hospital in that car to give birth to two kids!"

"Yeah, I'm not telling her that. She doesn't care," Rob says.

"She has to care. She has to take care of the car. I love that car!" I utter through quivering lips.

"Do you want to sell the Civic or not?"

"Yes, of course. We have to. It can't sit here unused for a year." Or could it? After jettisoning everyone else's stuff off to the nearest bidder, maybe I could keep my car? But I know that selling the car and renting out our house are strategic efforts that are funding the trip. I watch through the window as Rob talks to the woman out by the garage. They appear to have made a deal. *Judas.*

I can't take it. I go outside, tears rolling down my cheeks.

"Are you sure you want to buy this car?" I ask. The woman holds up the money by way of response. I turn to my Honda, openly weeping, and address it, "I love you. I'm so sorry for selling you. It's not personal." I stroke the hood. "You've been such a good car." The woman shifts awkwardly, door open, anxious to drive away. I catch Rob rubbing his temple, a *How-did-I-end-up-with-this-insane-woman?* look on his face. I turn and walk back into the house. I watch from the upstairs window as she gives Rob the money and he hands her the keys. She drives away in the Honda Civic my grandmother bought me.

I pull clothes from my drawers and place them into plastic storage bins, setting aside the odd T-shirt or pair of capris for the packing pile. I tuck silk dresses into garment bags and stack numerous pairs of heels and purses into boxes. I won't be needing heels where we are going. Slowly, I empty the drawers and closets and wipe them clean.

I move onto the kids' rooms and do the same with Oskar's school projects and slime collection, Isla's dolls and two-year-old stash of Halloween candy. At eight and five, they do not quite grasp why they can't take their entire rooms with them.

"Because we have to carry everything we take on our backs."

"But why can't you carry my rock collection?"

"And Beaks is part of the family! We can't leave him."

This trip was more like a foggy idea to them than a looming reality.

In the living room, I pull down frames containing pictures of Rob and me reciting our wedding vows in a garden on a warm summer day, photos of the kids swaddled in blankets, a few hours old, and candid shots from summer-long camping trips. I was acutely aware that I was pulling apart everything that I'd spent the last decade constructing in exchange for an idea that felt whimsical and risky. I march boxes of things down the steps and sit down on the last one. I can still see my dad hunched over the steps, carefully cutting and gluing the tiles I'd fallen in love with in a little shop in Spain. My mom, standing beside me, had said I should buy them. And so I did. She even schlepped them for me through plane changes and security checks back to Canada in her carry-on—all thirty-six kilograms.

I had returned to Europe with my mother when I was thirty. She had sent me to Europe at seventeen, triggering my passion to experience new places. So it meant just as much to me to accompany her on her first trip to Europe, many years later.

But I ran her ragged on that trip. I felt obliged to show her all the sights. We visited the Sagradia Familia Cathedral and the Louvre, and saw famous paintings by Pablo Picasso and Salvador Dalí. We chased buses and caught tours eight hours a day. I wanted my mom to see everything because I didn't know if and when she'd get back. (She tended to travel with my dad to places like Cuba and Mexico where there was a likelihood of warm weather and a wristband guarantee of free rum and beer.)

One night, after too much sangria, we decided to call home. She called my dad; I called Rob. I overhead my mom talking to my dad in the next phone booth.

"I'm going to have a heart attack. I can't keep up this pace. I'm so, so tired," she whispered. "I know, but I don't want to disappoint her."

I'd been so worried about letting my mom down; meanwhile she fretted about the exact same thing. She wanted to experience Europe, not necessarily to see every single sight.

After that, we slowed down the pace considerably. We ate pizza, drank wine, and sipped lattes in dimly lit cafés. We wandered the streets, nibbling on *pain au chocolat*. We attended a service at Notre Dame Cathedral, lighting candles for people we loved. We took the elevator, instead of the stairs, up the Eiffel Tower. We gazed out over Paris through sheets of grey drizzle, the way I had when I was a teenager. She let me read her travel journal—it was full of astute observations and colourful details about our trip. It turns out my passion for travel and writing could be traced back to my mother.

I would return to Canada and, soon after, start my own family, hoping one day share this passion for adventure with my own daughter.

Maybe this all started out as my mid-life crisis and an effort to evade my forties, and cling to bygone transformative travel experiences, but it's not how it turned out. Just preparing to leave was already an opportunity to step back and reassess life, to see if the values that we were buying into were the right ones, to explore another way of living. I wanted to see what else is out there. I wanted to escape routine, to wake up every morning and not know what the day would bring. I wanted to feel inspired and excited by the things I saw. I simply couldn't wait another fifteen years to do this. I wanted to experience this with my children. Now.

So I handed over the house keys to strangers—a doctor, his wife, and their son. As I passed the keys into their hands, I was about to say something about how much we love our home, and could they please take good care of it? That I'd changed my mind and we'd be staying after all and living with them for the year. But I knew from selling my car that if I opened my mouth, I was a goner. I'd be opening floodgates I would never be able to close. (Besides, I'd left twelve pages of typed *House Notes* on the counter—like they'll give a shit about my hydrangeas, oiling the deck furniture, or humanely trapping and adopting out the feral litters of bunnies and kittens that sometimes show up under the shed.) Instead, I climbed into a waiting taxi, a lump the size of Lake Winnipeg in my throat.

"Oh well," Rob says about my underwear.

"What do you mean, *oh well?* Maybe I should go back, tell them I forgot something and grab back the goopy gitch? I know, I'll email them."

Dear Matthew and Family,

Hope you are finding the house to your liking. Let us know if there's anything you need.

P.S. Don't look in the hamper.

Dear Matthew and Family,

Hope you are finding the house to your liking. Let us know if there's anything you need.

P.S. I'm really sorry about the dirty underwear I left in the hamper.

P.P.S. My underwear are not usually this dirty and gross. They are my period underwear.

P.P.P.S. There are some long bbq tongs in the drawer that you can use to extract said underwear from the hamper.

P.P.P.P.S. I don't need them back.

"This isn't about the underwear, is it?" Rob asks.

"No." I fan my eyes with my mittened hand, but the tears come anyway. "This isn't about the underwear."

I'd taken a leave of absence from my teaching job. We pulled the kids from school and watched them say goodbye to the friends and teachers they love.

We arrived at the airport, our lives for the next year reduced to a couple of packs. We were trading in the security of our home and possessions—things we'd spent a lifetime accumulating—for a year on the road. In planning the gap year, I'd only ever focused on the romanticism and adventure of it all. Now the reality of leaving was squeezing the air out of me.

Our parents are on hand to bid us farewell. Leaving my mom standing at security, as she tries to be brave and excited for us while her eyes are brimming with tears, and knowing that her heart is breaking because she won't see her grandchildren for a year, makes me question our decision to do this trip.

A year is a long time. I've tried to rationalize it to myself and say it's not that long. But a year is a long time. A lot can happen. A lot does happen. There are people we love dearly who will not be here when we return. Rob's right: this isn't about the underwear. I'm scared shitless.

But we are embarking on the adventure of a lifetime. We take the kids by the hand and board our first flight to New Zealand. *Please fasten your seatbelts. Cabin crew, prepare for takeoff.* As the plane lifts into the sky above the prairies, my mangy underwear becomes a distant memory.

LIFE IN THE NYLON CONDO

New Zealand was the first stop on the world trip and, as it turns out, one of the more expensive countries in the world to visit. The only feasible way to make our visit affordable was to rent an economical car that would double as a laundromat, grocery story, fridge, change room, and basement. And we would sleep in a tent. For two months.

"Yeah, yeah! Camping sounds great," I said when Rob suggested we pitch a tent throughout our stay in this little two-island country situated 15,000 kilometres away in Middle of Nowhere, the South Pacific.

As usual, in the planning stages I was only half listening and didn't realize Rob meant *only* camping. I assumed we'd break up the camping with stays in Airbnbs and hotels. Or that we'd break up the stays in hotels with a little camping.

But then, I tend not to get bogged down with minute details.

During that first leg of the trip, the flight to New Zealand would be a highlight for all of us and the last bit of luxury we'd experience for a while. Upon boarding the plane, the kids were immediately escorted backstage to meet the pilot. ("Daria, I think it's called a 'cockpit'," Rob says.) Meanwhile, they handed Mom glass after glass of quality Kiwi wine. Oskar almost peed in his seat when he returned and caught sight of the full video game console and hundreds of games he's normally not allowed to play. It had the only in-flight safety video I've ever watched because it involved battles, forests, mountains, sweeping music, and the entire cast of *The Lord of the Rings* telling us how to blow up our safety vests. (You can find the video on YouTube; I consider it to be four minutes well spent.) The in-flight three-course dinner, which included a salmon tabbouleh starter, a main course of seared hupuka in miso coconut broth with steamed shitake risotto and fresh coriander salsa, and rhubarb frangipane tart with vanilla bean mascarpone cream—all paired with the appropriate Kiwi wines—would be one of the best meals on the trip. If this is what they dished out in economy, I wonder what they served up over in business class? Lamb freshly slaughtered by the flight attendants? Black current chocolate ganache flown in on the wings of angels? The reclining seat was more comfortable than my bed. What an epic, albeit misleading, way to start our trip. Air New Zealand consistently wins the award for best airline. We would go on to take thirty flights on our trip. We'd often say, "Well, this definitely isn't Air New Zealand," as we passed stale sandwiches around the plane, removed oxygen masks held together with duct tape, or noticed the flight attendants wearing earrings eerily similar to those in my stowed luggage.

Upon arrival, Oskar pointed out that my eight-dollar latte was not listed anywhere in the $150/day budget. I was on my third one. (Whose idea was it to give the little shit an expense tracker app on his iPad, anyway? Oh, right, mine. Math home-schooling is already biting me in the ass.) If lattes were not in the budget, hotels would definitely be out, and for maybe the first time in my life I wouldn't be able to whine, plead, and bully my way with Rob. It hit me that we were on the road for a year and we were on a tight, immovable budget. *I can't coerce Rob into spending money we don't actually have*, I thought as I filled out more credit card applications. It was time to let go of the simple luxuries that one takes for granted in exchange for an opportunity to see the world.

We would camp almost exclusively for the next two months. We would camp for another additional month in Australia—but I didn't know that yet. On the plus side, if one must wake up in a tent, on a half-deflated sleeping pad *every single morning* for months, then unzipping the flap of the tent to expose long white beaches, looming mountains, or the wet, green rainforests of New Zealand is the best payoof—a pretty darn good payoff.

It's hard to stay annoyed about your cramped back when you find yourself engulfed in the dewy wildflower scent of Middle Earth, or when you stumble upon a colony of nesting penguins on a casual post-dinner walk. When we camped at Hot Water Beach at low tide, you could dig a hole in the sand along the ocean and release thermal water creating what is essentially a natural hot tub in which to soak your weary bones. A dolphin joined us for an afternoon swim at Porpoise Bay.

One morning, ten bad-smelling, burly, bearded men came tearing through our campground with their bodies half hanging out of their van. They were *Lord of the Rings* fanatics, and it turned out we were the luckiest people ever because we were camping in the realm of evil Saruman. Who knew?

Setting up and tearing down our soggy nylon home every day could be challenging, but this was the most intimate way to experience New Zealand's landscape, and an added bonus of being outdoors so much was that it really wore the kids out. They slept well, and on this leg of the trip, they seemed to be happiest and caused the least amount of collateral damage. We learned if you beat a stump senseless, no one is going to charge you for it. Not the case with a nightstand in a hotel. Hotels were always hotbeds for stealing and breaking things and being bored. Those free pens and pads of paper could incite the most hostile and vicious of battles. The Battle At Helm's Deep had nothing on Oskar and Isla fighting over a free hotel shoehorn.

A campfire could entertain and mesmerize Oskar for hours. He likes to burn things. (And blow stuff up, we later learned in Asia when a guy at a convenience store sold him explosives and gave him matches.) In campgrounds, the kids would chase each other around, making fast friends with other children. I'd meet the parents while trying to mash an avocado with a plastic fork in an outdoor kitchen, bathed in the orange glow of the setting sun. A community naturally forms in a campground. The most interesting conversations with people from around the world can transpire while chopping an onion or heating up yet another can of beans. I can't really say that I've ever met anyone while staying at a hotel due to the nature of the little closed-off rooms, but we met many young travellers, seniors, families, and couples while camping.

There was a lot of wine and barbequed lamb around those campfires in New Zealand. Sometimes we camped in TOP 10 Holiday Parks that had decent communal kitchens and swimming pools, and this was a real treat. But we always set up and slept in our trusty tent. Sitting around a campsite every night, often along the ocean and under the stars, drinking the local beer, talking about the day's adventures, was tough to beat.

Rob got up to go to the bathroom one night and claimed he saw a most extraordinary and intense cluster of light and stars in the sky. (I sometimes see another universe after a few bottles of malbec, but I don't wake everyone up to tell them about it.) The next day, he learned from another camper that in this part of New Zealand it's sometimes possible to see another galaxy with the naked eye. *A long time ago in a galaxy far, far away...* His *Star Wars* fantasies had been realized and he went on about it at such length that the next day we all set an alarm to get up in the middle of the night to try to see it, but it wasn't visible—but that might be because none of us bothered to get up. We decided Rob was crazy and should be treated accordingly. Smile and nod, kids. Smile and nod.

Camping did not, however, come without a range of challenges.

We often stayed in what were called DOC state campgrounds where the outhouses were so poorly maintained and smelled so rank, Isla would revert to the toddler stage, hold her head in her hands, and scream "no, no, no!" And I was in full agreement with her on this. But I learned it's not considered "cute" when a forty-two-year-old woman is lying in a fetal position due to the state of the bathrooms. Amazing how long you can hold a shit, given your options. And if this was the state of the bathrooms, there were certainly no amenities like picnic tables at many of these sites, and we were relegated to setting up our stove and cooking in the grass or on an old milk crate we'd scavenged. Is a table too much to ask?

I learned that New Zealand wasn't necessarily fundamentally against picnic tables, but rather that renting camper vans is the trendy and almost exclusive way (present company excluded) to tour the country, and almost *everyone* had a camper van. We were regularly the only tenters in a campground. Camper vans come equipped with their own tables, barbeques, and fridges. People would sometimes roll out of the fancier ones eating banana splits or holding the kinds of cocktails you'd get at a swim-up bar. You would often hear the swish of the broom as people swept out their mobile homes. Meanwhile, we'd often ask ourselves questions like: *If the meat has escaped its packaging and is floating in the cooler water, we can still eat it, right? When is the last time anyone actually saw the floor of this rental van? Do you really think the duct tape will hold this bumper on?*

The kids developed a serious case of camper-van envy. When one pulled in beside our tent, Isla would look longingly at it and start to drool, the way a dog does at a coffee table covered in bacon-wrapped hors d'oervres. They would beg us to rent a van. JUCY was the Cadillac of camper vans and our kids desperately wanted one of these gleaming apple-green vehicles decked out with more amenities than we had at home. We'd been ping-ponging around New Zealand with this French family we kept bumping into, who were on a journey similar to ours. Except for two important facts: they had the coveted JUCY van and they were cool.

The mom was a classic French beauty with dark hair and smooth skin, and she always smelled fresh. The children, with their creamy skin and tufts of shiny hair, were the stuff of fairy tales, and the dad—lean and bronzed—was always either cooking or surfing. They gave us a tour of their van one afternoon. Big mistake. I noted the shower, which explained their perpetually groomed appearance and clean odour. Coin-operated cold-water showers were the norm for us. (I feel that if you have to plug quarters into a machine in order to bathe, you should just give up on life. We are people, not laundry, for god's sake.)

The Frenchies probably had to hose off all of Isla's drool after the van tour. We found out the father was a chef and owned six restaurants in Paris. This must have been really slumming it for them. I explained to Isla that if I couldn't splurge on a latte or a bottle of malbec over seven dollars, then we sure as heck would not be getting a camper van!

One thing we discovered about taking life on the road was that when you're so busy surviving day by day, you forget about things you want or miss. You tend not to get preoccupied with comparing yourself to the Joneses, or, in this case, the Tremblays. (This was a rare exception because we kept running into these annoying, perfect people.) We found ourselves having to say "no" to a lot of things. There were constantly hard choices to make. Of course, we indulged in experiences or consumable things like ice cream and liquor, but we often had to stick to the budget. But my back-pocket trump card was always this: few kids get to ditch school for a year and travel the world. This is the experience of a lifetime. If you want LEGO and candy and more stuffies and a camper van, then we have to cut the trip short and head back to Winnipeg—where it is minus forty-seven degrees and there's a raging blizzard. In the end, telling the kids "*no*" to material items was a good thing. I noticed that they stopped asking for so much and maybe even appreciated the experiences a little bit more. In our life back home, I think we caved to our whims a lot more, but with this strict trip budget, we had no choice.

It rained a lot in New Zealand—which is unfortunate when you're mainly tent-bound. We woke up one morning just before we would be leaving to find that our tent was floating in a lake. Rob was so pleased that the nylon held the rising water out that he seemed oblivious to the whipping wind and torrential rain that flew in off the ocean. We rolled up our tent and tore down our makeshift kitchen as thick sheets of rain slid over us, making it hard to see. After two months of camping on the North and South islands of New Zealand, this felt like a fitting end to our visit of this diverse but rugged country. This was only the first of fifteen countries. It would not always be easy, but it would always be worth it.

The kids and I gave up and watched through the foggy windows of the van as Rob, who was ensnared in nylon, tried to fold the tent back into the pouch. Camping was his idea, after all.

After spending six weeks in the South Pacific, we were back to camping—this time in Australia. (I should also mention that housing in Samoa, where we'd just come from, is really just a step up from camping: the wall-less structures sat a metre or so off the beach and had mattresses the thickness of a pack of cigarettes.)

After visiting Samoa and Fiji, we had planned to go to Vanuatu where Rob had secured accommodations in a treehouse—are you seeing the pattern here? Cyclone Pam decimated the small country shortly before we were scheduled to arrive. After Vanuatu, Indonesia would be the next planned stop on our route. All flights out of Fiji were routed through Australia. Initially, when planning our trip, Rob had bucked at the idea of going to Australia, claiming it would be too similar to Canada and that it was dangerous. While I saw wild adventure, all Rob could see were crocs, snakes, sharks, and spiders. He earnestly believed if he went to Australia, he would never leave, or if he did, it would be in a casket with bite holes in his neck. But I made the argument that, since we were flying through and now had some extra time (having skipped Vanuatu), we should, at the very least, plan a layover. So we booked flights to Brisbane. It morphed into a month-long detour that became one of the most beloved parts of the trip.

Much to the elation of the children, Rob found a deal on a modest camper van—though it was more like a van that had a few features of a campervan. We meandered 1,600 kilometres up the coast of Queensland. Queensland is not the Outback—Australia's infamous arid and barren interior. Queensland is a stretch of lush coastline that hosts the Daintree (the oldest rainforest in the world and the only one that spills out into the sea), the Great Barrier Reef, and lots of surfing beaches with rich, sometimes dangerous, marine life. The kids loved Australia even more than New Zealand because the attitude, people, and atmosphere reminded them a lot of Canada—only with better weather, beaches, and kangaroos. Unfortunately, the kangaroos often took the form of roadkill or stewing meat at the grocery store, although a lively gang of them did come bouncing through our campsite at dusk one evening.

Isla was beside herself at the prospect of sleeping in a pull-out bed in a van. On the plus side, it really only slept two people comfortably. Crumpled up against the side windows, feet buckled into the back door wasn't our definition of a good sleep, so Rob and I let the kids have the van and we continued to sleep in the tent. Infer from that what you will. (Okay, I'll just spell it out. No more sex in family bathrooms while the kids were off on lengthy scavenger hunts where we never actually bothered to hide anything.)

Australia had a system of "freedom camping," which meant you could set your tent up in designated areas without a permit that cost thirty dollars. We loaded an app on our phone that would alert us to free camping sites when we were ready to hunker down for the night. With a budget of $150 day, not having to pay for accommodations was a huge saving. They weren't always the best campsites, sometimes being not much more than glorified rest stops along the highway, but other sites would be situated at the foot of a rainforest where the tent would be spackled with dew and sunshine that had filtered through ancient trees. Occasionally, we'd find ourselves camping on a secluded white sand beach. We realized in the morning that it was secluded because it's very difficult to extract your overweight camper van from fine sand.

We were often in the company of "Silverbacks," the term for retired, nomadic Australians who roam around the country in their motor homes; the equivalent of Canadian Snowbirds. The Silverbacks were always friendly and delighted to have children running amuck. Oskar and Isla were treated to chocolates, beef jerky, hard candy, or whatever other treats these folks had lying around on the floors of their vehicles. We interpreted this, more or less, as free babysitting.

Camping in Australia did not come without its challenges. One morning while Rob was hammering in the tent pegs, I noticed in the grass, moving along the tent towards him, a two-metre long reptile with glassy bulging eyes, scaly green skin, and sharp claws. I screamed, "Crocodile! Oh my god, crocodile!"

People sauntered over to see what the fuss was about, but no one seemed nearly as alarmed as I was. We learned that we were not anywhere near crocodile territory (although we'd just come from a crocodile-infested area) and this was only a Jumbo Monitor Lizard. *What? A lizard could be almost two metres long, and half a metre wide?* Google "jumbo monitor lizard" images. This is not something one wants to spot near her sleeping accommodations. It wasn't until it flicked its forked tongue and began to crawl off that I was convinced it wasn't going to eat us.

Then there was the Camping Lice Fiasco. Possibly one of the more difficult experiences of our year abroad.

If you're a parent, you've undoubtedly opened your kid's *Frozen* backpack and found that disturbing letter from the school announcing the presence of head lice at the school. "Please check your child accordingly." You gingerly sift through her hair, hoping you won't find any. Back in Canada, we'd always dodged the lice bullet. After what we experienced in Australia, it would have been a cakewalk dealing with the little critters privately, in the luxury of our own home, with a water source that doesn't involve a bucket and a stream.

No letter was sent to our camper van. How was I supposed to know to even look for them? So, by the time I spotted them, their breeding program was in its advanced stages.

We were in the shower at a campground when I looked down at Isla's head. Her hair was teeming with bugs. At first I thought that maybe she was just playing in the woods again and some bugs had crawled into her hair and we could wash them out. But closer inspection revealed that not only were there bugs, but they had laid eggs, lots of them, along every single shaft of her hair.

Is your scalp itchy as you're reading this? Because mine is itchy writing about it.

Since we were all sharing the same camper van and tent, if Isla had picked up hitchhikers, chances are we all had. I checked Oskar's head and, sure enough, he was hosting a little lice nest too, albeit not quite as bad as Isla's. But, by some stroke of good fortune, neither Rob nor I were worthy enough to be stops on the lice tour.

I trekked off to the chemist (that's what they call the pharmacy in Australia and I think it sounds cool and professional) to get the lotions and combs. We pulled into a holiday camping park that had showers and laundry facilities to begin Operation Lice Removal.

The lice goop had to stay in their hair for an hour—I left it in for three, so the kids were trotting around the campground in shower caps. And the only place to rinse out the goop that was now saturated with flecks of lice was in the shared showers.

We suspected people were tipped off to our lice operation when we hauled out the lice combs and started picking through the kids hair for two days, smack in the middle of the campground. Strips of used toilet paper littered our site. It didn't help when we'd gone through our fourth roll of campground toilet paper and sent Oskar to the bathroom to get more. He couldn't get the whole roll off, so he pulled out reams and reams of paper.

"Hey, kid, what are you doing?" one of the less friendly Silverbacks asked.

"My mom needs this to get the lice off the combs," he replied in earnest, under his mop of greasy, medicated hair. We noticed that when we began the tedious task of removing the lice, the campsite was quite full, but within a few days we were the only people left in that section of the campground.

To compound matters, the campgrounds in Australia are rife with wild bush turkeys. Who knew these brown, scruffy birds with red heads and a bright yellow ring around their scrawny necks would be so attracted to the smell of the tea tree oil in the lice medication? The whole operation took twice as long because I spent half my time shooing away six curious turkeys.

When I left the combs and shampoos in a sealed plastic bag outside for the night, so as not to reinfect our tent or the car, by morning the turkeys, unable to open the bag, had hauled off the entire thing. Those turkeys did not know wrath until they met a mother having to contend with lice in a campsite. In the end, it was back to the store with another fifty dollars to buy the second dose of treatment and more combs. And a turkey baster. If I managed to catch one, I vowed to snap its neck, barbeque it, and make all the other turkeys watch. How are these snoopy birds a protected species?

We finally reached Cairns, sans lice. It was almost the end of our time in Australia and we would be sending our camping gear back to Canada, as we were off to Asia, where camping was not part of the culture. While I tolerated, almost enjoyed, two months of tenting in New Zealand and another month of freedom camping up the coast of Queensland, Australia, I was about as happy to get rid of that tent as I was the lice.

MAP, SHMAP

We stood in line at the airport in Cairns, waiting to check in for our flight to Bali. The part of the trip that I was responsible for planning was officially beginning. God help us all. When we arrived at the front of the line, I cringed as I saw the sign. "In order to board the flight passengers must have onward tickets out of Bali." *Shit. Seriously?* It's not like we're going to defect to Bali or anything. We just want to soak up the sun and culture, maybe get a cheap pedicure, see the temples, and pet some monkeys. I didn't even plan to do any yoga—that's so *Eat Pray Love*. I would explain all of this to the agent when we got to the front of the line, like it was a misunderstanding we could clear up and not a government policy. Apparently, the Indonesian government doesn't agree with this free-spirited method of travel. They want you to have a clear exit plan. Who knew? And, after visiting Bali, I could see why one might not want to leave.

Rob turned to me doubtfully. "You booked something out, right?"

"Nope."

"You didn't look into the entry requirements?"

"Ugh, where's the adventure if you have to plan out every little detail?" I privately admitted this might be more than a minor detail. This is the benefit of reading the guidebooks and researching the entrance requirements of countries before arriving at the airport.

My utter lack of structure and Rob's rather obsessive organization have led to some of the most trying and challenging moments both in our marriage and on this trip. In my opinion, my lack of planning and refusal to organize every detail well in advance have also led to the most delightful and surprising moments of our journey. I think this is why we make such a dynamic team. But if nothing were planned (as I would probably have it), the trip would have undoubtedly been a year of total chaos, so Rob's skills are appreciated and valued. But if you plan every single destination and accommodation in advance, you can miss out on those under-the-radar magical moments that aren't always written about in guidebooks or reviewed on websites.

"Seriously? You're ordering spring rolls? That's your research plan for Asia?" Rob said as I sat on our couch, scanning the paper menu.

"No, I'm reading this novel too!" I said, hoisting up the book. It was a few months before our departure day. My New Zealand travel planning wasn't much better; I rented the TV show *Flight of the Conchords*. (I think Brett and Jermaine gave me a pretty good sense of what Kiwis are like.) I also picked up a couple of bottles of sauvignon blanc in order to properly familiarize myself with the New Zealand grape.

Meanwhile, Rob had been feverishly booking flights, accommodations, hikes, camping sites, car rentals, travel visas, and activities all over New Zealand, Fiji, and Samoa—the first legs of our trek around the world. He's a researcher, a mapper, a Guidebook Guy. We saw all the sights, but, honestly, it lacked a certain *je ne sais quois*—adrenaline, maybe?

I prefer less structure, what some might call flying-by-the-seat-of-my-ass. I was responsible for planning the Southeast Asia part of our tour. (I know, I know—I wouldn't trust me as far as I could throw a map either.) Most of my practical travel information about Thailand, Indonesia, and Cambodia comes from poetry books and take-out menus.

I've travelled a lot via this method, and one of the things I love most about travel is the unexpected adventure that unfolds when you throw yourself into new situations, embrace people, and sink your teeth into authentic experiences (as opposed to other people's experiences that are either critiqued or lauded on Trip Advisor and Expedia). Map, shmap, I say.

So there we were, at the front of the check-in line, waving people past as we fired up the laptop so we could book some flights and be allowed on the plane. Anywhere would do, really, since it was getting close to boarding time.

"C'mon, if we'd planned *every little detail*, we never would have detoured to Australia, you know!" I chirp.

Prior to leaving Canada, Rob said he didn't want to go to Australia. Had we pre-bought our tickets, preplanned every destination, we never would have seen koalas up close, snorkelled in the Great Barrier Reef, or incurred $1,200 in speeding tickets that were waiting for us back in Canada.

"Can we maybe just focus on the problem at hand for a moment?"

"Okay, I'm just saying Australia was a good idea."

"Focus."

"Okay. Just admit I was right, though."

Rob almost had an aneurism having to buy plane tickets as we were checking in for our flights to Bali. (Me, I get off on this kind of stress.)

"Can I have a snack?" Isla whined, teetering on top of a cartful of luggage as Oskar wrenched it back and forth.

Final boarding call.

"Hey, look at that! Fights to Singapore are cheap!" I said, pointing at the screen.

"Yeah, Singapore! Let's go there!" Oskar said. His travel destinations are usually based on the level of sophistication of the subway system. The boy, like his father, adores mapping and routing. For him, a subway is an intricate underground world that requires thorough exploration. Subway maps from all major hubs we've ever visited hang on the walls in Oskar's bedroom.

This is the final boarding call. Rob rolled his eyes, adjusted his glasses, and booked the tickets to Singapore. This is precisely the predicament in which he never wants to find himself. He'd prefer to spend days agonizing over flight destinations, prices, and routes. You'll note that I am no longer trusted with these boring tasks. Mission accomplished. (Also, important to note that while flights to Singapore were cheap, the city itself was not!)

So we had onward tickets (to Singapore!) and were permitted to board the plane. It all worked out.

I think Singapore comes up only once elsewhere in my portion of the book, in the chapter where I talk about the ways in which we almost died. So, here, I would like to point out that I was right, again, about the unplanned detour.

Singapore is a fascinating and unusual country to visit and consistently makes "Top Places to Visit in Asia" lists. It was celebrating its fiftieth anniversary of independence when were visiting. Gardens by the Bay, a nature park, is unparalleled in terms of city-integrated green space. A flower dome, cloud forest, skyway, and super-tree grove—with enormous electric trees that are part of a mesmerizing music and light show—were highlights in

Asia for me. Out of the fifteen countries we toured, Singapore was by far the most pristine and curated place we encountered—the complete opposite of more rustic and chaotic places like Bolivia and Samoa. A trip to Singapore is worthwhile for the food alone. Laksa, a coconut curry noodle soup, chile crab, satay, and chicken rice were cooked and served fresh out of stalls in festive open-air food courts all around the city. After cooking for months over a crackling fire, I was so ready for Singapore's culinary scene. It was also a city what knew how to court children.

LEGOLAND, just across the Malaysian border, but most easily accessible from Singapore, was a highlight for the kids. The first thing we noticed upon entering the park was how eerily devoid of people it was. Our experience with amusement parks told us there should have been long line ups and overtired toddlers having meltdowns everywhere you turn, but we had the place to ourselves. Either some sort of apocalypse had just transpired (but there seemed to be no evidence of zombies or blood), or the park was on its last legs. Isla rode the roller coaster eight times in a row. She didn't bother getting off between rides, as there were no lines and she was the only passenger. When I finally hauled her off the coaster to leave, she was green and on a first-name basis with all the workers. *Bye, Isla Blue! Come back soon!* They were genuinely sad to see their only patron that afternoon leave.

Five days in Singapore was enough to decimate our daily allotted budget, as Oskar would repeatedly point out to us. Singapore just takes everything to the next level. Most cities boast zoos, which we typically skip, but the famed Singapore Zoo encouraged visitors to participate in the Night Safari where nocturnal predators are in hunting mode and rip apart their prey. We had to settle for a very simple budget hostel without basic amenities like air conditioning so we could afford to take in all the sights. I had moments where I looked longingly at places like the Pan Pacific Hotel where people sipped cocktails with garnishes that we would consider a meal. I vowed to return with money and without children.

At midnight, temperatures are still soaring in the high thirties. But, as Rob and I sat in plastic lounge chairs on the roof of our hostel, twinkling white lights strung up around us, we clinked glasses to celebrate surviving another day, and I realized, for all the flaws, our trip is pretty perfect. Singapore was another delightful detour that was not on our official tour plan.

My poor planning skills didn't end at the airport as we boarded our flight to Bali. After booking tickets to Singapore, and while everyone slept peacefully on the flight, I started to get nervous about the accommodation and driver that I'd booked, or thought I'd booked, in Denpasar, where we would be landing.

We were leaving Cairns on June 19 and arriving in Bali on June 20 at 3:00 a.m. I booked the house from June 20 to 27—technically we were coming in on June 20—but it occurred to me on the plane that they could interpret this as the night of the 20th going into the 21st. This cheap Jetstar flight to Denpasar had no perks like movies, magazines, or free booze to distract me from spending four hours imagining the look on Rob's face when, upon arriving, we didn't have a place to stay.

"Okay Mom, where we staying tonight?" I imagined Oskar asking.

"Um, how about the airport!"

The last time on this trip that I'd been charged with finding us accommodation was in Franz Josef Glacier, New Zealand. Rob was driving and I found a hostel that the guidebook described as a "gem," but I missed the irony. They gave away free day-old pastry and soup every day at 4:00 p.m. so I figured we could call that dinner and save on our food budget.

People might not know this, but many hostels offer "family rooms" for people travelling with children. We regularly capitalized on this feature because they have wonderful amenities like libraries and book exchanges, kitchens, and lounging areas with televisions and ping pong tables. Some of the more glamorous hostels in hotter countries even have swimming pools. After suffering through a long bus or plane ride, the last thing we ever wanted to do was coop the kids up in a hotel room—not that the trip budget even allowed for that. Several of the hostels we stayed in even offered free organized activities like cooking classes, dance lessons, and walking tours. One hostel in Fiji held nightly frog races. Hostels are also filled with interesting travellers from all walks of life, from all over the world, who possess hot travel tips.

Franz Josef was not one of those places. We pitched our tent on a 4 x 4 piece of AstroTurf in the parking lot, up against the back of the hostel, where I actually saw someone urinating out of the window. *Not on the tent! Go left! Go left! Not on the tent!* The problem was that the place was overrun with twenty-year-old Swedes and Germans whose main impetus in life was to get laid, and they had the same ideas as I did about the free food. The partying kids finally left for the bar at 10:00 p.m. so we could put our children to bed, only to bring the party back to the hostel when the bars closed three hours later. The final straw was waking up to a station wagon that had wheeled in beside us, and having to step around a used condom that had been pitched out the window beside our tent.

"Well, that place was fun!" I said optimistically as we pulled away. I will probably never live down Franz Josef. I learned to specifically enquire about whether places accommodate families. Franz Josef will be *nothing* compared to our arrival in Denpasar if there's no guy named Wayan at the airport to pick us up.

When we landed in Bali at 3:00 a.m., miraculously, Wayan was standing there with a placard with my name on it. I owe the Travel Gods I'd been praying to on the flight for the last four hours one of my children. (I'll let them sort out who gets sacrificed via a few rounds of Rock, Paper, Scissors in the morning.) I had apparently, at some point through our stilted conversations and emails—there was a language barrier—mentioned our flight number to Wayan so he figured out exactly when we were arriving and would need the house. Thank goodness someone was paying attention. Because, as usual, it wasn't me.

After a two-hour drive, we fell into bed in the wee hours of the morning. It was so dark and we were so tired that we could barely tell where we were. This was another example of my fly-by-the-seat-of-my-pants booking. The French family we'd met in New Zealand had spent a few weeks here, loved it, and recommended it. I *never* would have found this place by trolling Booking.com or Expedia back in Canada, eight months ago.

We woke up in the environmentally sustainable, two-storey house to the sun rising over the rice fields that surrounded us. The kids played in the pool all morning as Rob and I sipped coffee on the deck. All was well. I needed a win after putting Rob through some kind of hell the night before at the airport. It turned out to be one of the best, most relaxing weeks of an often harried and busy trip.

I revelled in the fact that we were no longer sleeping in a tent. You could rent a beautiful but simple house in Bali for the same price it cost to camp in some of the holiday parks of New Zealand. I was ready for the next leg of the adventure.

We rented scooters and explored the funky and fun town of Ubud with its museums and temples. I noticed that Ubud hosts an inordinate amount of fortyish-year-old women wandering around wearing expensive yoga pants, sipping lattes, and looking for either love or their souls, no doubt inspired by *Eat Pray Love*. In the town square, on the evening we'd arrived, Isla was selected to be part of a colourful, albeit long, cultural presentation that gave a historical overview of Bali.

We visited the Monkey Forest where 600 monkeys run amuck in a forest filled with crumbling stone monuments that are considered sacred. Just before we entered the forest, a couple of monkeys came along and swiped Oskar's ice cream cone, teaching him the valuable lesson that you can't always have your ice cream and eat it too. Isla, having watched this, beat those monkeys back when they set their sights on her cone, and managed to hang on to her ice cream even when one of the monkeys climbed up on top of her head where she held the cone. Inside the Sacred Forest, a dripping-wet macaque monkey parked itself on Rob's back and he had to walk around with it on him for ten minutes with a bent head and grimace. His look said it all: *Like my wife's trip planning, I must tolerate this, but I don't like it.* For once, the monkey on Rob's back was not me.

BETTER A BROKEN BONE
THAN A BROKEN SPIRIT

We'd been travelling for seven months when we lost our daughter in Thailand. Now that I think about it, I'm surprised it took that long for it to happen.

One day, my son had a yen for street meat. I'm always in favour of procuring street food of any kind, so Oskar and I wandered over to the stalls that were lined up on the road right out front of our guesthouse. We embarked on a bit of an expedition to find our favourite supplier of meat—a guy who sold pork satay grilled on a charcoal barbecue hooked up to the back of his bike. He moved around a lot, but we were determined to find him—his sticks of greasy pork were worth the extra effort.

"Where's Mum and Oskar?" my six-year-old daughter asked my husband as she climbed out of the pool.

"They went for street food. They'll be right back." She ran off to find us.

The strangest thing has happened over the past seven months of travelling with our kids through numerous countries. The leash has gotten longer and longer. We often let them run off in pursuit of frogs and chickens and monkeys. They have forged makeshift friendships with children from all over the world.

"Mom, quick, gimme the keys. I met this Russian boy and he wants to see the back of our van!" Isla said, ripping through my backpack when we were camping in New Zealand. In Bali, local boys took Oskar off into the rice fields and taught him how to fly his red nylon kite. It was all pretty magical. They only real tragedy they encountered was The Great Monkey Ice Cream Heist.

Before we left on the trip, we talked about strangers and safety. The kids picked a (rather weird) "safe word"—butter (the idea being that if a stranger tried to lure them off to see a puppy or eat a Popsicle, they must know our family's secret word).

We certainly ate enough butter on our travels, but we never did have to use the word to stave off any bad guys. The kids were free to explore and play, and they developed a new kind of confidence in themselves, and in the world.

Then, my daughter went missing.

When Oskar and I arrived back at the pool, our mouths slathered in pork and peanut sauce, I asked where Isla was.

"Didn't she find you?" my husband asked casually.

"No?"

I jogged out into the street, expecting to see Isla in her little red bathing suit, her blue towel trailing behind her. She wasn't there. I went in one direction, my husband the other. My son and a family friend waited for her at the pool.

I was angry at my husband for letting her wander off after us. But I knew if it were me, I'd have done the same thing.

Sairee Beach on the island of Koh Tao is a charming and slow-paced town. We'd strolled along the narrow, pedestrian-filled streets past the shops and cafés many times over the past several days, and we all knew it well. Isla was used to being swept into the laps of sweet, elderly Thai women, treated to mints and cheek pinches. Even the transsexual burlesque dancers stationed at the corner of our street would wave and smile warmly at the kids as they handed out flyers for their nightly show. This small island was an easy place to let your guard down and get swept up with the simplicity of life.

Ten minutes had passed.

"Have you seen a little blonde girl in a red bathing suit?" I asked every person I passed. I asked the guy who sold us the skewers. He shook his head apologetically. The burlesque dancers kept a look out for her from their post. No one had seen Isla. How could no one have seen her?

Twenty minutes passed.

Trying to breathe through a hurtling wave of panic, I wondered whether I should start faxing Isla's passport and photo to the ferries and airports. But there were fifteen boats tied up out on the beach. If somebody had wanted to take her (because that's where my mind was going now), they weren't taking her to an airport—they'd put her in one of those boats and I'd never see her again.

After almost half an hour, I was back at the hotel when I looked up and saw a little blonde girl in a red bathing suit, a blue towel draped around her shoulders, skipping up the street towards me.

"Where were you? I lost you!" I threw myself around her.

She looked at me, perplexed, and brushed the tears from my cheeks, the way I'd brushed tears from hers at least a hundred times on this trip. "I wasn't lost. I knew where I was, Mom."

"But I didn't!"

A young backpacking couple were standing a few yards behind Isla Blue, keenly observing our reunion as I hugged my daughter yet again, still unable to stop the stream of tears. They hesitantly stepped forward.

"You're her mom, then?" the twenty-something girl asked in a thick Irish accent.

"Yes," I said, wiping the snot from my face with the back of my hand.

41

"We just wanted you to know we asked her if she was lost or needed our help. But she said she wasn't lost, that she was okay." They smiled at Isla. "But we followed her anyway—at a distance. She went half a mile, almost to the end of the strip, before she turned back. She kept peering back at us over her shoulder."

"I went to the restaurant way down there where we have breakfast every morning," Isla chimed in. Her eyes were bright and excited, like she'd been on an adventure and had solved a great mystery. "Can we get some satay now?" Isla pleaded.

"Thank you for staying with her and watching out for her," I blubbered through more tears. By then Rob had returned, shaking his head and tousling his daughter's hair. Amid our family anarchy, I never got the names of these kind strangers. I would have sent them a note confessing I had feared the worst in people, but they reminded me it is more likely that, anywhere in the world, people will watch out for our kids rather than try to snatch them. And at least twice on our travels I had reunited teary, wide-eyed children with their mothers.

We went to see our street meat guy, Isla hopping along ahead of me. Of course, he wasn't there. We can never find that guy when we need him.

After I published this essay in the *The Globe and Mail* travel section, a number of people commented in the feedback section that our kids should be taken away because we are "idiots," "terrible people," and "must be smoking up." While all of this may be true, I'm not sure what that has to do with our parenting.

There were incidents on our trip that make us look like even worse parents than this. Rob writes about them. He's supposed to be writing a travel memoir, but it reads more like a volume of evidence that Child and Family Services could use to haul us away for questioning.

If you're one of those judgmental, perfect parents, maybe skip the chapter about the pink dolphins. Actually, maybe skip the whole book. But if you're the kind of person who revels in other people's screw-ups because it somehow makes you feel better about your own inadequacies as a person and a parent, then we are your new favourite writers.

Maybe other parts of this book will make us look like cool, adventurous people—but not likely. Anyway, this is not one of those parts.

Our neighbour, Susan, has an expression: "Better a broken bone than a broken spirit." We have definitely borrowed this philosophy in raising our kids.

Day-to-day parenting, when you are at home and comfortable in your surroundings, can be challenging enough. *For the love of Pete, who smeared peanut butter on the flatscreen? Why are there pantyliners all over the cat? The Christmas tree is for presents, not where we shit.* And we've all sat in the emergency ward with our kid for ten hours after some careless accident that probably could have been prevented.

When you are constantly foisting yourself into new situations every single day—amid cultures you don't understand and languages you don't speak, when you are not always well rested and your mental faculties are short-circuiting because you've been trapped on a bus for forty-seven hours—things can, and *will*, go wrong.

We had just arrived at our cabin overlooking the ocean in Thailand. It was yet another off-the-beaten-track recommendation we'd received from an angry German in Samoa. We were starting to see an emerging pattern of unforeseen "quirks" that accompanied these suggestions from fellow travellers. When the boat arrived, there was no dock. The watercraft got as close as it could to shore without grounding itself when the guy in mirrored sunglasses behind the steering wheel barked at us to jump out and take our bags with us. A little wary of the idea, we hopped out of the boat and sloshed our way to shore in thigh-deep water, trying to keep our backpacks dry by hoisting them above our heads.

We were staying in a secluded cove on the ocean, accessible only by this boat that had just dumped us in the waters near the shore. Once on land, we had to shimmy through a cave and up a whole lot of stairs to get to the cabin. It was rustic, with its rolling electricity, off-colour water, and wild pigs that had learned to navigate the stairs quite well and seemed intent on breaking down the cabin door. But the simple accommodation was perched on a cliff overlooking the ocean, on the cusp of a perfect crescent-shaped beach.

It had been another long travel day of waiting for a boat then bobbing along the ocean, navigating our way to this island. This was quickly becoming our new routine; between the often inaccurate transportation schedules, coupled with hot weather and hauling our heavy backpacks, travel days were always exhausting and usually involved lots of waiting around for cars, buses, or boats. Card games and Fanta, however, usually got us through.

By the time we arrived at the island, Rob and I were ready to crack a beer and watch the sun make its leisurely descent, leaving a crimson canvas of clouds in its wake. One of the perks of this trip, for me, was my growing appreciation for watching the rising and setting of the sun.

Addie, our seventeen-year-old neighbour from home, babysitter, family friend, and interloper who had joined us for the summer, decided he wanted to explore the beach and the small surrounding cliffs.

Having Addie join us on the trip was great fun for all of us. As a precocious and imaginative seventeen-year-old, he was old enough to stay up late and get into heated discussions about civic politics back home or the nuances of the same book we'd all read on the trip, but young and energetic enough to have chicken fights in the pool with the kids for hours. He was free-spirited and unfazed by some of the dodgy situations in which we found ourselves, including that we didn't always know where we were headed or where we would be sleeping. Although, we did have to police his diet a little, as seventeen-year-olds tend to think they can survive on Coke and chips. There are few people we would have invited to join us for part of our journey but Addie was one of them, and he proved to be an excellent addition to our adventure. The kids were getting a little bored with us anyway, so bringing one of their favourite people in the world onto the trip for a few months renewed their energy. It pleased us immensely that upon graduating, Addie would go on to have his own adventures to Nepal and South America.

When Oskar came out of the bathroom, he asked if he could catch up with Addie and explore with him.

Our balcony had a clear view of the crescent-shaped beach and I could see Addie walking along the shore. We let Oskar go, reminding him that he wasn't allowed to swim without one of us present. I should note that he was visible and we had been dropped off by the last boat of the day—so, unlike Isla, there was no chance that he would go missing.

He ran off and I could see both of the boys as Oskar chased Addie to catch up. It seemed like the perfect playground for a couple of kids, and there were lots of children swimming and playing on the beach.

Addie had a good head start on Oskar. He was sauntering along slowly and had reached a group of rocks on the far side of the beach. Oskar was striding across the sand to catch up. A few minutes later, I could see them standing on the rocks across the bay, three metres apart. Perfect, they were reunited. Or so I thought. Rob and I sat on the porch and toasted surviving yet another long boat- and bus-filled travel day.

Suddenly, I heard blood-curdling screaming and frantic yelling. I'm pretty sure any mother will understand this. There were lots of kids yelling and playing and screeching on the beach, but one scream stood out so clearly to me among the others.

"Rob, did you hear that?"

"Yeah, kids yelling."

"No, *that!*" I said, indicating a high-pitched screaming. "I think it's Oskar."

"There's tons of kids yelling. He's with Addie. He's fine," Rob said.

There was the scream, again. It could have been any of the thirty kids playing and running around on the beach. I was looking out over the rocks where I'd last seen Oskar. There was no sign of him or Addie.

"He's fine. You're helicopter parenting," Rob said, cracking another beer.

I got up and bolted down the stairs, through the cave, bumping into a wild pig, and ran out onto the beach. Maybe I was being crazy, but I knew it was Oskar. Rob eventually sauntered after me, beer in hand.

Addie was strolling towards me. Oskar was not with him. I saw Oskar twenty metres behind Addie, sobbing and shaking as he walked, still trying to catch up to Addie.

I ran past Addie, who saw me and then Oskar for the first time. They had never connected—even though to anyone observing, it clearly appeared that they had.

Addie was wearing headphones, his music cranked, and never heard Oskar calling out to him, just three metres away.

Oskar's face was red and smeared with tears and snot. He was shaking. I held him tightly.

"I tried to jump across the boulders to get over to Addie, but I slipped. And I slid down the side of the rocks and I was clinging to the barnacles on the side of the boulders so I wouldn't fall into the water," Oskar explained, his stomach scraped and scratched.

Some of my own sharpest and most poignant childhood memories are those where I had survived precarious situations. When I was eight and biking with my brother and his friend, we got locked in a cemetery. We'd been riding along the maze of paths, not knowing that the cemetery gates locked at 8:00 p.m. It was growing dark when we arrived at the entrance to find the chain locks in place after 9:00 p.m. I was terrified we'd have to spend the night in a cemetery, fending off the ghosts of all the dead inhabitants.

Luckily, we found some bushes to squeeze through. We jammed our bikes through the branches too because we knew we'd be in big trouble if we returned without them. We finally arrived home very late and very scratched up. I remember telling my dad with pure horror, "We almost got locked in a cemetery all night."

"But you got out," he said, pouring himself another rum and Coke. Translation: sometimes you're going to do dumb stuff and land yourself in hot water; use those survival skills.

Or never let your children out of your sight in the first place. Like that would ever happen circa 1983.

As Oskar held on to the barnacles on the side of that boulder (he wasn't far from shore—swimmable for him if he weren't panicked and clinging to a rock for dear life), it was a valuable lesson in survival. He needed to remain calm. Knowing that would have helped him figure out how to climb back up or get down, but thankfully some kayakers glided by and he dropped down into their boat. Once, again, people who weren't his parents to the rescue!

We run ahead of our kids with a snow plough these days, removing every single possible obstacle that might cause them stress or challenge them to rely on their wits. When travelling, you can't remove all the obstacles because it's harder to anticipate them. It wasn't just the kids having to survive bizarre situations; we did too, and we often did it together.

When some boys in Bali came by and offered to show Oskar how to fly his silk and wood-framed kite after watching us hopelessly try to get the thing airborne, our response might have been, *Absolutely not! We don't know you. It's too dangerous. You might throw our kid down in a field and beat the crap out of him.* Instead, we watched the kids forge a fast friendship, even though they didn't speak the same language, and get the stubborn kite into the air. The strip of red nylon fluttered precariously up in the pearly sky as the kids passed the string back and forth. Moments like those are what this trip is about, but they do not transpire without risk.

While *The Globe and Mail* saw value in my article and published it, I was faulted and flogged by some readers, although others were generous in their defence of our decisions and what we were trying to achieve in giving our kids freedom. At what point do we take off the bubble wrap and give kids the space to bond with others, negotiate their own way in the world, and endure the consequences of their decisions? If you jump between rocks, you might fall.

Whenever I tell the story about Isla Blue getting lost, she always interrupts and adamantly insists, "I wasn't lost! I knew where you were. I knew where I was. Stop saying I was lost! Grmph!" She's absolutely right. This is part of her personal landscape, her story, her adventure.

Better a broken bone than a broken spirit. Leaving the comfort and safety of home and entering into unfamiliar territory, with often uncontrollable circumstances, truly forced us to test this belief. I think that it still holds up. Isn't that one of the ultimate purposes of travel—to thrust yourself into new situations in order to challenge your thinking and beliefs, and perhaps to develop new ones?

I heard Oskar's calls. Deep down, intuitively, we know when our children need us and when we need to give them space to grow. Sometimes it backfires and falls apart and we mess up, but in both cases—with Oskar falling and Isla wandering off—I learned there are good people out there to catch our kids if we aren't around. That's the kind of world I want to live in. And I think I learned that that's the kind of world I *do* live in.

"Knock, knock."

"Who's there?"

"Child and Family Services. We'd like to talk to you."

SNAKY SITUATIONS &
DITCHING OUR WESTERN
SAFETY STANDARDS

We were assigned an adventurous tour guide (by "adventurous," I mean "on a death mission") in the Amazon, who, somehow, thought it was a good idea to take us, armed only with sticks, searching for anacondas.

"So, uh, do you think it's a good idea to poke deadly snakes with wooden sticks?" I asked as he pulled the boat up to the grassy shore.

"It's okay, it's okay. Don't worry. They don't have the poisonous bite."

"But they're still dangerous, no?"

"They wrap themselves around and kill slowly. They only go after the smaller things like animal." I look at Isla—aka, snake food—curled up, sleeping in my lap. She seems to suffer from boat narcolepsy.

"Okay, so, you're *sure* it's safe?"

"Yeah, yeah. Safe. I take people all the time. This is part of Amazon experience." He believed in earnest that this was an experience not to be missed deep in the jungle of Bolivia, but we didn't do things like chasing polar bears with sticks back in Canada.

I don't think it was our intention to get ourselves or our children killed when we embarked on this trip, but we kept finding ourselves in these *Holy-crap-did-that-really-just-happen?* situations. We started to realize how the safety standards are all over the world are very different from those in North America—in terms of food, water, transportation, and just general *staying alive*. What would seem downright dangerous and unacceptable here in Canada is just a normal day in other countries. There were so many examples of this that after a few months I stopped keeping track, or maybe I just stopped noticing.

We pulled on the rubber boots we'd been given and got out of the boat, wading through grass that was two metres high in places, taller than me. We had to pick the kids up at times for fear of losing them in a field potentially riddled with deadly snakes.

Another guide across the plain waved excitedly, and our small group walked over. We assumed we'd get a look at an anaconda. I still wasn't sure how I felt about this.

"We found cobra!" the guide exclaimed. He had a very pissed-off snake pinned down with a pronged wooden stick. *A cobra? What the hell?!*

"Don't get too close. They are fast. Bite and attack!" our guide cautioned.

"Okay," I said, slowly backing away from the writhing reptile, its tongue flicking out of its flat, scaly head in anticipation of busting loose and sinking those razor-sharp teeth into some pale Canadian flesh. "Why are we still here?"

The guides were delighted that we'd found a cobra. "There's an antidote."

"Okay, good."

"But we are three hours boat ride from a hospital." *Okay, very reassuring.*

After a few hours, the heat had taken its toll on Isla and she was totally over the expedition.

"If you follow the path we came, the snakes are scared away and you are fine," the guide explained.

Rob left the safety of the guided group, and, carrying Isla, waded through the long, dry grass, back to the boat where there was warm juice and melted chocolate tucked in our backpack.

Oskar was keen to see more snakes, and so he and I stuck out the rest of Snake Fest and saw another wild cobra. We never did find any anacondas that day, and I feel more than okay about this.

In retrospect, maybe we should have skipped that excursion— especially since it involved us being face-to-face with a couple of deadly cobras. But so far, in life, the kids' exposure to snakes had been only through the small glass enclosures in zoos and at pet stores. They got to see some large, deadly snakes in their natural habitat, and that was what this trip was about—seeing the world as authentically as possible. By the end of the year, we'd have snorkelled alongside hammerhead sharks in the Galápagos, peered at tarantulas up close on a night hike in the Amazon, watched elephants roam a reserve in Thailand and orangutans swing from trees in Borneo, and swum with a rare kind of jellyfish that don't sting in New Zealand—we'd had to reprimand the kids for having jellyfish fights. These encounters with wildlife became almost common during our travels.

There also were many "Snaky Situations." You must weigh the benefit of the experience and the "when in Rome" mentality with the risks and dangers of the situation. Even the short return plane trip we took to get from La Paz, Bolivia, into the snake-infested Amazon was eighty white-knuckle minutes that I will never get back. It's a loopy flight because the plane flies from the fifth highest-altitude airport on the planet, through the Andes mountain range, down into the sea-level Amazon. I looked out the window at one point and thought we were absolutely going to smack into the side of a mountain. I gently closed the blind and thought about crossing myself. Due to the altitude shift, puking was a common experience on this shaky flight. We were warned that on any given flight, up to half of the passengers would make use of their sick bags. The alternative was a winding eighteen-hour bus ride down into the Amazon via roads and one-way highways that veer through valleys and along sheer cliffs. Flat tires and reversing along sharp turns with death-defying drops to allow cars to pass is the norm. A short flight full of puking passengers seemed like the better option.

Ideally, you get to be a position to *choose* which risks you want to take and which ones you will skip, but often, the nature of travelling in other parts of the world, where the standards are very different from Canadian ones, lands you in situations that you cannot control. The only way to truly avoid danger, or "the unexpected," as our travel nurse back in Canada suggested, is to just stay home. She seemed genuinely appalled when we named some of the places we were planning to take our children as we sat in her office, inquiring about vaccinations. She was not a traveller. It smacked me as a bit odd that she would hold this position. It's like having someone who reviews books that doesn't read, or a fashion designer who lives in a nudist camp.

After having just arrived in Kuching, Borneo, Oskar was leading the way through the airport about three metres ahead of us when, all of a sudden, the airport floor started to buckle and crack right where he was walking. A long section of the floor erupted and pushed upward half a metre right beneath his feet. Yes, you read that correctly, the floor of the airport *erupted*. Oskar and the other travellers around him ran back towards us. We thought perhaps a bomb had gone off. Or there was an earthquake. Only those kinds of incidents could cause a floor to do what we'd just witnessed. Some security guards sauntered over, told us to move along, and hung some yellow tape, offering no explanation for why THE FLOOR OF THE AIRPORT JUST BUST OPEN.

What was more baffling was that nobody, other than foreign travellers like us, seemed remotely alarmed. They were hardly even curious. It was treated like a normal occurrence around here, even though it felt like we'd entered the bloody *Twilight Zone*.

The following week, when we flew out of Borneo through the same airport, the area was still taped off with no explanation or any attempt to repair the floor. What is even more unnerving is that the more we travelled, the more these weird scenarios—where strange, unsafe things would just happen out of the blue—became the new normal for us.

We were sleeping on a bus travelling from Singapore to Kuala Lumpur when the vehicle started rumbling and careening out of control all over the highway. My heart lurched into my throat and I thought for certain that we were going to crash.

The bus jarred and shook and there was a large thud. The vehicle rolled to a stop. I looked out the window to see that part of the engine had fallen out onto the highway. "Well, at least we didn't crash," I said, always the optimist. The bus had come to a stop in the middle of four lanes of dense traffic flying down the highway. Speed limits aren't really a thing in many parts of the world. It was 2:00 a.m. I'd hate to see this road at rush hour.

One of the elderly, less informed passengers looked out the window and saw liquid coming out of the bus and thought it would be a good idea to alert everyone that the gas tank was leaking and the bus was going to blow up. This incited mass panic, of course. The traffic whipping around us would not so much as slow down, let alone stop, so that we could disembark the bus, which was apparently going to explode. Death Option A: Blow up. Death Option B: Try to get off, but get run down by a car that is blazing by at 160 kmph.

The bus driver eventually managed to get out of the bus, light some flares, and determine that the liquid was only water. He stopped the traffic long enough to get everyone off the bus, which almost caused several more accidents.

It felt like a real-life game of *Frogger*, getting ourselves, our half-asleep children, and our belongings off that bus.

"Will they send another bus soon?" I asked the driver.

"Oh, no, I don't think so," he laughed. Silly woman.

"So, now what?"

"We find our own rides."

"You mean, we hitchhike? At this hour?" I tried to suppress my irritation. He shrugged and went about the fun task of trying to extract everyone's bags from underneath the bus amidst all of the traffic.

Sending another bus was, apparently, entirely out of the question and laughable. There were no other buses. The ones they had barely worked. We then stood on the side of the road, in the middle of the night, with our luggage and all of the other passengers, at the mercy of any cars or buses who would stop to pick up stranded travellers. Most of them were full or didn't bother to stop.

While we waited, I struck up a conversation with a woman who teaches in an international school in Singapore. She'd been in the country six years and had done this bus trip four times already this year; three of the four buses had broken down. In fact, she was surprised that the bus had made it this far and she had been getting hopeful that we might make it all the way without a breakdown. She'd splurged for a more expensive ticket with this company because it had a better reputation, but the truth of the matter was, she explained, that the bus companies can't afford to service the buses properly or regularly. Three-quarters of the buses will break down on the highway. This doesn't seem like a great business model.

In Samoa, we found ourselves in yet another precarious situation. I woke up in the middle of the night to find that the mosquito netting was suspended in a little ball above our bed instead of where it should have been, *around* the bed, protecting us from the bloodsuckers. Even if they hadn't given Isla and me the "baby size" netting for our double mattress and it hadn't popped right off like a cap from a beer bottle during the night, there was still a gaping hole in the middle of it anyway. I looked over at Isla, who was sleeping beside me. There were at least five fat mosquitoes feeding on her pudgy little blood-filled cheeks. I pressed them down one by one with my thumb, careful not to wake her. The mosquitoes were too fat and engorged with her blood to even bother trying to fly away. Her face was splattered with blood stains.

You know the expression, "These days you can get anything you need anywhere in the world"? People usually throw it around when they forget to pack something like deodorant or a razor. I'm sure that's the case at resorts and other well-travelled places, but there are places in the world, we learned, where you cannot get things that you need.

We were having a run of bad luck. I'd bought mosquito spray, lots of it, along with wax strips for my legs in the capitol city of Apia the night before. (My experiment to see how long I could go without hair removal was wearing a little thin. Feral dogs were starting to root around for treats on my legs.) We checked into a hotel for one night, as we were taking local transportation to more remote parts of the island first thing in the morning. We went to the hotel buffet for dinner, which consisted of lots of unrecognizable, deep-fried foods, slabs of Wonder Bread, and pasta out of cans. When we returned, our hotel room had been cleaned—or cleaned out, was more like it. The plastic shopping bag containing the bug spray and wax strips was gone. Stores were now closed. We were catching a bus to take us to a boat that would ferry us to an island first thing in the morning.

I hoped we could pick up some more bug spray (and wax strips) before we caught our morning bus. But our ride hit the road before any of the stores opened. I assumed we could find some spray when the bus dropped us off at the dock.

You can get most things anywhere in the world, except on the island of Samoa. There were little stands that popped up on the side of the road every few kilometres, but they were small and sold whatever random things they felt like selling: Nutella, Coke, ciga-rettes, Radler. (Incidentally, I'd been letting the kids drink Radler because it was poorly labelled. I thought it was lemon pop. It was at one of these stands that I picked up a can and realized that the kids were getting an occasional treat of citrus beer. The mild buzz they experienced probably explains the bouts of mellow behavior. And here I thought they were adjusting to the travel schedule.) They did not have any mosquito spray. This was odd, considering the whole island was afflicted with the chikungunya virus. It should be the *only* thing they sell. Maybe they were sold out.

We boarded a bright red, spray-painted bus called the Tropical Storm that was full of mainly locals and rolled along the coast blast-ing reggae tunes at a deafening volume for two hours. It dropped us off on the side of the road in the middle of nowhere. We had to battle our way through a bush, down to a rickety dock where a boat would pick us up. The dock was barely floating. Suffice it to say, there was no store selling mosquito spray. We'd booked this night on a private little island because it offered the opportunity to sleep in *fales* along the ocean, under the stars. Fales are unwalled sleeping structures in Samoa. It seemed romantic enough in the guidebook write-up, but not so much when there is a debilitat-ing mosquito-borne disease lurking all around you. No Internet, no civilization, and we had no bug spray. The woman who owned and ran the island offered me some homemade bug spray, but it seemed to be made of some fairly toxic, undiluted household cleaners. Hmmm, get the mosquito virus, or douse my kid in Mr. Clean? We opted to wear long sleeves and pants and stay under the mosquito netting at dusk when the bugs came out. Except our netting was meant for a crib and had a hole in it. Thankfully, we didn't catch the virus, but we learned that we must have bug spray at all times.

Travelling between the two islands of Samoa was another har-rowing experience. We got on the ferry, and once it reached capac-ity, they packed on another seventy-five people. There was not a life jacket in sight, and the one and only life preserver, which looked like it had huge bites taken out of it, serviced the two hundred people on the boat.

I told my kids to climb over the sleeping fat guy and go sit on top of that preserver. My fears were not unwarranted when, still quite a ways from shore, water started to pour into the back of the boat. I panicked and told the kids they were not to let go of that life preserver under *any* circumstances. No one else seemed very concerned about the prospect of the boat sinking as they dozed, their bodies lolling along with the motion of the waves. It was reminiscent of the airport floor buckling in Kuching, or the engine falling out of the bus in Singapore. Just another ordinary day.

We could probably easily write a sequel to this book by filling it just with the weird or unsafe things we encountered on our year abroad.

If you'd have told me three years ago that my five-year-old would be cruising around on the back of my motorcycle, I probably would have laughed in your face. *Umm, no, my kids are schlepped around in $600 Britax luxury car seats that I extensively researched for safety prior to their purchase.* These things can withstand impact from a semi. I insisted that all the grandparents purchase them as well for the few times a year they'd be hauling them around. This, combined with their all-organic diet, vitamin D, and fish oil, would ensure they were brilliant, healthy, well-adjusted children.

Well, let me just say that the entire continent of Asia is in direct conflict with this parenting style. If we were going to see anything of interest—namely temples and ruins, though Dairy Queen if the kids had their way, and *luwak* cafés (where you're charged a fortune to drink coffee made from pooped-out coffee beans eaten by Asian palm civets) if I had mine—we would have to travel by motorbike. Said children would have to ride on the back of these motorbikes with their parents—one of whom can barely drive a car properly, let alone an ill-maintained bike.

I'm not the greatest driver at the best of times, so the learning curve for the motorcycle was a little steep for me. On my first day, I mixed up which way you are supposed to turn the hand throttle for gas and the brakes on a motorbike that I felt was a little punchy to begin with. Isla, our bike, and I had a bit of a scuffle with the pavement and wiped out. We were going slowly enough, but I think Isla sensed the doom that was coming with her mother at the helm and bailed off the bike; she was not injured at all. I, however, was all scraped up, again, in a crumpled heap under my bike. A guy came running up to me with a bottle of iodine. I held out my leg.

"No! Mom, you're allergic to iodine!" Oskar bellowed through his helmet from the back of Rob's bike.

"Righto! No iodine!" So many darn things to remember all the time.

I managed to wrap my head around the bike controls and got used to driving in Asia's dense traffic, where they have an aversion to stop signs and traffic lights. Isla reluctantly became my passenger again when she was confident I'd sorted out the difference between the brakes and gas.

There were some other unusual obstacles to contend with. In small towns, we'd have to dodge monkeys foraging for food all over the roads, and if you were cruising too slowly, they would try to accost you. On another occasion, the road crossed an airstrip and we had to wait for a plane to pass.

Another time we found ourselves in a situation when the only transportation was the back of a truck. I called for three different drivers and each time a pick-up truck would appear. I was finally told that there were no cars; it was only trucks. We visited the island of Gili Air in Bali where there were no vehicles at all, only horses and buggies. At any rate, we'd come a long way from those Britax car seats.

As for that organic diet back in Canada, in Asia we often procured our food from street vendors, and about fifty percent of the time we had no idea what exactly we were eating. Pork? Chicken? Possum? Roadkill? It was often grilled or fried and very tasty.

The thing about travelling for a year is, after a while, you become acclimatized; your standard of "normality" starts to shift, and you stop noticing all the strangeness. That may have been one of the greatest gifts of this trip: the general acceptance that anything is possible. You lose your first-world, organic safety, for just general "staying-alive" standards and allow yourself to be immersed in the experiences themselves. This is how the rest of the world lives, *every day*. They have no choice but to take this leaking ferry, or unserviced bus, probably many times a month. They aren't just *visiting* places with mosquito-borne diseases. They *live* in places where a child dies of malaria every thirty seconds. Here we fret about if we should take our expensive anti-malaria pills because they might cause sunburn or make us nauseous. We would often see and hear tourists complaining about food, accommodation, flights, or the poor standards of other countries. In the beginning, we were probably guilty of that too. As the trip wore on, however, we had a lot of conversations with the kids about how lucky we are to live where we do, because broken-down buses and over-capacity sinking boats are the norm for many people in the world, but you don't hear them complaining about it. In Bolivia, shining shoes is such a shameful job that shoe shiners must conceal their identity beneath balaclavas. It was Oskar who made the observation about the masked faces and his eyes welled up when he learned the reason why. It was a realization that made him sensitive and sympathetic towards the plights of the less-fortunate. He now spends time on Kiva making micro loans to people in countries around the world for projects that will help them support themselves. We have learned that people in the most trying circumstances just get on with the business of life. In Fiji, the kids and I participated in a kava ceremony with an elder and then we were allowed to tour the village and see the local school. Oskar noted that the houses did not have front doors. The elder explained that they were not necessary as everyone is welcome into one another's homes. If we did that, Isla said, all of our stuff would be gone!

As visitors, once you move past the challenges and differences, and ditch your judgments and high standards (not that our standards were ever really that high to begin with), you start to embrace and fall in love with places. The quirks become the charm.

FILTH & FAITH

We celebrated our tenth wedding anniversary in Kuala Lumpur, Malaysia. Rob found a deal on a dreamy condo for a few days in a hip district of the city. Oskar and Isla Blue were joyous as they swam in an open-air pool with a spectacular view of the city and devoured Apple TV—unusual luxuries for us. We hoped they wouldn't get too used to it. Rob and I had a rare night out while Addie babysat, which meant introducing the kids to the "stomach float"—a dinner of Coke and ice cream—while rearranging all the white leather furniture into a tower from which they would play video games and throw Doritos at us when we returned.

Rob and I revelled in the evening away from our children! We were with the kids almost 24/7 for the entire year so our time alone was a real treat. We ate steak and got tipsy on fancy cocktails in a trendy part of town that was packed with restaurants, bars, and millennials who were trying to get laid.

I'd bathed for an hour in the tile bathroom, got my hair looking glossy again, and was wearing my best outfit: flip-flops and a fraying Patagonia black halter dress. Wearing the same two utility dresses for an entire year really creates the urge to get out a pair of scissors and cut them into teeny, tiny pieces and set them on fire. The standards sure had dropped, but it was one of the few times on the trip when I felt clean and civilized, and not covered in sweat, grime, sunscreen, bug repellent, drool, or puke.

As we walked back to our condo, we remembered we were flying into Borneo first thing in the morning and we'd better stock up on bug spray. Story of our lives on this trip. One moment we could be having a romantic dinner in an exotic city; the next, we could be trolling around in back alleys looking for late-night convenience stores to buy mosquito repellent because we were flying into the jungle.

I once read a compelling piece of advice about marriage: *One of the best ways to keep your marriage fresh and make it last is to experience new things together and go on adventures together.* We'd been married ten years and we were certainly on an adventure. (That's the politically correct term for a year-long exercise in filth and minimalism.) In fact, we'd been on many adventures. We might not even like each other that much anymore for all I know—but we don't really have enough free time to think about it.

Rob and I had hiked the West Coast Trail for our honeymoon. It was an extremely sexy way to kick off our life together. We spent twelve-hour days hiking seventy-five kilometres in five-and-a-half days. Bathing standards were loose: if it happened at all, it was in the ocean or in waterfalls. I don't think we bothered with the soap, since we were carrying everything on our backs and every ounce mattered. If the options come down to soap or coffee, I'm always going to choose coffee.

We didn't have sex because by the end of the day we were tired, soaked, and sore. "Sweaty" and "crusty" summed up my underwear situation—no one was going to voluntarily go digging around in there. Instead, we treated one another's oozing blisters. I think maybe we kissed once. For a picture.

"This sucks," I complained on kilometre nineteen one day. "Whose idea was this?"

"Yours."

I remember that one morning Rob tried something someone had told him about called a "tidal flush." I'm not going to go into mechanics of it here or put it in any notes at the back of this book, but you can Google it. Waking up to find your new husband trying, unsuccessfully, to take a shit in the ocean is certainly one way to kick off a marriage. To this day, he is still laments that he was unable to perform the tidal flush because his "sphincter wouldn't loosen" when there was a giant wave coming at him.

Our honeymoon was five days of sheer hell where I threatened to beat Rob senseless with my walking stick if he whistled one more time. But after it was over, I loved it. We had established right from day one what our life together would be like. (We later went to Tofino and Hawaii to do the proper honeymoon vacation that involved more sex and fewer failed attempts by Rob to poop in the ocean. Although, I suspect he rose early in the mornings to go and master the technique, much to the disdain of the B&B owners.) But I don't remember the details from those trips nearly as clearly as I remember climbing endless ladders, crossing swinging bridges, tripping on gnarled tree roots, slogging through the sand, and gazing up into the green canopy of old-growth trees— the glory of the West Coast Trail.

We had to encourage and push each other to continue. In some ways, I think that trek was a pretty good metaphor for marriage. Sometimes it was incredible: we watched whales playing in the water just off the coast, came across colonies of sea lions basking in the sun, and we stood in waterfalls, letting the icy-cold water run over our faces and bodies. Sometimes it was terrible pain: you were wet and dirty, blisters were leaking pus, calves were cramping. Lots of times it just *was*. You'd be slogging through sand or forests and it was monotonous. You focused on putting one foot in front of the other. Marriage can have both epic and difficult moments too. And there are stretches of marriage that are monotonous. Lots of them.

My wedding ring is at the bottom of the ocean off the coast of Samoa, thanks to a stomach virus that forced me to lose ten pounds, resulting in extremely skinny fingers on this adventure. I hope, at least, that some grouper used it to propose to his fiancée. My wedding vows suffered a similar fate. They are locked away on a dead laptop. We each wrote our own vows. My vows were about keeping a sense of humour, having adventures together, and not getting stuffy and boring once we were married.

Lately, as we roll deeper into our forties, people have been telling me that their marriages aren't exciting anymore; they're not having as much sex, and life is getting stale. One friend was seriously mulling over whether she was even going to stay with her husband. Nothing was inherently wrong—she was just bored.

I haven't felt like that yet. Being with Rob still enthuses me. Sometimes I look at him and think, "Man, this guy, like a bottle of malbec, is getting better with age." He, of course, will tell you that his knees hurt, his back aches, and that he's basically on his last legs. But one morning, when we were camping at Rainbow Beach in Australia, I took my coffee down to the beach to catch the early morning sun (and maybe escape the children for a few minutes). Off in the distance, a barefoot jogger was running along the shore towards me. Silhouetted by the sun, the ocean kicking at his feet, he was lean and strong and sexy as he bounced along the sand at a solid pace. I felt a bit guilty gawking at this guy, but as the jogger approached, I realized it was Rob and I got butterflies in my stomach. It was the same feeling I had when we got married ten years earlier. Rob says it's just indigestion. Maybe we're just lucky. But part of me attributes this continued admiration and affection to the fact that we've gone on a lot of adventures together, and now we're on this big, fat journey with our kids. It's hard, and we are always tired, and almost every day there is some debacle that needs to get sorted out, but we're living up to those vows. And it's never boring.

When you've been with someone for a while, you get sucked up into that domestic world of *Who's making dinner?* and *When was the last time anyone vacuumed around this place? I need to load up on better panties; these ratty ones aren't doing it for you anymore, are they?* If you have kids, it gets even more chaotic. *I'd love some intimacy, but Oskar just recreated a Picasso on the bedroom wall with the contents of his diaper.*

The gap year was another metaphor for our marriage. There were moments so beautiful and surreal that will forever be woven into the fabric of our family, but there were moments that were so hard—as in, suck-the-life-out-of-you-why-are-we-doing-this?-I-want-to-give-up-and-go-home, hard. And, of course, there were long stretches on buses, planes, and highways that were tedious and underwhelming. But, as with marriage, you stay the course, because when it's all said and done, you know marriage is not a highlights reel; it is comprised of a collection of experiences, many of which will end up on the editing room floor.

I believe the gap year profoundly strengthened our marriage.

For ten months, we had no time apart. We spent 24/7 with one another, with only a few exceptions. The big, burning question everyone wants to know is how we fit intimacy into that year. Short answer: you really don't. Okay, well we did, but family washrooms at campsites are not something to be proud of. In Australia, the kids could not understand for the life of them why we opted to sleep in the tent when we had a camper van. When Addie joined us, we occasionally splurged or struck a deal and the kids got their own room.

Something extraordinary happened on our trip: I don't think we had one argument or disagreement. Every day was a battle—whether it was with our kids, the weather, insane border cross-ings, trying to procure travel visas, extracting head lice, locating a misplaced kid, and just generally trying to figure out what the heck we were doing. We *had* to be on the same team. There was no choice. A crack in our fortress risked the entire thing falling apart.

Not only were we constantly experiencing new adventures together, but we had to plan and make a multitude of decisions together every single day. There just wasn't really the time or energy to engage in arguments.

Who's taking Isla to gymnastics? became, *Holy shit, we've been at this corrupt border crossing for three hours in the blistering heat—let's just bribe the guards, everyone else is*; or, Rob, *I will give you all my money if we can just swing by this vineyard for a couple of hours.*

We constantly had "decision exhaustion"; it was relentless, always figuring out what we were doing next. We were often too tired to argue. Hell, we barely had the strength to crack a bottle of beer at the end of the day half the time.

Mainly, we had to stay united so we could battle the Little Terrorists. Well, one was an outright terrorist, while the other was more like an under-the-radar anarchist. We had to be a united front; there could be no fractures, otherwise they would jam their little fingers into the fissure and hijack the entire trip, reducing Rob and me to rubble. If Oskar got his way, we'd relocate to Gili Air, an island that boasts no rules or police presence. If Isla Blue had her way, we'd reroute back to Canada in the dead of winter.

So, we worked as a united team to create the best experience possible. Sometimes we screwed it all up, but at least we screwed it up together. When things did go wrong and one of us made a faulty move (e.g., forgetting my wallet four hours back at an ice cream shack in New Zealand; Rob backing the rental van straight into a deep ditch), we usually laughed about it and sorted it out. *Those six German guys over there look like they could lift a car?* We knew that mistakes happened a lot, and it could be either one of us who messed up at any given time. (It was usually me.)

The gap year was great for our marriage. Adventure was great for our marriage. Evacuating our comfort zone as a couple was great for our marriage. I believe we put that piece of advice about experiencing new things and going on adventures to the test while on our year abroad. It holds up as the best piece of marriage advice I've ever heard. And it doesn't necessarily have to be an elaborate, year-long trek around the world. Racing cars, rock climbing, or having sex in your kids' treehouse would suffice. Do something, anything new together and maintain a sense of humour about it when things don't go as planned. That's how we survived, how we continue to survive.

I hope to be on another grand adventure for our fifteen-year anniversary. I should probably let Rob know one of these days.

As we arrive back at the condo in Kuala Lumpur after our tenth-anniversary celebration, the kids hurl pillows at us and say they need us to go back out and get them more Oreos and Coke. Happy Anniversary.

BACK ON THE ROAD

I sat in a Winnipeg airport restaurant, picking at a chicken Caesar salad as the kids and our parents chattered around me. My stomach was in knots. We were resuming our world adventure today and I was too excited, nervous, and consumed with mixed feelings to eat. Rob was at the airline desk checking us in.

We were saying goodbye again to everyone—except Rob's dad.

There was an aura of sadness about our departure this time for so many reasons, but mainly because Rob's dad was no longer with us. Part of the reason we'd planned the trip now was because our parents were healthy and we worried that as we got older, it would be hard to travel for this long when our aging parents might need our help. Hell, we'd probably need care in a couple of years ourselves. Sometimes, in life, things don't work out according to plan.

It was seven months into our trip. We had been in Bangkok, Thailand and were supposed to fly to Siem Reap, Cambodia, the morning of August 30th for the next leg of our tour, which also included Vietnam and Myanmar. We woke up to a barrage of messages and emails to call home immediately. Rob and I looked at each other; we knew something bad had happened. When Rob called home, he learned his dad had passed away unexpectedly. We cancelled our flights to Cambodia and booked airline tickets home.

That endless flight from Bangkok back to Winnipeg was grim. We felt profoundly sad, lost, and aimless. Rob's dad had died; we abruptly stopped our world trip. Isla, not quite grasping the severity of the situation, was elated to be going home to see her grandparents. The news hit Oskar hard. For years, he'd been planning to be a mathematician and professor, just like his Opa. In my head, I started to question whether we'd made the right decision at all in travelling. It was my idea. We'd missed out on the precious last months of Rob's dad's life. My overriding emotion was guilt.

To add to the situation, we felt removed from life back home. We'd been riding around in tuk-tuks, small, open-air, three-wheeled motorized vehicles, the night before, and wandering the overcrowded streets of Bangkok, eating street meat. We were so immersed in our travel life and now we were abruptly and unexpectedly flying back to Winnipeg. It felt like our tuk-tuk had barrelled into a brick wall at full speed.

Our house was still rented, so we couldn't return there. The kids were pleased we would stay with my parents where there were significantly less rules and a lot more bowls of chips and candy lying around.

After we'd been home for two months, we were living in a haze of sadness and paralysis. The kids went back to school for the start of the school year and they quickly came to appreciate my less-structured, road-schooling program a whole lot more. I wasn't scheduled to return to work for another three months. I knew that if we didn't get back on the road and finish our trip, we would regret it for the rest of our lives.

But leaving the comforts of home the second time around took so much more gumption than the first time, because we knew how much energy and stamina were required to do this trip. The first time, we were naïve about this gong show onto which we were embarking. We were oblivious to the long travel days, the overwhelming amount of planning and decision-making, the volatility of a five-year-old when all structure is removed. There was something really beautiful about the naïveté, but now, we were still emotionally reeling from the loss of Rob's dad and we were foisting ourselves back into this chaotic travel life. The world had changed for us, and we knew what lay ahead.

As we got on that plane to South America, we were well aware of how challenging life could and would be on the road. It's like having a second baby. The second time around you know exactly what you are getting into. It doesn't mean you don't do it, but you brace yourself for the sleepless nights, tantrums, and the work. The joy and bliss will always trump the exhaustion, but you don't go into the whole thing like the blind fool you were the first time.

Just as you might do with your second child, I didn't take quite as many photos or keep every single boarding pass on part two of our trip, but we appreciated going back and knew there were exciting experiences in store for us. We just had to make the leap.

We'd rerouted to South America on short notice. We'd been in Asia for a few months, so we felt like we had really gotten our heads around the travel, border crossings, visas, food, and culture of Asia. We had done a fair bit of reading and had a rough route mapped out of where we were going to go next. Rob and I were both especially looking forward to visiting Myanmar and Cambodia. But somehow it didn't feel right to fly back to Asia. Besides, that would be taking the easy path, a path we never seemed to choose. Because we were starting from Winnipeg, we were given the opportunity to change our route and explore an entirely different part of the world and we seized it. Suddenly, we were heading to South America, a continent we knew little about. We'd had our heads out of the travel game, as we'd been focused on the passing of Rob's dad, and this would become painfully evident as we tried to board a plane to Brazil.

It took a lot of effort to get back to the trip. I got the distinct feeling that Rob's and the kids' enthusiasm was waning somewhat. Isla was so happy to be reunited with her grandmothers and her stuffies that she insisted she wasn't leaving. I felt the weight of being the driving force, firing up the enormous travel engine. The wind had quite literally been taken out of our sails. It would have just been easier to stay home, but I knew that I'd forever have the sense that we hadn't finished what we started. We were budgeted and packed and planned—sort of. There was nothing holding us here except our own sadness and Isla's stuffies. I knew deep down that if we could just get back on the road, it would be okay.

And here we were at the airport, starting from scratch, about to board a plane to Brazil. Or so we thought.

"Dar, they aren't going to let us board the flight." Rob said.

"Huh?" I asked through a mouthful of Caesar salad.

"We don't have travel visas."

At this point, I thought Rob was joking. In light of the recent death and our trip's derailment and spending two months back in Winnipeg, I thought this was a pretty lame joke on his part. Then again, it was a good sign that his sense of humour was returning. But as I studied his face, I knew he wasn't kidding.

"Can't we just get them online?"

"It takes ten days."

"We always get them online. Check!"

"I did. Not this time. Not this country. We can't leave today. We have to rebook, go another day."

"Well, let's just find a flight into a country where we can get visas on short notice, anywhere in South America will do. Let's just go."

Our bags were packed; we were mentally prepared to leave. Come hell or high water, I was going to get on a plane. I was not leaving that airport in a car.

It was 8:00 p.m. already. Rob got on his computer and started looking for flights. "Anywhere, anywhere," I kept saying. "We'll figure out an itinerary when we get there." I was desperate. I thought if we didn't get on a plane, we never would. We'd get sucked back into life here. This dream we'd planned for years would end now.

My dad and the rest of the grandparents were standing around in disbelief with looks that screamed *Are you guys idiots?*

We'd travelled for seven months without issue. Well, okay, we had *lots* of issues, but not visa issues. Rob was always on top of this, but coming back home to mourn the death of my father-in-law really pulled us out of the travel game in a big way.

"We're not getting on a plane tonight," Rob said, slapping his laptop shut.

I got up, walked across to the other side of the terminal, sat down on a trolley, put my head in my hands, and wept. I knew that it wasn't the end of the world and we'd be leaving soon, but my heart sank with the thought of our trip getting interrupted yet again, this time on account of our own stupidity. We'd been through such an emotional thrill ride these past few months. This was the straw that broke my heart. Everything else had been handled stoically and in stride.

My parents took our luggage and the kids back home. Rob and I went straight to a beer vendor and bought a twelve-pack. We sat in my parents' driveway in Winnipeg and drank it all. We were never leaving this city. Eventually, we saw the humour in the situation and my tears turned to laughter.

The next day, Rob booked us flights to Lima, Peru, where they had less stringent entrance requirements. It was on the other side of South America, but we had planned to make our way to Peru eventually anyway.

The passing of Rob's father reminded us that the people we love will not be here forever, so we made sure we incorporated our parents into the last part of our tour. At Christmas, we would fly up to Mexico City and take a four-hour bus ride to San Miguel de Allende, where Rob's mom was spending the winter. This city, a

UNESCO World Heritage Site, was cultured and quaint and offered a welcome breather after visiting more rustic and undeveloped places like Bolivia and the Galápagos Islands, after frenzied border crossings on foot in blistering heat. We abandoned the chaotic pace of relentless scheduling, to which we'd grown accustomed, and for a week, we allowed ourselves to be absorbed by the charm of San Miguel via my mother-in-law's condo rental. Actually, we unloaded the kids in Renate's small condo while Rob and I stayed at her friend's place a short walk away where we were introduced to the noble heritage of fine Mexican tequila. We wandered the narrow cobblestone streets and took in the markets, Christmas traditions, and artistic culture of the colourful town. I was starting to see the appeal of the Canadian snowbird trend and why people might wait until their children leave the nest to enjoy tranquil travel experiences. With my mother-in-law and her friends, there seemed to be less meltdowns about things like an absence of peanut butter.

Near the end of our trip, my parents would fly down to Ecuador and spend two weeks touring the country with us. It took them multiple flights to reach Quito, Ecuador, another UNESCO World Heritage Site at an altitude of 3,050 metres. It speaks to their sense of willingness and adventure that, in their seventies, they would fly to South America to join our shit show.

The kids were happy to see my parents, for it would mean more treats and that life would perhaps be a little cushier for a few weeks. My parents took the kids on a bus tour of Quito, nestled high up in the Andes and often dubbed "The Most Beautiful City in South America," with its colonial architecture and stone streets. The bus allowed them to hop on and off at their leisure for as much ice cream and churros as the kids could consume. Rob and I, of course, remained committed to the three-hour walking tour.

My poor mom, ever the good sport and wanting to travel how we did, turned green on the coastal bus ride that had the same level of thrill as an amusement park roller coaster. Afterwards, they promptly hired a driver to take us to our destinations.

We checked into some hot springs, basking in private pools of thermal water, visited the largest market in South America in the region of Otavalo, and stayed on a farm in the lush hillside that housed a llama that enjoyed kissing people—especially my dad. Overall, we had to balance our travel style with not getting my parents killed. They had to accept not wearing a wristband that entitled them to free drinks at a swim-up bar. It was a healthy exercise in compromise.

Going home when Rob's father died was difficult on so many levels, but some good came of it. We were granted some time to plan and incorporate family into our year abroad. As difficult as it was to get back on the road, I know Rob's dad would have wanted us to finish the year. Two years later, we would spread his ashes in the mountains on yet another family adventure.

WHAT HAPPENS ON THE ROAD, STAYS ON THE ROAD

I was on one bank of the creek and Rob was on the other. He pitched Isla towards me and I caught her by the shoulders and pulled her up into the long grass. Oskar was able to jump across the stream of water unaided.

We walked along a cornfield, checking behind us to make sure we hadn't alerted anyone to our mission. As we rounded a bend, there was a large black bull lying in the middle of our path. It rose and shook its horned head. It seemed none too pleased about human visitors interrupting its lazy afternoon.

"Let's get out of here. The guy didn't mention anything about a bull!"

We had just spent upwards of $1,000 scratching Machu Picchu off our bucket list. We walked up the steps to the crest of a hill perched 2,500 metres above sea level in the Andes. Where one would expect to find only trees, mountains, and clouds, an Incan citadel is tucked away in the valley. The draw of Machu Picchu, and the reason your breath catches in your throat a little when you first lay eyes on it, is that it defies expectations. There should not be a stone city here, and yet there it is. I'd seen many photos of Machu Picchu, but the allure of the site lies partly in the journey to get there and in how it modestly reveals itself in this impossible land-scape. The Spanish never did find the well-hidden Machu Picchu, and so they couldn't pillage and destroy it the way they did the rest of the Incan Empire.

Even the kids break from walloping each other to take in one of the New Seven Wonders of the World. But they quickly get down to brass tacks, realizing the potential of this place as a venue for hide-and-seek while we went about hiring a guide.

Unfortunately, the guide we hired was academic and dry in her delivery of information, and the kids don't suffer university lectures, in broken English, in thirty-five-degree heat very well. *Structures were built with a technique called "ashlar." Stones are cut to fit together without mortar. Remarkably, not even a needle can fit in between two stones.* Isla managed to busy herself posing for individual photos with a busload of Japanese tourists. She was very popular with Asians. Some of them, in fact, seemed more enthralled about their selfie with this little girl with wispy blonde hair than they did about the ancient city in the background. *Hidden among the cliffs and lush vegetation, the ancient city of Machu Picchu remained secret until the twentieth century, and not even the Spanish conquistadors in search of treasures were able to find it.* Oskar discovered the practice of photobombing, and busied himself with seeing how many Machu Picchu memories he could insert himself into.

It had been an uncharacteristically hot day for Machu. We eventually cut the tour guide loose and passed several hours during the muggiest part of the afternoon eating Oreos and playing UNO in the shade of one of the 500-year-old walls. I'm pretty sure this wasn't your usual Machu Picchu experience. But by the end of the day, as the sun started to sink behind the mountains, the hordes of tourists drained the valley, whisked back to Cusco via tour buses, and we had the place mostly to ourselves.

We would learn over and over again on our trip that sometimes days at the most coveted places don't unfold quite as you planned, and that a bleaker, unexpected detour can offer experiences you will spend the rest of your life thinking about. Such was our day in Ollantaytambo.

After Machu Picchu, we had settled into the quiet town of Ollantaytambo, Peru. From our hostel, we could see the sun setting, casting a warm orange glow over some local ruins that I wanted to visit. When we inquired about entrance fees, we learned that we had to buy an expensive three-day pass for hundreds of dollars that provided access to *all* the ancient sites in the area. The outrageous price tag was even harder to justify considering that the novelty of visiting high-altitude Incan ruins in the baking heat, quite frankly, was starting to wear a little thin with our five-year-old.

I was lamenting to our hostel owner about how we'd like to see the ruins, but couldn't spend that much money when our kids would be exhausted and whining within an hour, and our entire daily budget was only $150 for the four of us, inclusive for food, accommodation, and travel. Besides, we still needed to make up what we'd overspent at Machu, not purchase more passes. Whether or not to do something, weighing out the cost versus the value of the experience, would become a recurring theme on our trip.

"That pass is too expensive. Another effort by the government to rip off tourists!" he huffed. "I'll tell you how to get in without paying." Parental instincts should have kicked in, but I really wanted to check out these ruins. And that's how we found ourselves pitching our kids across creeks, confronting bulls, and running through cornfields.

We had jumped across the creek and were walking along a footpath next to the babbling stream, as per the instructions of our hostel host. Cornfields stretched out along the other side of the path. The bull was sunning himself on the trail when we appeared. He rose, shook is head, and started down the path towards us. The kids and I instinctively bolted back in the direction from which we'd come; since Rob was up ahead, closer to the bull, he disappeared into the cornfield. The kids and I arrived back at the creek, thinking that we'd put enough distance between us and the startled bovine, and waited for Rob. As the minutes ticked by, I started to fear something had happened. When we heard rustling in the corn stalks, I clutched the kids, hoping it was Rob and not the bull. I had Isla in my arms, ready to throw her back across the water.

I had had a traumatizing cow-related experience as a child that has resulted in some serious trust issues with all livestock. When we were visiting my great-aunt's farm in Saskatchewan, we were encouraged to play with some newborn calves. When the horned mother cow saw us petting her babies, she charged with unflinching speed and ferocious determination, chasing my nine-year-old brother clear across the farm right towards the front door of the house. We all watched in horror, certain he would be trampled. Thankfully, he made it inside. When we finally reached the house, my dad chased the cow away and banged on the locked door. My brother refused to answer, convinced it was the cow. All the adults were relieved that my brother wasn't hurt, and agreed that this was unusual behaviour for a cow. The experience, however, would leave me wary of bovines even into adulthood. The incident was an unfortunate blow to the good reputations of cows everywhere, as they are apparently very docile, domestic beasts—until they decide to hunt you down.

Thankfully, it was Rob who emerged from the cornfield, arms in the air, mouth agape, annoyed that we'd all bolted and left him standing there to face the animal alone. "Women and children first," I muttered. I had never really believed in that mantra until it applied directly to me.

We waded through tall stalks of corn, giving that bull, wherever it was—I hoped not in the cornfield—a very wide berth. We finally emerged from the field and came to an ancient stone wall. We peered over it and, sure enough, we were at the outskirts of the Ollantaytambo ruins. All we had to do, according to the owner of our hostel, was wait until the coast was clear and lower ourselves down over the wall and into the ruins; *voilà*, we'd save a few hundred bucks. A security guard roamed past and then disappeared. The area never seemed to be completely empty of tourists, so when there was a lull, Rob scaled down the wall, Oskar and Isla scrambled after him, and then I plunked down onto the dirt path. We ignored the looks from the other tourists, pretending we'd been checking out some other section accessible only via scaling the walls.

"That was so fun!" Oskar said, eyes wide, sweeping the fine red dust from his shorts. We high-fived and got on with the business of touring what was the last Incan stronghold in the Spanish conquest of Peru. The kids chased each up and down the steps that had been carved into the hill and fortified with stone.

I didn't think about what that particular adventure was teaching our children until we were in an admissions line at a museum the following week.

"How come we're paying? Why don't we just sneak in?" Isla asks, pulling at my hand. She is extremely loud. People comment on this all the time. So when she asks why we're not sneaking in, thirty people around us stop and look to see who the hillbillies are.

"Of course we're paying, Isla!" I say, waving her off as though that's a preposterous idea and she's just an imaginative child.

"We didn't pay last time. We ran through that field and climbed over the wall and sneaked in! Remember?" I do my best to ignore her. "How old should I say I am? Five? Four? It's cheaper if I'm four, right?" I kept forgetting to buy a gag for her at the markets. Sometimes it's the difference of forty dollars at an expensive park when you capitalized on the "free under five" clause.

While I home-schooled Oskar and Isla Blue on this trip, there were many lessons that were learned that were never intended. And I couldn't help thinking, *We are really screwing up our kids.*

Oskar and Isla took surfing lessons in Thailand and we rented them surfboards. This also fulfilled the Lying, Cheating, and Stealing component of my curriculum.

"How much for the board?" I inquired of the tanned, shirtless guy lying beside a dozen unused surfboards on the beach.

"Five dollars an hour."

"The guy up the beach said five dollars for the morning."

"What guy?" Oskar asks, his brown, sweaty hair matted to his forehead. "We didn't talk to anyone."

"Yes, we did. Be quiet." I explain to Oskar later that I was bargaining, but really, it's just lying.

Eventually, we had to shamefully admit to the kids that lying is wrong and we shouldn't be doing it. We started paying the proper entrance fees for their actual ages. I'd like to say that we did this because we are remorseful and somewhat moral people, but it just got too hard to pass Isla off as four when, by the end of the trip, she was closer to turning six and a little on the tall side. The nature of travelling for a year constantly put us in a position where we had to balance doing the right thing and modelling good behavior against MacGyvering our money wherever we could so we could afford this trip.

When Rob cashed in his travel points to get us a suite at the Hilton in Bogotá, Colombia, the kids were very excited to be staying at a fancy hotel and not our usual accommodations: sharing a hostel room with a hairy guy from Belgium who snores (a hostel that was booked for the express purpose of capitalizing on the two free "welcome" cocktails served daily at 4:00 p.m.).

"Okay, you can go and wait in that hotel over there," Rob said to me as we were getting out of the cab. Taking a cab was also a treat, as we generally always relied on public transportation.

"Huh?"

"I booked for one adult and two children. It's fifty dollars for an extra adult." I trekked over to the Marriott across the street while Rob and the kids checked in; I would later be let in through a side door, like the help, which is how I felt many days on this trip.

In the blue-lit lobby bar of the Marriott, I ordered the cheapest wine I could find on the drink menu: a thirteen-dollar glass of pinot grigio. Now we are saving thirty-seven dollars on the room, twenty-two dollars if I go ahead and order the oysters. For a few moments, I sipped my pinot and fantasized that I was travelling alone, on a normal trip, maybe to a writers' festival, not on a world trip with my family. I would arrive in my room, turn on CNN, order room service. But when I crossed my legs, one of my flip-flops fell off and I noticed the bottom of my foot was caked in dust and dirt. My eye travelled up my leg. My shins were coated in hair, thanks to a broken razor that I hadn't had time to replace. My thigh was still festooned with scratches after a fall into the space between the bus and the bus platform as we tried to get off the overcrowded vehicle, in the pouring rain, with giant packs and kids in each hand.

Who am I kidding? I can't pull off this fantasy.

I down my wine, pay my bill, and walk back over to the hotel to meet Rob and the kids.

"This room is awesome!"

"You should see the pool!"

"There's free cookies in the lobby!"

I fill the Jacuzzi tub with water. I tear the wrapping off the complimentary razor and pull it down my leg. I feel almost human. But, out of the corner of my eye, I see Oskar loading coffee, whiteners, shampoos, moisturizers, shoehorns, pamphlets, a bible, and pretty much anything else that isn't bolted down into his backpack.

I close my eyes and sink down into the soapy water.

We've taught him well.

LOST IN TRANSLATION

The night we arrived in Bolivia, we found ourselves in an otherwise empty street with the military, fully decked out in black riot gear, wielding batons and plastic shields, charging up the street towards us. They were chanting while their boots hit the cobblestone in unison. The free cocktails that we'd received in other countries was a less harrowing way to welcome visitors.

South America is an extremely worthwhile continent to visit, but nothing about the four countries that we toured was easy. It all starts the second you open your mouth.

When you visit a country and you don't speak the native language, it doesn't matter how articulate you are, how smart you are, how many university degrees you have (almost five between the two of us); you are rendered stupid. You can't give or receive even the most basic information. And having a conversation about the current unstable political climate of a country is entirely out the question.

That first night in Bolivia, we debated whether we should report to our nearest embassy and get the hell out of this crazy country. We cowered in a doorway as the riot squad passed. Protesters were converging from the opposite direction. Eventually, once we made it to our hostel, we learned from the cheerful host that we just need to stay out of everyone's way and take in the passion of one of the most socialist countries in the world. Civil protests are the preferred method of communication and the riot squad is sometimes the government's response. They don't exactly have a 311 number you can call to complain about water security, increased bus prices or a corrupt government so people take to the streets to communicate their displeasure.

I see the appeal of travelling to destinations where they cater to tourists and speak English, and where they don't wear riot gear. I see the advantage of learning some basics of the native language prior to visiting a non-English-speaking country. But we stayed in fifteen countries during our year abroad, and we couldn't learn ten new languages. Time constraints aside, I'm just too old, lazy, and brain-damaged for that. Every time we'd run into French travellers, I'd struggle to conjugate *avoir* and I was reminded how much work I have to do resurrecting a rarely used language for which I supposedly hold a university degree.

We'd already travelled in many countries where English wasn't the native language, and we managed to get by. It felt like we were finally just learning the basic phrases in the Asian countries we were visiting—*please, thank you, bathroom, coffee, beer, do you want to buy our children?*—when it was time to move on.

I loved South America for many reasons, but it was easily the least forgiving as far as language (and landscape) was concerned. We were *gringos*, and we would have to accept our fate and endure many challenges.

In South America, not only did we not speak any Spanish, we also kept finding ourselves in off-the-beaten-track places like the high jungle where no one spoke so much as a lick of English. The most menial task of buying six ingredients at a market so that you can make dinner was exhausting. It eventually came down to pointing at things and handing over my money, hoping for the best.

In one market, apparently I needed to speak cow. A carcass of a whole cow was splayed out on the table, and a guy was sitting beside it, half-asleep, clutching a meat cleaver. I didn't know how to say "steaks" in Spanish (should've looked it up). I didn't even know where exactly to point on that cow to get steaks. Change of menu. I went to the chicken lady one stall over. There were dead chickens suspended from the ceiling; I held up four fingers and pointed to my breasts. The woman handed me four chicken breasts. No Spanish necessary.

I was usually the one to go to the market to get supplies, but I recall Rob going one morning and getting charged five times as much for half the fruits and vegetables I'd bought the previous day. The ability to negotiate and to ask questions is taken away when you don't speak the language. I found this to be mentally and emotionally taxing.

We were heading into the Amazon, which meant we needed to get our yellow fever shots. We'd planned to get the vaccine for free at the airport upon entering Brazil. Some countries greet you with fruit drinks and leis; others, with the riot squad. Brazil says "welcome" with free arm jabs, and we fully planned to capitalize on this because those yellow fever pokes would have cost the four of us $800 back in Canada.

You may recall an oversight in entrance visas—this time not on my part but Rob's—prevented us from being allowed into Brazil. No Copacabana Beach and no yellow fever shots. We had rerouted yet again, this time to Peru.

We arrived in Lima, and while the hostel handed us a free pisco sour and a schedule of the free cooking classes on offer upon arrival, the country wasn't offering free vaccinations. I asked where we could get the shots at the front desk of our hostel and the girl wrote down directions to a hospital ten blocks away.

We walked the ten blocks, the kids complaining the entire time. It wouldn't have been a problem if we were going to waterslides or an amusement park, but going on an urban hike through busy, uneven streets only to be rewarded with painful arm jabs is a tough sell. It also didn't help that we'd taken a free walking tour of the city that morning. The tour was supposed to be ninety minutes but ended up being almost four hours, thanks to a very zealous tour guide and a long line-up for "the best churros in Lima" that was part of the tour. This is no exaggeration and illustrates wonderfully the complete disregard for time they have over in South America. How does an excursion run long by two and half hours? Isla has refused to ever do another walking tour again, and she was none too pleased about the trek to the hospital to get the yellow fever shots. Oskar, forever the opportunist, suggested we get them some candy, thinking that if we stuffed some sugar in her mouth (and his), we wouldn't have to listen to her complain.

We finally found the hospital, but when we tried to enter, the security guard wagged his finger, stopping us. I didn't have the language skills to find out why. And even if I did, this guy was dismissing me for the gringo that I was. I told Rob and the kids to wait and I would try to get in from the other direction. The guard shook his head again. Denied. I put on my hat and sunglasses and tried again. Denied. It was starting to feel like an episode of *Mr. Bean*. I tried to get in when he was talking to someone or wasn't looking. I hid behind a statue and tried to bolt past him, but he shot out his arm. What was this guy's problem? Everyone else seemed to be allowed to come and go as they pleased. But not us.

A woman finally took pity on us and led us to a side entrance where there was no security guard and we were allowed to go in. I tried to ask her what the problem was and she prattled on in Spanish. To this day, I have no idea why we couldn't get through what looked like the front doors of the hospital. Riff-raff policies in place, I suppose.

Past the gates was a maze of buildings and courtyards and

bandaged people wandering around with IVs. I parked Rob and the kids on a bench and began my goose chase amidst this myriad of buildings.

Back at the hostel, I had written down on a piece of paper, in Spanish, *Excuse me, where do we go to get yellow fever shots?* Between my lack of Spanish and asking people who didn't know themselves where to get the vaccinations but who gave directions anyway, I toured every single pathway and corridor of the entire massive complex. Think about how hard it is, sometimes, to navigate your own hospital in your own city when you need an MRI. Doing this in a foreign hospital, which was really more like fifty small buildings plunked together and connected by a random maze of pathways, when you can't read the few signs that do exist, was near impossible.

I was triumphant when I finally found the clinic and slapped down my note. The woman at the desk smiled apologetically.

"Lo siento, sólo hacemos las vacunas contra la fiebre amarilla los lunes, miércoles y viernes," she said. I shrugged my shoulders and mustered my best, sweetest *I-have-no-idea-what-the-hell-you-just-said* look. She went outside and came back a few minutes later with someone in a lab coat.

"The shots occur only on Monday, Wednesday, and Friday, she wants to tell you." Of course, if you are an astute reader following the nuances of this book, you will have guessed that it was Tuesday.

"Vuelva mañana," the nurse says.

"Come back, tomorrow," Lab Coat translates.

The next day, the hostel offers free ceviche cooking classes, which, of course, we opt to take. By now, we capitalize on anything that is free. The cooking lesson is listed as an hour so, of course, it takes three. We have to go to the market to buy all of the supplies, which also includes a tutorial that we cannot understand on how to determine if fish is fresh or not. Isla refuses to ever eat fish again after almost gagging on the soup. I thought it was delicious.

Under even more protest from Isla, we head back to the hospital in the late afternoon. This time, however, it is much quicker. We know which entrance to go in to avoid that annoying security guard, which building to go to, which triage nurse to see. I give her my piece of paper. *We are here for our yellow fever shots.*

"Sólo hacemos las vacunas contra la fiebre amarilla entre neuve de la manana yla una de la tarde. Ya son la dos."

I stare at her blankly. I jab my arm and say, "Fiebre amarilla."

She pulls me over to a sign on the wall. This time Rob is here and I ask him to use his phone to translate. By now, we've managed to get a SIM card and some data, making life much easier. Since we are in a major city, the phone works; we were often in places where there was no phone reception or Google Translation services.

"They only do yellow fever shots between 9:00 a.m. and 1:00 p.m.," he says.

"Are you kidding me?" I sigh. "They could have told me this yesterday!" Between nine and one we were at the fish market with Pablo, massaging groupers to determine if they were fresh or not.

"Well, they probably did and you just didn't understand," he points out.

We head out of the hospital and buy ice cream from a truck that is parked out front. Ice cream, we are finding, can take the edge off of any frustrating predicament.

"How's your day?" the woman behind the front desk of the hostel sings.

"Well, not great. We've spent two days unsuccessfully trying to get yellow fever shots at the hospital."

"Oh, well, why don't you go to the children's clinic around the corner?" she asks. "They do them there." I guess the woman who was behind the desk when we arrived felt it would be a character-building experience to send us to the massive hospital complex instead of the small neighbourhood clinic.

We walk one block up the street, turn the corner, walk another block, and find the clinic. Within ten minutes, we've all had what I'm pretty sure, but can't officially confirm, are our yellow fever shots and it costs only $70 total. I can understand why people might want to pay $800 to get this all sewn up back in Canada.

In light of the experiences we were about to have in the Amazon, the yellow fever effort was worthwhile. But as we travelled through South America, incidents like these due to the language barrier started to pile up.

At some point on the trip, I got the idea that I was an art expert and that I was going to fill our house with art from around the world. We'd sent home boxes and boxes of tiles, ceramic bowls, painted coconut shells, and cheeseboards from Australia, Fiji, Bali, and Thailand. But on top of my limited language skills, I speak "art" about as well as I speak "cow."

We arrived in Manizales, Colombia, after a long bus ride from Ecuador and I discovered that there was an art gallery around the corner from our guesthouse. A painting in the window caught my eye as the cab rolled past. It was of two owls, a red one and a blue one, painted on canvas.

The next morning (after taking advantage of the free salsa dance lessons offered in the basement of the guesthouse—where I crushed Antonio's feet mercilessly), we were on our way to get groceries when we strolled past the gallery. I decided to inquire about the owl painting.

The woman in the gallery didn't speak a word of English. As usual. And after three months of travels in South America, my Spanish had expanded to about fourteen words that did not include the nuances of purchasing art. But I could count to seven and order a bowl of chicken and rice like nobody's business.

The woman was wearing white pants and a white shirt. She could have been an artist or a cleaning lady. No real way of knowing.

The painting had been moved to the back of the gallery.

I'd like to think that the misunderstanding that ensued had

more to do with the language barrier than my complete lack of knowledge about art. Rob will vehemently disagree.

When I acted out, via charades and hand gestures, that I was interested in purchasing the painting and having it packed and shipped to Canada, she nodded enthusiastically. She got on her cell phone and handed it to me. Her son, who spoke English, was on the other end. He would come down to the gallery to translate the deal.

I sat on the steps in the hot sun, waiting for her English-speaking son to arrive while Rob and the kids schlepped off to the grocery store to get what would probably be our ninety-fourth jar of Nutella.

Emilio, a twenty-year-old kid arrived and he translated for his mother. We agreed on a price that wasn't exorbitant, but certainly chewed up our budget for a day or two. She left to have the painting packed.

Emilio, spoke English better than anyone I'd encountered in South America so far—even better than our English-speaking guide at Machu Picchu. (I still had a mild headache from concentrating so hard for three hours and that tour was months ago.)

"Where'd you learn to speak English so well?" I asked.

"Mostly from watching *How I Met Your Mother*," he replied.

"Really?" Maybe I could learn Spanish by watching *Game of Thrones en español*? But then, all I'd really learn is how to dismember people and ask my brother if he wanted to get it on.

His mother was unable to get the painting packed as the post office was closed. We made arrangements for them to drop the piece off at our hostel later that day.

We inquired about buses and they asked us where we were going. We explained that we were heading to a nature reserve just outside the city. They had an exchange in Spanish.

"My mother wants to know if you'd like us to drop you off?" Emilio asked. "We are going in that direction anyway." Art dealer *and* Uber service!

"Oh, wow. Okay. That'd be really nice." The next thing I knew, we were all piling into their SUV.

"Did you get any info about the painting?" Rob asked as we were pushed up against each other in the back seat.

"No, of course not. Language was a bit of a barrier, in case you hadn't noticed. I'm still sweaty from playing charades. But Emilio and I had a lovely chat about his education and the shows *How I Met Your Mother* and *The Big Bang Theory*."

Rob decided to get a little information about the painting from Emilio.

"Did your mother make the painting?" Rob asked. Emilio translated the questions for his mother.

"No," he replied.

"Oh, who painted it?"

"It's, how would you say it, like a digital art or a print."

"Does she represent the artist?"

"She doesn't know the artist. It came from a store."

"What kind of store?"

"Like a homewares store."

"A homewares store?"

"Like Home Depot or something," Emilio says.

Rob turns to me incredulously. "You're shipping a *Home Depot* painting back to Canada?"

"How the hell was I supposed to know?"

"Um, you ask."

"How come it's on display in the art gallery? I like owls..." I mutter.

"My mother was going to paint it, do her own version of it. That's why it was in the gallery."

"See, it's not just me," I bark back at Rob. "The Art Dealer liked it too! I'm going to see if she can send us her original version of the painting. We'll have a painting of a Home Depot painting."

"For the record, I wanted to take the bus to the Eco Reserve," Rob says flatly, removing himself from the conversation.

She said she'd love to do the painting for us. We agreed on a price for the art and shipping, and exchanged contact information.

I was reminded again and again over the course of the year how taxing day-to-day survival could be when you don't speak the language. To try and engage in more complicated transactions that concerned healthcare or culture were beyond challenging. It gave me an acute appreciation for what migrants around the world constantly face—and often not by choice.

We are still waiting for the painting. And I still don't speak Spanish.

BABY TURTLES
& PINK DOLPHINS:

THE ROAD LESS TRAVELLED
DOESN'T ALWAYS LEAD TO
MISADVENTURE AND SCREW-UPS

A lot of this book has been devoted to talking about when things went wrong on our trip because, quite frankly, that's how it felt a lot of the time. We stumbled onto unique and unforgettable experiences—experiences that would make all the challenges and debacles worthwhile.

We simply couldn't map out an entire year of travel. Well, Rob probably could, but not me. I think many people don't do the gap year because a) the planning is too overwhelming, and b) they are not naïve idiots, like us. To avoid being entirely overwhelmed, it helped us to approach this adventure a month, sometimes even a week, at a time.

You wouldn't plan out *every single* day and moment of your life a year in advance when you're at home, right? (Well, some people might, but I suspect that would lead to a very dull, albeit safe existence). So, why would you endeavour to do that when in foreign, often developing countries where you have no idea what kinds of outrageous circumstances are lurking, waiting to take you down and thwart plans you had the gall to make in the first place? Many people ask if we planned out the whole year. We met many long-term travellers who did. We prefer to remain in a state of uninformed chaos. Besides, aren't you setting yourself up for disappointment when things don't go according to plan? If there is no plan, I believe, the delight is much greater when things actually work out! I would also argue the unexpected moments are often the sweetest.

Many of the places we discovered were recommended by other travellers. When you have time, no real agenda, and are open to anything, some very extraordinary experiences present themselves.

Of course, you have to deal with the weird stuff first. For example, Samoa is, in general, a very strange country. They don't really know what to do with tourists. I took a photo of a sun setting across a field one evening and a boy came and asked me for money because his family owned the field on which said sun appeared to be descending. I tried, to no avail, to explain that you can't charge people for taking pictures of landscape. I eventually handed him some money to make him go away, which I suspect was perpetuating the problem.

There were many more instances like this in Samoa. We were travelling to go swimming in a public waterfall and some people had set up a makeshift road barrier, with a toll booth. If we wanted to see those waterfalls, we had to pay them because the road passed by their land. Charging tourists random fees was starting to feel like standard operating procedure.

We visited a tower in a rainforest; it was one of the few government-sponsored attractions and our arrival there seemed to surprise the heck out of the person processing our entrance fee to the tower—the only thing that came close to resembling a national park or a reserve. A chain-smoking guy in civilian clothes, claiming he was employed by the park, accompanied us up the tower. The tower turned out to be a bunch of rickety ladders bungeed together and fastened to a tree whose heavily-leaning stature suggested it was none too pleased about the arrangement. The ladders led to an even ricketier platform in the tree canopy. Climbing this thing was probably not advisable, but up we went anyway.

The cigarette guy was unable to answer a single question about bird species or plants. After we'd been up in the tower for only a few minutes, he told us to wrap it up because he had to get back down. *To what?* I wondered. *Isn't this your job?* There were no other visitors in the park. Getting down was probably wise, as I wasn't sure the structure could even support five people.

When we returned, he required a hefty tip, and to this day I'm still not sure whether he was employed by the park or just some random guy who joined us and then charged us for his company. I suspect the latter. I'd seen begging in almost every country we visited, but the setting up of fake toll booths, impersonating tour guides, and charging for pictures of your field demonstrates economic imagination on the part of the civilians. The people of Samoa feel that the government is capitalizing on tourism and they are not compensating the citizens, so they are getting creative. Kudos to them, I say. In my estimation, based on the one government-sponsored activity we could find, the government is definitely *not* trying to capitalize on tourism. I can't even confidently say that they care either way if people visit their country or not. I respect this flippant attitude, especially after coming from New Zealand, one of the most tourist-driven countries I've ever visited. You couldn't spit in any direction without your gob landing on a foreigner veering all over the road in a camper van they don't know how to drive.

However, for a country with such a bizarre approach to tourism—and maybe because of it—some of the best travel experiences we encountered were in Samoa.

In order to embark on said experiences, we had to rent a car, but it was impossible to buy insurance.

"But what if we hit something?" Rob asked at the car rental. "Or someone hits us?"

"You'll have to pay," explained the towering 6'5" transgender person who was renting us the car.

"But how much?"

"It would depend on what you hit."

"Well, who decides?"

"I look at the damage, tell you how much it will cost to fix, and you pay."

This seemed like a bad idea, but there were no other options so we rented the ten-year-old beater car anyway. (We'd already experienced the local bus system and it wasn't an efficient way to tour the island.) It was a pretty lazy, slow-moving island and we hadn't seen all that many cars, so we figured the odds were with us. We made the person sign off on the dents that were already on the car while they scratched their head, appearing baffled by this procedure. It seemed like they should be generating the paperwork, though, not us.

Car aside, we had some wonderful and unexpected adventures in Samoa. We found the most spectacular swimming hole in the world, To Sua Ocean Trench, a deep, turquoise pool of water enveloped in in lush green vines that drip down into the seawater, drawing butterflies and birds. This place makes every "Best Swimming Hole in the World list," and is featured on the cover of this book. And yet, there is no one there. Go figure!

We arrived at a little resort called Taufau, in Lalomanu Beach, that might be considered "basic" by some people's standards, but it knocked my socks off.

Food was served communally at big tables in a dining fale, so you had no choice but to get to know the people seated next to you. It is a really different approach, compared with the boxy little hotel rooms you find in North America. We befriended a lovely young French couple who were exceedingly tolerant of our miscreant children.

We met another family from Sweden at Taufua—also travelling for a year; they were ten months into their adventure, while we were only two months into our escapade. I think we looked at one another with envy. They were wishing they could turn back time; meanwhile some days I searched and searched for the fast-forward button on my backpack. (At ten months I, too, would want to turn back time.) The kids became instant friends, and so did the adults. We exchanged a plethora of information about life on the road. *You guys get any good infections yet? How do you get streaks out of underwear in a hostel sink when you're out of soap? Did you get charged money by that random guy out front when you tried to throw your can in the garbage?*

After spending a week at Taufua, the beautiful but simple Samoan "resort," we came to know everybody who worked there. There was a guy named Bruce who runs the hospitality and dining fale, and he was one of the warmest, most beloved people we would encounter. We learned from him that a tsunami had destroyed the resort in 2009 and nine people died, including the father and children of the woman who owns the resort, as well as many guests. Isla befriended and played every day with a little girl on the beach who was the only tsunami survivor in her family. Her parents and siblings had been taken by the wave.

And yet, the owner rebuilt. They were so positive and warm and kind; you'd never know the place was destroyed a few years ago. Only as you drive up the coast do you see the tsunami carnage: abandoned houses and desolate resorts everywhere—wreckage from the wave.

Taufua is full of guests who keep returning because you can't help but fall for the spirit and charm of the place. There is a genuine love for people and life that you feel here, a desire to create an authentic experience and connection between locals and guests that seems to be born out of tragedy and an appreciation for life.

we loved it so much that we kept extending our stay. The fales dotted the white sand along the ocean and offered divine views of the sunset as all the kids splashed in the ocean together. We had a week of unexpected bliss.

As we pulled away, clutching a wood carving our hosts had given us as a gift, surrounded by most of the staff and Jon, Oskar's new Swedish friend, I had a lump in my throat and tears in my eyes. I said we'd be back, but I know we live half a world away and it wasn't likely. At least not for a long time.

We were headed to another special place in Fiji that our new Swedish friends had recommended. The Yasawa Island Chain draws tourists and travellers from all over the world. A big yellow catamaran shuttles visitors to various islands along the chain. It would have been good to have known in advance that three of us are not "boat" people before spending five hours, heads between our legs, faces in paper bags, trying, unsuccessfully, not to puke. Scrubbing vomit off sandals was not something I would miss when the trip ended.

We are likely the only travellers who showed up in Fiji with aspirations to camp. After two months of camping in New Zealand, the children and I had no interest in setting up a tent, but Rob could not seem to part with the nylon condo. After New Zealand, largely amid rainstorms, I lobbied hard to cut the tent up into little pieces and use it for our children's craft projects as part of my education program. Rob managed to find a humble little island "resort" that was one of the only places in Fiji that permitted tents. So, of course, we were going there.

After that rough catamaran ride, we arrived at a stunning secluded bay with azure water that lapped onto a white sand beach lined with palm trees. Most people were ferried over to the five-star resort next door, the Blue Lagoon, named after that controversial Brooke Shields film that was shot at a nearby location. But we, and a few other passengers, would be staying at the much more rustic lodge next door, the Oarsman. As we stepped off the boat, a woman handed us fresh fruit cocktails and we were serenaded by a couple of guys with guitars and bellowing voices. It felt a little like a humble person's *Fantasy Island*, without Tattoo and the creepy guy in the white suit. The kids, sucking back their third glasses of the free-flowing watermelon juice, loved the place already.

The woman who ran the Oarsman showed us a grassy spot beside the ocean where we could pitch our tent. Then she threw us a pitying look, one that that would become all too familiar on this trip, as though she just couldn't fathom why we'd show up in Fiji with a tent. There were no other tents or campers to be found anywhere. Unless you watch *Survivor*.

"We're not so busy right now. For ten dollars more, you can have this cabin." She pointed to a simple cabin with an ocean view, just behind us. She pulled out keys and unlocked the door, and Oskar and Isla leaped onto the bunk beds as a way of accepting her offer. While there was something romantic about camping in the South Pacific, the prospect of ditching the air mattress was too appealing.

"You can stay in the tent," I said to Rob as I unpacked. "We'll come visit. Promise."

We stayed on this island for eight days. We were booked in only for a few nights, but we kept extending our stay here as well. The boat arrived every day and new travellers came and left, usually staying only for a night or two before being boated away to another island. Most visitors buy six-day packages and spend two nights each on different islands. The Yasawa Chain is a series of twenty volcanic islands that make up the western part of Fiji. The rustic nature of some of the accommodations and the lack of civilization draw many backpackers, flashpackers (a fancy, flashy version of the traditional backpacker), and tourists who want a more remote holiday. Although, more luxurious resorts are popping up, as these stretches of white beaches situated on clear water, away from civilization, are attractive.

People were quick to point out upon arrival that this was definitely one of the less-fancy lodges to be found along the Yasawa

Chain. I'd guessed as much if they were willing to let us pitch a tent. It was particularly challenging if people came from a luxury place called Octopus Resort, which everyone seemed to rave about. It had drinks with umbrellas delivered by buff, shirtless guys, five-course dinners served along a romantically lit pool, and a kids' club where you could drop your kids off so you could go get loaded and not have to parent your ill-behaved offspring all day. I won't lie: on a year-long trip with kids, that seemed pretty appealing. But the self-righteous mother in me, who surfaces only when I'm jealous of other people's circumstances, questions why you'd go on vacation with your children only to dump them off at a resort day care. What some people pass off as parenting! (And, um, how do I get in on that action?)

We liked the Oarsman, a lot, but maybe because we were not on a two-week, all-inclusive vacation, expecting all the frills. (In fact, on any given day, our expectations were to not die or get injured. So the Oarsman was looking promising.) We planned to sleep in a tent and were given a cabin. We learned that the Oarsman was a community project and the proceeds were used to fund a hospital and school back in their community, a place we would later have the opportunity to visit.

The staff offered to take us to their church on Mother's Day. We're not religious, but it was something to do on a lazy Sunday. Isla was particularly over the moon when she found out we'd get to wear traditional Fijian dresses, as we didn't exactly have modest clothes appropriate for a Sunday service. Oskar was excited we would be going to church in a speedboat. (Fast boats do not make us puke, just the slow ones that bob along with the waves.) Isla and I were sporting traditional Fijian attire head to toe, and we all boated off to church on Mother's Day. (I posted a picture on Facebook and my online friends were quick to point out that floor-length, purple floral-print cotton is not a good look for me. Noted.)

After church, we were taken into the community to see how a

traditional Fijian feast is prepared. A pig was killed. We could hear it. I tried to downplay the pig's death to Isla by saying it was excited it was going to be part of the feast. The pig was put onto a fire, and hot rocks and coals were placed in and around it. We were later served the freshly killed pig for dinner. Delicious. The kids were shown how to weave baskets, while the fittest guy I've ever seen climbed high up a tree to pick coconuts so we could sip on fresh coconut water. It gave us a deeper glimpse into the Fijian culture beyond umbrella drinks and catamaran cruises.

On our second-last day, the woman who ran the Oarsman came to us with a proposition: "Would you like to use our private island for the day tomorrow?" I spit out my coffee. Those were not words I expected to hear in this lifetime.

Rob and I looked at each other suspiciously. *You have a private island? And you want to let us use it? You know our children will burn it down, right? They're like those* Lord of the Flies *kids—except they have parents, but sometimes they behave like they don't.* "We'll talk it over with them and let you know later."

We walked away and pondered this offer. *Maybe they're just sick of us and our urchin children and trying to get rid of us?* The classic "overstaying our welcome" was finally paying off. This was a strategy we should further exploit. *This is too good to be true. We need to clarify that this is actually free and we don't get slapped with a $5,000 bill at the end.*

"We'd love to use your island for the day," I said. "It's free, though? Right?" I felt awkward clarifying, but we were on a tight budget and we couldn't afford expensive misunderstandings. A fair question, as Turtle Island was only a short boat ride away and celebrities paid $14,000 a night to stay there.

"Yes, no cost. Sometimes we rent it out to honeymooners from other resorts, but it is available tomorrow. We will take you there at 10:00 a.m. Okay?"

"Okay..."

Being the hillbillies we are, we saved our scraps from dinner that night and snuck a few extra buns so we would have food on the island the following day. There were no stores at the Oarsman, as all food was provided.

We did not need the scraps. The next morning, they packed us an elaborate picnic lunch of sandwiches, fruit, cakes, juice, and beer, and boated us out to the island. Now we were getting really suspicious. This smacked of trying to fatten us up. They said they would pick us up around dinnertime. Hmmm.

So, we lazed around on our private island in the South Pacific, eating sandwiches, sipping juice and beer, and reading about Harry Potter's latest adventures in the various hammocks that had been suspended among the palm trees. *This can't be our life, this can't be real,* we thought.

The island, with its bleached sand, surrounded by cobalt blue water and colourful fish, was peaceful and divine. And then Rob noticed tiny black blobs emerging from the sand.

For the first time ever, Harry Potter was abandoned. All around us, baby turtles were hatching. They scuttled towards the ocean. Isla and Oskar were so excited, watching, waiting, and escorting as many baby turtles as they possibly could to the water, protecting them from birds and predators. We cautioned the kids not to carry the turtles to the water, but to let the turtles make their first life journey themselves.

I had a barfy Hallmark moment watching them. As these baby turtles, smaller than the palm of your hand, slogged through the hot sand and made it to the water, they'd get swept away by the waves to begin their new life. I was teary watching Isla and Oskar with these turtles, because, like the turtles, I felt that the kids were growing up. We were showing them what was possible and I knew they would be making their way out into the world too. That was part of the reason for doing the trip: to show them what is out there, what is available, what is possible. From a very young age, I wanted them to know that there is more than the small city from which they hail. One day, with mixed feelings, I will watch them float off like these turtles.

Eventually, all the turtles made their way to the ocean and we returned to Harry Potter. At suppertime, the boat picked us up and our magical day came to a close. No blood was shed. Maybe a little by J. K. Rowling. It turns out that the people at the Oarsman were kind folk who appreciated that we spent much of our time in Fiji on their island, and wanted to show their gratitude. Nothing pleases me more than to write about these special people and this special place. I hope they get at least two more bookings out of it.

We did make a two-day pit stop at Octopus Resort because we kept hearing over and over again from other travellers how it was not to be missed. We laboured over the decision to go there because the fee for one night was our budget for four days. But we might never be in Fiji again, so we booked a few nights. It was posh and fancy and, most importantly, had the kids' club. Ironically, our kids were bored after about an hour and signed themselves out. So long "parent time" back at the cabana. They were there long enough, we think, to pick up the nastiest case of head lice we've ever seen.

It turns out that the humble Oarsman, and our day on their private island, was, in fact, the *real* experience not to be missed.

In Bolivia, we visited another community-run destination: Chalalan Ecolodge, in Madidi National Park in the heart of the Bolivian Amazon. It was recommended by our good friends who lived in Bolivia for four years. The trip there involved a dizzying plane ride over the Andes and into the Amazon basin, followed by a five-hour boat journey up the Beni and Tuichi rivers. We stopped for a picnic lunch on shore where our guide pointed out jaguar tracks, but thankfully no jaguars. We did see a number of capybara, the world's largest rodent—roughly the size of a pig—along the shores. Worth Googling. (A few of them escaped the Toronto Zoo and managed to survive for a month on the lam before being located and returned.)

At the Chalalan Ecolodge, deep in the jungle, we hiked and saw troupes of rare monkeys and toucans, to which the kids exclaimed, "That's the Fruit Loops bird!" The biggest treat, however, was when our guide learned how much Oskar loved fishing. He took us out in a boat, where Oskar caught three deadly piranhas that the chef at the lodge whipped into a delicious dinner.

It was here that we were introduced to the Competitive Traveller in the form of a snotty English couple who had a checklist of wildlife and birds they needed to see. At the end of the day, we'd swap notes with these obsessive people about who had seen what out in the jungle. *Had we seen this blah, blah, blah rare monkey? No, but we'd broken up sixty-seven brawls between our kids in the jungle, you childless asshats.* The next day, they made the rookie mistake of losing the lens cap of their $6,000 camera out on a hike. We found it. I really wanted to see them sweat out the prospect of not getting good pictures due to a smudged or scratched lens. Remember, if you didn't get a photo, it didn't happen. In the end, we returned the lens cover because we are good, moral people.

It became a full-on war with them that we'd never win. How the hell would we ever see the monkeys with Isla screeching that she could not walk anymore because her underwear kept getting stuck in her sweaty bum? Never one to back down, I tried to compete with them anyway—mostly because she had perfect blonde hair and a blow dryer. I pretty much hated anyone with a blow dryer by this point on the trip. I started lying about what we'd seen, making up animals and birds. *That purple bird with the giant head and the yellow horns sure was a sight to behold. Only three of them left in the world.*

These kinds of travellers can actually be found *all over* the world. They are to be avoided at all costs. They mainly exist to make you feel bad about your disorganized travelling shit show, to check clichéd things off their travel bucket list, and to expand their roster of Instagram followers with innovative hashtags like #blessed, #dreamlife, and #nofilter. Meanwhile, we use tags like #sendhelp and #haveyouseenourdaughter?

As it was such an arduous journey to get to the Amazon, we decided to extend our stay and take a boat ride down into the Pampas, part of the Amazon's basin. Thankfully, these peaceful river boats didn't seem to make any of us sick, although they did bore the younger ones a little.

The shores were packed with birds and wildlife—it felt like we were in a Disney movie, or maybe a dumping ground for all the illegal exotic pets that are confiscated at airports around the world. A monkey jumped aboard our boat and hung around for a while, acting suspiciously like Marcel, the monkey from *Friends*. We started counting the different species of birds along the shore and we got to about seventy in only a few hours. There were also lots of caiman and capybaras lounging along the river.

A major highlight, especially for Isla Blue, was the pods of pink river dolphins that swam alongside the boat. Our guide told us there was something in their diet that made their skin turn pink, just like when we eat beets it makes our ... never mind. When I came home and researched this fact, I learned that their smooth skin turns anywhere from a milky to a vibrant pink because as the dolphins grow to adults, their skin becomes more translucent and their blood vessels show through their skin. Sometimes when my kids ask a question and I don't know the answer, I just make it up. I'm pretty sure tour guides are not supposed to do this.

On our second day, our guide took us swimming in the river. Within a few minutes, the curious, playful pink dolphins joined us. I was swimming with Isla and my first encounter was when one probed me in the butt with its pointy nose—the most action I'd had in a while.

The dolphins bumped and rolled up against us. One dolphin was particularly enamoured with Isla, perhaps because she was so small and it thought she was one of them; she actually was roughly the size of a dolphin. It lay across her feet as she stood in the river and let her wrap her arms around its slippery pink body to give it a big dolphin hug. This was actually the second time a wild dolphin joined us to swim. And a penguin cruised up to examine us when we were in the Galápagos Islands. These kinds of wildlife experiences were becoming almost superfluous.

While we were playing with the dolphins, Oskar nervously pointed out the caiman watching us from the shore, lips pulled back, teeth gleaming. They look like crocodiles, but they lack the angry and hungry temperament. Our guide assured us that they rarely attack humans. *Rarely*. It wasn't the best assurance I'd ever heard.

It was so hot that we let the kids run around drinking endless amounts of Fanta as we watched the sunset. I woke up at 5:00 a.m. to see one of the most glorious sunrises of my life. A massive, steaming red ball emerged on the horizon, bathing the foggy grasses and trees in crimson. We were so close to the equator and the power of the sun was palpable, especially when compared with the frozen white world we hailed from.

Our Pampas experience was dampened when we learned that the reason the area was so rife with wildlife was because the animals' normally vast natural habitat was being destroyed due to the creation of sugar cane fields. The animals were being forced into a small strip of land only a few kilometres wide on either side of the river. Sadly, a natural zoo had been created.

While the animals in the Pampas were being robbed of their habitat, the Galápagos was a protected wonderland for wildlife where humans could catch a rare, close glimpse of unusual animals, unthreatened, in their natural environment.

One of the dangers of a trip like ours is that you almost become immune to the wonder. This isn't necessarily a bad thing, but while we saw many kids excitedly squealing over iguanas and penguins and trying to upload selfies with giant tortoises in the background, my kids were a bit blasé. They weren't being spoiled with material things; they were being spoiled with experiences. By the end of our trip, we'd had so many unique wildlife encounters that it was actually getting hard to impress the kids.

Look, a purple-spotted, fire-breathing dragon!

Didn't we see one of those in Asia?

In the Galápagos Islands, we saw blue-footed boobies padding around (a wildlife experience on my personal bucket list), land and sea iguanas stacked onto one another like dominoes, and sea lions lazing about. We were constantly stepping around these creatures on paths, as they rightfully possessed the attitude that they were here first. We took a snorkelling tour and swam alongside rays, sharks, sea horses, and a sea turtle that loomed larger than Oskar.

All these experiences, individually, would have been trips of a lifetime. But when you are travelling for a year and you are so close to all these amazing locations, it's hard to pass any of them up. We often agonized about whether we could afford to go to places like the Amazon or the Galápagos, but it always came down to *When are we ever going to be here again? I will not buy new shoes for two years.* Even as I write about this a year later, I feel like these moments were pure magic. I think we spend a lot of time writing about when things go wrong because it makes for more interesting reading. But when I reflect on the journey today, these once-in-a-lifetime moments are the pillars of my memories for that year abroad.

YOU, ME & MY DEPRESSION MAKES THREE

Is she okay?" the waiter asks, gesturing at me. My head is cradled in my hands while tears stream into my salad.

"She doesn't like the kale," Rob says.

"Pardon?"

"Just kidding, she'll be all right. Not the food or anything. But she could probably use another glass of malbec," he says, sliding my empty glass towards him.

"I'm sorry, I don't know what's wrong. I can't tell you why I'm crying. I just feel so … sad." We'd returned home from our world trip and in the months that followed, I fell into a deep sadness and I couldn't see a way out.

I could distract myself and hold it together well enough during the week, but by the time Friday nights rolled around, when Rob and I would sometimes head out for dinner, I could no longer contain my gloom and I'd turn into a sobbing mess. "The Friday Night Cry," Rob dubbed it.

Perhaps I'd have understood it better if I'd ever suffered from depression before, but this was new to me. It sucked.

We'd just come off of the adventure of a lifetime and had experiences that I never could have dreamed possible. I should have felt jubilant, grateful, and fulfilled, but I felt down, empty, and lonely. I normally like people. A lot. It's Rob who would prefer to remain locked in the dark basement, eating Cheetos, and watching *Star Trek* reruns. All of a sudden, I felt awkward around people and started avoiding conversations unless absolutely necessary. Interactions made me anxious.

I had this overwhelming feeling that I didn't fit in anywhere anymore. I felt like I couldn't find the door to get back inside my life. I was on the outside, looking in. I had trouble sleeping and some nights I wouldn't sleep at all. I used to haul back a rib-eye steak the size of a small board game, but now I could barely get a side salad down. Suddenly, I wasn't hungry.

It would take me many months to understand that the root of my depression seemed to be the incongruence between what we'd experienced and how we'd lived for the past year with reintegrating into the routine of everyday life back home. The things we had experienced brought new insights and values that were clashing with old ones. I was trying to slip seamlessly back into my old life and finding that it doesn't quite work like that.

For the past ten months, we had been making decisions daily about transportation, food, activities, destination, and budget. We would finally make a decision about one aspect of our day, only to be immediately slammed with another, and they were often big questions and decisions: *Should we blow the budget and take a forty-five-minute plane ride into the Amazon, or stick to the budget and take the eighteen-hour-winding-kids-puking-everywhere bus ride? Campsite is closed. Where are we sleeping? Is there a liquor store within walking distance?*

We lived in a perpetual state of mental exhaustion from constantly being barraged with choices.

For example, when we ventured into the Pampas, the low-lying area in the Amazon basin, we'd done our research and decided not to take malaria pills. Our reading said it wasn't necessary. Rob is very German and very meticulous in both his research and his not wanting to contract malaria. Malaria is on his "Ten Worst Things That Could Happen in Life" list. I'd travelled to malaria-riddled countries in Africa twice, and while I obviously wouldn't *choose* to get the disease, I'd consider a strike by the malbec grape growers in Argentina to be equally alarming and near the top of my disaster list. (Also alarming would be getting chased down the street by a man wearing a panda costume or a five-foot-long reptile right outside our tent. Wait, that all happened.)

Even when you make educated and calculated decisions, you're second-guessing them half the time. Thankfully, we did not get malaria in the Pampas, or anywhere, for that matter, though the decision to not take the pills was only one of the huge number of taxing choices that concerned our safety, health, or finances that we constantly faced. When combined with the physical stress of carrying everything we needed on our backs, and the schlepping of often sleep-deprived, hungry kids to fifteen different countries, it was often a grueling existence. But at the end of the day, when we'd finally arrive at our destination and the kids were in bed, Rob and I would sit on our balcony overlooking the ocean, or in the rooftop lounge of yet another hostel amid drunk twenty-somethings who were making out, and we'd crack a beer, clank bottles, and congratulate ourselves that we'd made it through another day. We became accustomed, maybe even a little addicted, to existing in a permanent state of major decision-making. It was exhausting. But it was also exciting.

Coming home felt pretty dull. *What kind of sandwiches should I make for the kids' lunches? Liverwurst? Ham? Shall I sign up for the 4:30 or 5:30 fitness class? Ooh, ooh, where should I fill up the car with gas?* I kept hoping to see one of those lice letters in the kids' backpacks; I could take those suckers down like nobody's business. That would liven things up around here a little.

Life became a lot easier, but I think being in that heightened mental state of decision-making, then to coming home and not having to make any meaningful decisions for weeks at a time, contributed to my depression. This was the first and most immediate transition that I had to make upon returning home. My weekly sobbing into a salad bowl clearly meant it was not going well.

By Friday night, I realized that nothing during the week had challenged me either physically or mentally. The first-aid procedures we had to administer in a week alone on our trip were incredible. Now, no one so much as cut their finger, let alone fell off a bus platform (me, in Peru), got nipped by angry dogs that may or may not have had rabies (Isla, in Colombia), had a wet, disease-ridden monkey jump on his back (Rob, in Bali), or stabbed himself with a rusty nail (Oskar, everywhere we went). I think Rob was experiencing some serious first-aid-kit withdrawal. He kept trying to apply iodine if anyone had so much as a hangnail.

The second major source of my saddened mental state was that the trip broadened my awareness. My values and how I looked at the world were different now.

For one thing, I realized how little we actually need. Carrying your life around on your back for ten months is a humbling experience. Suddenly, you're shopping for shampoo in some mini-mart in Penang and all you give a shit about is finding the smallest bottle possible, with the least amount of packaging. The lip glosses and eyebrow tweezers I packed were jettisoned after the first day. Entrance visas and malaria meds would take precedence. Not all of us learned this lesson, unfortunately; my daughter still managed to carry around 14 stuffies. When they became too cumbersome for her to carry, after only a week, while I was somehow already down to two pairs of underwear, Mr. Wrinkles and Boobs, the beanie boos, took up residence in my backpack where the waterproof mascara should have been. Meanwhile, Oskar honed his hoarding skills. I was always equally nervous and amazed at what might emerge from his backpack at airport security.

While the children didn't necessarily embrace the lessons of minimalism, even they realized that we had to carry all our possessions. For the better part of a year, I was constantly evaluating how to get rid of things, how to lighten the load, not replacing items as they ran out. My sanity and my spine depended on it.

When the kids' birthdays arrived, we scoured the markets for things that were small or, ideally, consumable. Oskar's love for explosives was probably triggered when we got him a collection of fireworks. He set off Roman Candles on the beach and we wouldn't have to carry them around after they'd been lit. *Brilliant! Explosives it is.* Isla likes stuffies. *Think she'd settle for these edible finger puppets? Better yet, let's give her those packs of Oreos they were handing out on the plane while she was sleeping and say that they're edible finger puppets.* In the markets of Asia, the kids did occasionally buy themselves LEGO knock-offs and other toys that seemed cool. They soon realized the toys were usually missing parts or didn't come remotely close to meeting the promises made on the packaging.

For my birthday, I was granted a day of tastings at wineries in the Marlborough area of New Zealand where we were camping. A day of boozing! A consumable and experiential gift. *How lovely; I'm in!* When the winery staff pouring the tastings found out I was travelling with my family for an entire year, and that I was given one day away from my children *and* it was my birthday, they waived the tasting fees and the wine flowed even more freely. "Tasting Rooms" became "Getting Sloshed Rooms" which became "Get-that-Canadian-woman-out-of-here" rooms. My family showed up to find me completely blitzed, feeding cheese cubes to a goat in the garden out back at one of the wineries.

Over the course of the year, we had a lot of *experiences* that made me more happy than material things ever could. I don't just mean jetting into the Amazon to swim with pink dolphins or boating through caves lit up by glow-worms in New Zealand. Those moments were incredible, but there were long stretches of time that, apart from the fact that we were halfway around the world, were not at all exciting: riding out a rainstorm by reading in our tent, or playing cards to kill off the hours of a never-ending bus ride. Those were some of the best moments on the trip. We bought very little—only essentials. We had to constantly tell our children "no" when they wanted things (often stupid things, like inflatable ocean toys) because we couldn't transport it, or couldn't afford it. Experience became the new currency of our happiness. We were a team and we relied on one another, and J.K. Rowling, to get through tough days. We always experienced the ups and downs together.

When we came home, we were back in a world of constantly acquiring things. Happiness seemed connected to buying stuff. Before I left, mine did too. A pair of Fly boots, a new laptop, or even a fresh lip gloss always made a dull week a little better. But buying things didn't make me feel happy anymore. I hated even going into stores. They made me depressed because they were filled with all sorts of things that I didn't need or want. I was an experience addict. And even when the urge to purchase started to creep back, I was on a pretty strict budget for two reasons: 1) we'd just come off this expensive trip, and 2) I knew already that I wanted to do something like this again.

But our trip was over, and while I relished the memories, I was back in our old life, suffering a voracious, insatiable thirst for experiences. This all contributed to my depression.

I, of course, came to realize that you do not need to jet off to exotic places to have experiences. In fact, the best ones can happen in your own backyard; screening an outdoor movie, or attempting a new hike, or hitting up the wine sale at the local liquor store. Perhaps one of the greatest gifts of this trip was that it jolted us out of our ordinary schedule. Sometimes it's easier to stick to your old routines, but the world trip reminded us to test new trails, hit more local music festivals, and just do more. Since coming home, we started growing our own food and running a weekly farmer's market. It took me a little while to figure this out.

Yet another problem was creating a vortex of sadness for me. Through our travels, I started to realize that you don't necessarily have to live a conventional life. Before we left on the trip, it seemed like such a radical thing we were doing; packing up and renting out our house, selling off our car and many of our belongings—it all seemed a little crazy. And many people told me as much.

But when we were on the road, we'd met all sorts of people leading intriguing lives. Software developers working from camper vans, teachers working in international schools, people who've sold off all their possessions to travel indefinitely, seniors rewarding themselves with a life of adventure after working for thirty years, and young people travelling the world before embarking on their careers.

We met a married couple in Fiji who were originally from California. Jim (whose name I've changed, or perhaps can't remember) worked in advertising and he'd run Arnold Schwarzenegger's ad campaign for governor, but he and his wife got sick of the rat race in Los Angeles. So they sold their house and all their belongings. And now, they were professional house-sitters. They travel the world, taking care of people's properties. When we met them, they were scrambling to secure their next house-sitting gig; it was a different kind of rat race.

In Colombia, we met a couple from Canada who worked from the road—they'd been driving through South America, living out of a camper van for the better part of three years. There is a whole network of people just like them. I caught a glimpse of other, less conventional ways to live and I was very drawn to it.

The biggest trigger of my depression was that when we came home, we weren't a tight family unit any more, sharing our days and experiences together. Everyone was off doing their own thing, and that bond we had created was loosening a little. We were becoming a normal family again and I missed the closeness. In Thailand, Rob and I didn't necessarily want to throw out our backs jumping across giant red rubber balls, getting whacked in the head by foam rods, and pitched, upside down, into a lake on a wipeout course. The kids didn't necessarily want to spend two days hiking up hills in New Zealand. But, for that year, we all compromised, shared, and participated in one another's passions. We could get through anything and everything together. Now, the kids were off at school for most of the day, and then we'd be jetting them off to swimming lessons, birthday parties, or play dates. I missed the endless stretches of time that we had spent together.

I also realized I was harbouring a lot of guilt. We'd visited fifteen countries, eleven of which I'd consider "developing." One thing that will stick with me for a long time is how hard people have to work just to scrape by. We saw people selling everything from plastic bags filled with soda pop to mismatched pairs of used runners. In Colombia, when the bus stopped for a bathroom break, a guy hopped on and gave the most heartfelt pitch for the toothbrushes he was peddling. There always seems to be someone hustling hard to sell something, and it's not just to make a bigger buck, but to survive. I should have bought a toothbrush.

At the start of the trip, I used to love bargaining and getting a good deal. That's what we do when we go to Mexico on vacation, right? Get souvenirs as cheaply as possible. But after months of seeing people work so hard to just barely survive, and sometimes getting a glimpse of where they live, bargaining lost its appeal. Fifty cents is nothing to me, but it's a lot to someone who lives in a country where the daily wage is eight dollars. In whittling down prices, I started to feel like I was screwing with people's livelihoods. I appreciate where I was born. Not only do I not have to struggle relentlessly every day just to survive, but also I get to do what I love, and, occasionally, I even get paid for it (assuming you purchased this book and weren't a cheapskate who borrowed it from your pal!). This feels a bit superfluous in a world where people walk around for fourteen hours a day selling cups of chopped mango. I am very, very lucky, and I still can't even cut a mango properly. Coming back home made me realize all this. Our lives are downright luxurious. We live in a society that teaches us to constantly want more, rather than appreciate and celebrate what we have. I struggled with this and still do.

A few months after coming home, Oskar started crying when he saw a guy pushing a shopping cart with all his belongings past our house in Osborne Village. We'd seen much more dire scenarios on our travels and, living in the Village, he'd seen this his whole life. I asked him why he was so bothered when we'd also seen this so many times before we left on the trip. Oskar said he didn't think the world was fair. Why do we have so much when there are people with so little, pushing shopping carts down the street, rummaging through garbage? It was a moment of realization for him about how much we have and how lucky we are. With this, I knew that I was not the only one looking at life differently and experiencing the post-trip blues.

The waiter sets down my glass of malbec. I wipe my eyes. It's going to be okay. I'm caught between two worlds, between home and away. I'm caught between values. Initially, my response was to start planning another trip, but I knew that wouldn't solve the problem. I had to find a way to reconcile the old with the new.

We'd been given this rare gift to step outside the box. Once you do, you start to realize how much is out there, and how it's possible to live life many different ways. Your heart and soul start to fill up and expand with new understanding, and suddenly you look at life a little differently, but the problem is that you don't quite fit back in the way you did before. That's what growing, as a person, is all about. I guess it's supposed to hurt a little.

YOU CAN DRINK
THE WATER AT DISNEY

We'd been back from our world trip for about a year. It was spring break and we were en route to a ski resort in Montana. The car was jam-packed with downhill skis, boots, warm clothing, and, of course, my slow cooker. One should never travel without a Crock-Pot. You never know when the opportunity to roast a chicken might present itself. We'd been relegated to returning to more typical family holidays that fit our work and school schedules (even though I was already secretly plotting another world trip that would involve us, a camper van, and the entire coastlines of North, Central, and South America—and maybe even my slow cooker).

As we drove through the valleys of Theodore Roosevelt National Park in North Dakota, Isla announced she had to go to the bathroom, so we pulled into a rest area. I was taking in the burnt-orange striations of Painted Canyon from the viewing platform when Isla asked for the toilet paper. I looked at her quizzically for a moment before I realized that most of the places we'd visited on our year abroad in her young life had required her to bring toilet paper with her to the bathrooms.

The following spring break, we were contemplating a Disney vacation. Had we learned nothing from our world trip? We could tour eleven countries for the same price tag as a week at Disney. Disney is pretty much the antithesis of everything I value. It lacks authentic learning opportunities, culture, and art. (My general travel rule is to visit only places where you can get good art. Although, just because I desire good art does not mean I have the ability to recognize it. Still waiting for that Home Depot painting.) Yet here we were, entertaining this Disney madness. The debate of whether to take our kids to Disney could be the subject of an entire other book. Ultimately, though, Rob and I had both gone as children and loved it and thus decided to book a trip. (Wait, does that mean that since I got lickings as a kid I should be doling those out too?) I do believe that the experience was at least tempered, and possibly ruined, by our year abroad.

As we were booking FastPasses, creating itineraries, and watching our money get sucked down a Magic Kingdom vortex before we'd even set foot on the premises, Isla asked if we needed shots. Nope, no Japanese encephalitis or rabies at Disney, according to the guidebook. As we checked into our Princess room (oh yes, we drank the "upgrade-your-room" Disney Kool-Aid), Oskar asked, in earnest, if the tap water was safe to drink.

Why are my kids so weird? I wondered, but our travels had taught them not to take basic things for granted. We had to remind them now that there were places you could visit that offered clean drinking water and didn't require vaccinations. There were places you could visit where the bus that was supposed to take you from your hotel to the front gates of a theme park wasn't going to lose its engine in the middle of a busy highway. And we were going to those places! While these cushy holidays consisted of ski gear,

Space Mountain, and my Crockpot, the focus of our world trip had often been the basics: safety, food, health, education, and just generally staying alive.

Disney has an underground tunnel system, they call it, so that your magical experience will not be interrupted by the sight of trash being removed or food being delivered. Garbage is vacuumed, at a hundred kilometres an hour, from bins into an underground compactor every fifteen minutes. You will not see food being trucked in or prepared because this is all done secretly underground. Disney doesn't want you to think about where your food comes from as it magically appears in front of you. In fact, Disney is so curated that the reason the elaborate tunnel system was created in the first place was because founder Walt was once bothered by the sight of a cowboy walking through the futuristic Tomorrowland in order to get to the Western-themed Frontierland. Egads! The illusion had been broken. (And here we'd figured out a route to circumvent the often-present riot police in La Paz, or how to bail out our own boat in Samoa lest we not make it to shore.) A misplaced cowboy or the sight of garbage being emptied wouldn't have registered with us.

While every part of me wants to rail against Disney and everything it stands for, it was nice that my children could experience this dreamy world. At the same time, I also want them to understand that this is a destination for the seriously privileged. Disney had created elaborate tunnel systems because they didn't want you to ever have to think about the basics of life; by contrast, our world trip taught us never to take those things for granted. In many countries we visited, we saw people working hard, even fighting for things we don't think twice about.

On our extended travels, the kids took a genuine interest in where food came from, because they saw it come from so many different places. In Asia, they would tear around busy markets looking for fruits they'd never heard of—like the stinky durian that smelled so rank it was banned on subways in Singapore. Dinner in Peru would be whatever part of the heifer the Spanish-speaking butcher hacked off for us to be cooked up back in the kitchen of our hostel. In New Zealand, we'd buy fresh feijoas by putting our money into honour-system boxes at unmanned stalls along the winding roads. We stayed at a B&B where the farmer took the kids out in a wagon pulled by his tractor to the orchards to pick apples. Five-year-old Isla commented that the apples didn't have stickers. Oskar and Isla were so smitten with the markets they'd seen all over the world that they started growing their own food and selling it at a makeshift stand at the end of our walkway, the way that kids would sell lemonade. They still run their Sunday markets. We've always had a family farm in Dugald, Manitoba, but it took travelling the world to ignite a genuine interest in that farm and growing food.

The restaurant experience, we learned, is different all over the world. We were staying in the high jungle in Bolivia when it happened to be Oskar's birthday. For his celebration dinner, all the boy wanted was a burger, but he was disappointed to see that burgers were not listed on the menu. We ate local food that was often foreign to us. Sometimes we didn't know what we were eating—guinea pig, on one occasion, I learned after the fact. So Oskar was craving a little bit of home. When the server found out it was Oskar's birthday and conveyed this to the chef, he insisted on making this Canadian boy a hamburger for his special day. The chef schlepped off to the market, bought some fresh steak, and ground it into chuck. They didn't have proper burger buns, but they improvised with two slabs of freshly baked bread. It took a while, but the chef presented Oskar with a hamburger. It wasn't a typical North American burger, but it still stands as the best one he's ever eaten because he knew the story behind it and the effort that was taken to make it.

Our family still talks about Stars Bar in Gili Air, Indonesia. It was the kind of place where you can send your kids over to the bar to purchase a beer for you while you waited for your dinner—and we definitely capitalized on this lax liquor law. We'd spent the day snorkelling, and by the time we arrived at the restaurant we were all famished. We waited an hour and a half for our food, even though there were only a handful of people in the restaurant. The kitchen doors flung open about every half an hour, a waiter emerging with a tray of food that wasn't ours. A couple of cats frolicked around on the counter where the cook was preparing meals. Finally, the doors swung open and our food came out. We watched the waiter pick fries from our plates and toss them into his mouth as he brought our dinners over. The lemon crepe contained bananas. Later, when he collected our plates to take them back to the kitchen, he picked at the scraps of uneaten food. Registering a complaint about the many infractions didn't enter our minds. We got our food. And we didn't get sick. We'd chalk that up as a good day.

In Asia, we gnawed on skewers of unidentifiable meat and drank smoothies served out of plastic bags, all prepared right in front of us on the street. Food and where it came from was an integral part of the journey— and it always varied; it wasn't always good, but it was always a pivotal part of the adventure. While the Disney approach is to shroud the origin of food and magically serve it up in swanky places like the *Beauty-and-the-Beast*-themed Be Our Guest restaurant, the origin of food was one of life's basics that we unexpectedly came to cherish on our long-term travels.

One of the nice aspects of short vacations is that it is a break from work, school, and life. The focus is rides, ski slopes, and water parks. Long-term travel must incorporate daily-life activities like cooking, work, and school into an often rigorous travel schedule. I understand completely why the Western world has structured society in such a way that vacations function as a break from life. Only after returning home can I see how incorporating daily life with travel, while rewarding, is a mammoth undertaking. I can appreciate the efforts that Disney goes to—providing meal plans, transportation, and entertainment—so that you won't have to think about the basics.

One of the questions I get asked the most about our trip is how we managed to educate the kids when we pulled them out of school for a year. A thought constantly loomed in my head that I was somehow messing them up. That they would return home not only maimed by those feral dogs that had chased us down that hiking trail in Colombia, but that they would be dumb and behind in school to boot!

At the beginning of our trip, I was pretty rigid about spending a few hours each morning doing schoolwork. I picked up books back in Canada so we could work through subjects such as spelling, reading, writing, and math.

At first, the kids were keen on our school sessions because they realized that an entire day of school back home could be packed into just a few hours every morning. I'd volunteered in their classrooms, and sometimes by the time they finished singing "Oh Canada," discussed the date and weather in French, and announced birthdays, it was practically time for recess.

As we pressed on with our adventure, the school hours became harder to enforce. I would fret when we'd miss several school days because we were on the move. Attempting spelling on a boat rolling on the rough South Seas was a recipe for puking. When I did carve out school time, Oskar and Isla weren't always interested—especially if there was a kangaroo or an unsupervised surfboard nearby. I'd get one of them on task, and the other would be off chasing frogs. Poisonous ones, in the case of Australia.

Classrooms often took the shape of a breakfast nook in a hostel, a picnic table at a campground, a desk in a public library, or a counter in a local bar. Over the course of the year, the learning shifted. It became apparent that it was happening organically—usually when I wasn't running a classroom or even looking. Isla hated when I pulled out her reader. One of my bigger anxieties was that she was going to return to Grade One not knowing how to read. But while she refused to read on demand for me, I found her sounding out the words on a placard in a park one rainy afternoon. She was, in fact, figuring out how to read. She sounded out the words because she wanted to know what the sign said about the colourful butterfly that was pictured. She could give a shit about finding out what the kid in her reader was up to. Especially when all the things he was doing rhymed: *spoon, lagoon, moon.*

Oskar, Isla Blue, and I were seated at the long breakfast table in our hostel in Cusco, Peru, battling altitude sickness and trying to squeeze in a little schoolwork. Isla kept running off to capitalize on the free drinks as Oskar and I worked through his math problems. A curious traveller sat down next to us with his cup of coca leaf tea and inquired why two kids were doing homework in a hostel in Peru. I explained how I was road-schooling the children through our world trip, but today's math lesson was a little underwhelming. In fact, math in general is underwhelming for me. The young man introduced himself as Gerhardt, a math professor from Berlin, and asked if he could try a few math activities with Oskar. I was on my feet to get some of that free coca leaf tea and test the hammocks out back before he even finished his sentence. This passionate math professor had a captive audience for the next forty-five minutes, playing games that taught Oskar about the power of prime numbers.

Even though I had packed Canadian curriculum workbooks that covered the core subjects, Oskar was honing his writing skills more by posting restaurant and hostel reviews on interactive sites like Zomato and Trip Advisor where other travellers could "like" destinations, post comments, and ask questions. Here are a few of Oskar's Zomato restaurant reviews:

Gelato Secrets, Ubud, Bali

The ice cream was flavourful and fresh. I had mango sorbetto in a homemade waffle cone. The waffle cones were crispy and homemade. There was a wide selection of flavours such as lemongrass sorbetto, local Bali dark chocolate with sea salt, salted caramel, and Oreo. The atmosphere was open air with wooden chairs, seating right by the main temple in busy downtown Ubud.

Devilicious, Ubud

Devilicious in western Ubud, with its fun style serves both western and Indonesian classics. I had a pizza with fresh, sweet pineapple and a mixed fruit juice. The fruit juice lacked flavour and sweetness, but the pizza was excellent because the crust was handmade and the ingredients were fresh. The service was attentive but the food was a bit slow.

Oskar naturally learned the capital cities of countries we flew into, like Fiji and Samoa. Ironically, once we got home, he would fail a test on naming Canada's ten provinces! The trip also allowed him to discover his passion for navigation. Rarely do we take city buses in Winnipeg, but use of public transportation on the trip opened up the world of mapping and routing for Oskar. He could often be found scanning the subway map in a large city like Kuala Lumpur, formulating the fastest route to a museum or market. Upon returning home, Rob ordered the subway maps of major cities we visited to decorate the walls of his room.

Oskar also exhibited a keen interest in the expense tracker app that Rob used to keep us within our very stringent budget. We loaded the app onto Oskar's iPad and started handing him the receipts. One afternoon in Auckland, I was savouring an expensive but much-needed latte after a particularly arduous day of driving when Oskar asked me to hand over the coffee receipt. After I reluctantly coughed it up, he pointed out that he could not find my eight-dollar latte anywhere in the $150/day budget. (I whispered to Rob to please remove that app from his iPad before he discovered the bottle of cheap malbec I'd slipped onto the grocery bill.) These kinds of learning opportunities transpired spontaneously while we were on the road.

We could never get our hands on enough books. That was always the joy of arriving at a hostel with a library: we could swap out our novels and comics. I was such a literary snob at the outset of the trip, but now, in a pinch, I'd blast through a Danielle Steele novel if that was what was on offer on the shelf. Reading filled many hours on beaches and buses. The kids also kept journals that covered their trip highlights.

Physical education took care of itself in the form of swimming, snorkelling, hiking, and surfing lessons. There were some unusual experiences along the way, such as adventure parks, a wipeout course, a bike excursion on the Galápagos Islands that required the careful dodging of enormous tortoises, and an afternoon at trapeze school on an island in Thailand. We did a number of challenging overnight and backcountry hikes in New Zealand. Isla also spent some of her ice cream money from her grandparents to go parasailing over Lima, Peru. (Does that even count as physical activity?)

By the end of the trip, I wasn't doing a whole lot of formal schooling anymore. A few days a week we'd sit down for some math, spelling, or journal writing, but it largely happened organically and authentically. When we returned home, I was happy to learn that the kids were not at all behind in school. In fact, they were a little ahead. Socially and behaviourally, well, that's probably another story.

That first summer back, about six months after we'd returned to our normal life, we sat on the deck, swarmed by bloodthirsty mosquitoes. We were grateful to be home, but we still talked a lot about our adventure and found ourselves starting sentences with, "Remember that time when…" The sentence would be finished with a memory of Isla falling into a sewer, or Oskar being flipped out of the side of a poorly constructed waterslide onto the pavement, or how the kids watched R-rated movies on buses while Rob and I slept. I guess the Family Life part of the curriculum was also inadvertently covered. Historians refer to human history in terms of BC and AD. Sometimes I chronicle our lives as BT and AT. Before Trip and After Trip.

As I flatten a mosquito on Isla's arm, Oskar mentions that it's nice not to have to listen to us debate about whether we need to take the malaria meds or not. The mosquitoes in Winnipeg are annoying, but we don't have to worry about dengue fever or any other debilitating illnesses. We don't have to think quite as much about food, water, illness, safety, or education.

For me, the appeal of our journey was that we learned not to take basic things for granted. At Disney, they don't want you to think about anything except when to show up for the Aerosmith rollercoaster. On our trip, we had to think about everything. On that spectrum, our everyday life exists somewhere in between. As I pour myself a glass of wine and scan the shelf, I spot the pristine Disney photo album with its glossy pictures, not far from the torn, stained, and dog-eared *Lonely Planet* guidebooks. I realize how lucky we are to have had all of these experiences. Rob opens his part of the book by referencing my bragging about having visited six continents. I understand now, more than ever, that this is a privilege, not an accomplishment.

As more time passes, and we've been slowly pulled back into our old life, no longer in survival mode, I can finally start to think about what some of those experiences meant, and begin to understand how they impacted us. Our instinct as humans is to find meaning in our encounters.

I think back to the Waitomo Glowworm Caves that we visited in the first few days of our trip, back when we were still so clean and full of fresh anticipation. As our boat glided through the glassy waters of the damp cave, millions of stringy worms suspended from rock above our heads emitted the tiniest bluish-green light. The glow of one worm would have easily been missed, but together, the effect of those millions of little lights was magical; we felt like we had entered a secret universe.

This journey was a collection of a million moments that were inspiring, heartbreaking, boring, frustrating, ugly, and happy. Individually, many of those moments might not stand out or offer much meaning, but cumulatively, they have created our secret universe. They've become part of who I am, who we are as a family. They will forever connect us to one another and to the world.

The night before we flew back home, we sat in a dimly lit restaurant in Bogotá, Colombia, eating burgers and drinking beers and Coke. We clinked our thick glasses together. *To our last night.* That was it. This crazy adventure was officially drawing to a close. We were all sort of speechless because it's hard to know what to say in a moment like that. I know that being away and travelling the way that we did for a year was making us all miss and appreciate home that much more. We knew that something rare and special, maybe even once-in-a-lifetime, was coming to an end. I was ready to go home, and yet I never, ever wanted this year of travelling with my family to end.

How do you put that into words?

DON'T TRY THIS AT HOME

DON'T TRY THIS
AT HOME

ONE FAMILY'S (MIS)ADVENTURES
AROUND THE WORLD

ROB KRAUSE
&
DARIA SALAMON

TURNSTONE PRESS

Don't Try This at Home
One Family's (mis)Adventures Around the World
copyright © Daria Salamon and Rob Krause 2019

Turnstone Press
Artspace Building
206-100 Arthur Street
Winnipeg, MB
R3B 1H3 Canada
www.TurnstonePress.com

Turnstone Press gratefully acknowledges the assistance of the Canada Council for the Arts, the Manitoba Arts Council, the Government of Canada through the Canada Book Fund, and the Province of Manitoba through the Book Publishing Tax Credit and the Book Publisher Marketing Assistance Program.

This book is a memoir and reflects the authors' experiences as they have recalled them. Names, events, dialogue and characterizations may have been changed, compressed or recreated for the purposes of telling their story.

Cover photograph courtesy of Daria Salamon and Rob Krause

Printed and bound in Canada.

Library and Archives Canada Cataloguing in Publication

Title: Don't try this at home : one family's (mis)adventures around the world / Daria Salamon, Rob Krause.
Names: Salamon, Daria, author. | Krause, Rob, 1968- author.
Identifiers: Canadiana (print) 20189067675 | Canadiana (ebook) 20189067683 | ISBN 9780888016539 (softcover) | ISBN 9780888016546 (EPUB) | ISBN 9780888016553 (Kindle) | ISBN 9780888016560 (PDF)
Subjects: LCSH: Salamon, Daria—Travel. | LCSH: Krause, Rob, 1968-—Travel. | LCSH: Voyages around the world. | LCSH: Voyages and travels—Anecdotes.
Classification: LCC G440.S25 S25 2019 | DDC 910.4/1—dc23

MANITOBA ARTS COUNCIL
CONSEIL DES ARTS DU MANITOBA

Canada Council   Conseil des arts
for the Arts   du Canada

Funded by the Government of Canada
Financé par le gouvernement du Canada | Canada Manitoba

DON'T TRY THIS AT HOME

Cast of Characters

Daria

Starting Age: Whatever you think you think it is, minus ten.

Known for such uplifting catchphrases as, "We're all in this together," and "By 'we,' I mean 'you,'" Daria is the "ideas" person of the household and the one responsible for initiating the year off to travel the world. Being the only family member who has travelled to Africa, she is often overheard singing, "Who's been to six continents? Just me! Not you!" and responds to any familial dispute by holding up six fingers in front of her face.

Oskar

Starting Age: 8

Having heard the phrase, "You are what you eat," this young go-getter fine-tuned his diet to comprise only the singular food item known as Skittles, in the hopes that he would eventually be able to eat his own hands. It's forward thinking like this that allowed Oskar to develop unique solutions to some of the world's most pressing issues before reaching the age of four. His phosphate-reducing method of doing laundry (by forcing your sister to flush your underwear down the toilet) is presently in its test phase in four municipalities throughout Canada.

Isla Blue

Starting Age: 5

The self-anointed ruler of the household, Isla Blue is the proud world record holder for longest nonsensical tirade that contains

the phrase, "dumpster diving muskrat." During the course of these travels, however, she was taken aback by the inability of the rest of the world's inhabitants to recognize her as supreme ruler of all things on planet Earth. Presently, she is working on incorporating multilingual expletives into her outbursts in order to change that perception, and hopes to—nay, will—assume her role as All Powerful Overlord by 2024.

Rob

Starting Age: Don't get me started.

Lovingly referred to as "Spirit Crusher" by his familial members, though he prefers to go by the more prosaic moniker of, "The only one with any sense of reality." After years of suffering stroke-like symptoms each time Daria uttered the word "trip," Rob is now an Elite Platinum member of his local hospital's Emergency Ward Rewards Program and has earned one free use of a defibrillator. His long-term goal is to take a nap sometime before 2021.

"EAT, PRAY, NAP"

In the weeks that led up to our year off, I was enthusiastically quizzed by friends who were excited by our decision to take the kids out of school and journey around the world for twelve months.

"What do you hope to achieve during your travels?" they asked.

"Won't this be a great opportunity to set some wonderful life targets?"

"I would love to be able to focus on my chi and realign my life force like you're going to do."

Er, what?

For someone who was never very goal-oriented (as indicated by my spartan work resumé), these inquiries caught me a little off-guard. Did this trip actually need a purpose?

The thought of it being some spiritual journey where I would find my inner Deepak Chopra or Chewbacca had never occurred to me. The concept of the trip, and the push towards it, did not garner

much of my attention in the early spring months when we (read: Daria) first began discussing the framework for such an undertaking. I just did a lot of affirmative head-nodding and sometimes an added, "Sure, sounds great!" to what I thought were conversations revolving around colour schemes for planting perennials at the house that year. How easy it is to tune out sometimes ...

When August arrived and Daria began to seriously contemplate booking flights and renting out our house, my fine-tuned sense of deduction, accompanied by a few rapier-honed questions along the lines of, "What the hell are you talking about?!" allowed me to glean that she, meaning we, were actually pursuing this path.

A year, huh? Interesting.

It's not that I didn't want to travel for a year; it's just that my personality tends to lean towards inertia, a trait undoubtedly driven by my slow evolution into a middle-aged man-sloth. These days, my idea of a great night out is just staying at home. In the basement. Playing a unilateral game of hide-and-seek with my children. Hence, I'm not going out of my way to quit my job and uproot my family. Neither am I actively trying to expose myself to insects that will delicately place their egg sacks behind my eyeballs so that their young may graze upon the textured pastures of my brain. I have noticed that as I grow older, it certainly has become easier to stop challenging myself. This is because with two children, my world is challenging enough. Children also change the dynamic of taking on such an adventure. There is no more reckless indifference towards what might befall you as you travel, because I am now responsible for ensuring that my children are not put in harm's way. Something that I may take too seriously, which, in turn, causes me to be consumed by the fear of "what if?" Congruently, I am also the "fixer of problems" in our day-to-day lives. At home, this means that I'm the one who figures out where the blue star socks are hiding and retrieves the underwear that was stuffed into the deep recesses of the toilets' pipes by our children. This is trying enough in my home environment where I know the

parameters of what I'm working with. The possibility of unknown debacles that could potentially endanger the safety of my family is a whole other level of parental anxiety that we urban sloths tend to shy away from. In the end, I acquiesced to Daria's plan and her continual prodding because, as a sloth, I am also not prone to fighting back or standing up for anything. I am just hoping for a nap, and maybe some fruit.

Don't misinterpret my hesitation, though. I have indeed travelled, so not all of my time has been spent lurking behind the drawn curtains of my house.

When Oskar was three and a half and Isla was nearly one, we decided that they were old enough and we were smart enough to do a two-and-a-half-week camping trip to Utah. I was a little worried, as most of my previous car-camping experiences were either with my father when I was in university or with him and my mother when I was much younger. For me, camping with my father was transformed into a spectator sport, in accordance with his campsite management style/tent-side dictatorship. He would allow me to attempt a task for about three seconds, whether it was putting in tent stakes or lighting the stove, but would then quickly put both of us out of our collective misery and commandeer control over said undertaking. Because of this, I never actually learned how to do anything and was left with the impression that all of the routines associated with camping (like putting up a tent) were well beyond my abilities.

Later, Daria and I would have some backcountry trips together, including multi-day canoe excursions and, most notably, a six-day hike along the West Coast Trail in British Columbia. However, though each trip was fun and always seemed to work out, we still never felt like we actually knew what we were doing. This was especially true on the West Coast Trail, our first true backcountry hike, for which we had packed enough food to feed a high school marching band. Our canoe trips were equally ill-prepared, as we based most of our meal planning around the fish that we would catch, yet neither of us knew how to kill or filet a fish.

For advice, I looked to a close friend who had two older children that had travelled extensively with him, including on a number of camping trips. He reassured me it was all doable. "Going camping with kids is just like being at home but waaaaaay more work."

Indeed, it was a herculean amount of effort but it was also completely gratifying, even amidst the flood of comical moments fuelled by my inexperience; and in one instance, literally fuelled by the white gas used in our camping stove. (I thought it would be wise to refill the stove's reservoir over a still-smouldering fire pit, resulting in flames that shot over my gas-drenched hands faster than a middle-aged man can cry for his mother.)

That trip led to longer and more complicated ones: the Black Hills in South Dakota, camping in California for four weeks, and then camping to and from Atlantic Canada for six weeks. With each successive road trip, it felt like the risk of accidentally snuffing out my entire family diminished. That's not to say that these trips were not without incident—injuries occurred, things were lost, and meltdowns were endured, the latter generally resolved once we found Daria's misplaced bottle of wine. However, all of these tribulations were offset by the oceans and lakes that were swum in; the bridges and cliffs that were jumped from; and the waterfalls, forests, and mountains that were traversed.

Our success on these excursions naturally led us to believe that we could do this type of travel for an entire year, which, to a majority of the populace, seems completely idiotic. Why would anyone want to spend a full year, non-stop, with their children? Amongst our relatives and friends, there was also a level of incredulity regarding our plans. For most people, spending two or three weeks on summer vacation with their brood is quite enough, thank you very much. And I get it; it's really hard sometimes—strike that—a lot of the time. However, Daria and I were already acclimatized to/ traumatized by spending extended periods with our kids since we both work primarily from home and have no workplace at which to hide. As a teacher, Daria also has the entire summer off. It's not

that we believe that we are superior parents or that we have a better grasp on how to deal with kids; we are just around our children so much already that we have been forced to accept that they aren't going anywhere anytime soon.

Thanks to these past family vacations, as well as my own childhood experiences travelling with parents and relatives throughout Germany and Europe, the prospect of such an extended trip never intimidated me, and neither was I adverse to experiencing new places, cultures, and people. Though, how much enlightenment one gains from being squeezed in-between Winnebagos in a national park is debatable. Or from German culture, for that matter, when it's simply distilled to sausages, beer, and Lederhosen. Even so, heading into any of those trips, there was never any discussion of *What will I learn from my soon-to-be-new neighbours from Sheboygan, Wisconsin, who are nestled next to us at our overcrowded campsite?* or *How will these delightful pork products develop my spirituality?* On those more recent forays out into the world with my family, we were just going on vacations where we could yell at our kids in the great outdoors instead of yelling at them within the confines of our own home. In some regards, this was a plus, as it forced me to get a little exercise as I chased them away from our car after discovering the pine cones, bark, and national park knick-knacks that they had stuffed into the tailpipe.

The closest that I had come to any sort of spiritual journey was when I was nineteen and had travelled on my own across much of western Europe for nine months. That is, if you can classify trying to lose my virginity as a spiritual journey. And, to be honest, it became more of a spiritual pain-in-the-ass than anything. My lofty goal of having a meaningful first sexual encounter, one that would not make me cringe when I remembered it later in life, failed throughout high school and the first few years of university. It seemed that no one was interested in sleeping with me; after all, the marketplace needs to want what you are offering, and nerdy, pimple-faced, punk rock kids were seemingly not in high demand.

So that idealistic cornerstone of my teenage years was exchanged for the "Will-somebody-please-have-sex-with-me?" ideology that, interestingly enough, I have once again adopted in my marriage during middle age.

Suffice it to say, the focus of that trip was on finding cities, towns, wheelbarrows—whereever and whatever—that offered the greatest opportunity to get my weird life hurdle out of the way. It did become a defining time in my life, however, as I did do a lot of soul-searching over the course of those nine months and learned a lot about myself. First and foremost, I discovered that after nine months of travelling, I was still a virgin.

Our upcoming year off, though, did not harbour the same "spiritual" undertone as that of my teenage travels, as I am glad to report that I am no longer a virgin. In fact, our gap year had no quest driving it at all, which was something that began to weigh heavily on me as the months progressed and it became apparent that almost everyone else we encountered on our year abroad was guided by some such vision. Travellers of all sorts—across age groups, solo trippers, pairs, and families—kept punctuating our journey with their array of enviable travel goals. Their objectives were spiritual and cultural: learning a local language or immersing themselves in the history of a great civilization. We listened with interest and awe at how people were so motivated, organized, and so, well, intelligent in their planning and their lives in general. It created a continuous source of unease that fed into my loop of Travel Anxiety, as well as my personal anxiety, for that matter. The best response I could muster to counter these A-level travellers was that the learning methods that I had incorporated into our travels were guided by the theories of one Henri Dutrochet, known as "passive absorption"; which, I subsequently had to clarify, was not to be confused with the common malady found in many middle-aged North American men known as "doing sweet dick all."

Sometimes, however, the ambitions of our fellow travellers were somewhat murky. In Samoa, we stayed in a group of beach huts

that were vacant except for a German couple, whose travel mission was to amass a list of complaints about the exciting new frontiers they had visited, solely to blog dismissively about these "horrible" places, and a lone Russian man in his mid- to late twenties. Our Russian friend would only materialize around dinner, when you might catch a quick glimpse of him scurrying back to his hut with a loaded-down plate featuring that night's offerings from the kitchen. The rest of the day, and night, he remained in his hut, blinds closed, doing *something*. At first, we surmised he was just catching up on past episodes of *Downton Abbey*, or perhaps the Russian equivalent, *Yorgi Dosvidana!?*, that he had downloaded onto his computer. We soon realized that there was no sound or telltale video flicker whatsoever emanating from his hut. So what was he up to? Playing Manifesto Monopoly? Meticulously rechecking his application for Uni-bomber post-graduate work? Planning the next great Mexican fiesta for the Samoan winter solstice? Whatever it was, he was immersed in something so completely that it occupied every waking minute of his day. This guy had a plan, a true mission. One day, Vladimir woke up in his Moscow dacha, fed his pet bear (vodka, naturally), put on his ushanka, and said, in broken English (of course), "Today, I stop being Russian stereotype and find true calling by living in Samoa hut alone!"

His new life vision—especially if it involved the Uni-bomber part—may not have been in the best interest of humanity, but clearly he had travelled to this remote part of the South Pacific with the motivation to discover his true self. At the end of his sojourn, he would undoubtedly have something to show for it—a plan, which he could later offer as an online adult education course through his local community college, entitled, "Gap Year Travel for the Tentative Terrorist: What Not to Pack When Packing Plastic Explosives." I laud you, future insane-terrorist guy. I wish that I had had just an inkling of those aspirations for my year off.

But alas, I had none. One can hardly say that "Hoping to come back home sane and in one piece" or "Not causing irreparable

II

harm to my children" were commendable cornerstones for a trip around the world, but they were the best I had. In the end, I'm not sure that I succeeded at either one.

What's worse is that our lack of goal-oriented travel sadly extended to, and thus affected, our children. We were not just lazy travellers, we were crap parents for pulling our children out of school to tag along for a year of, well, nothing. Of course, that's not how it was sold to their school when we asked for permission to have them take a year off. It was all, "cultural this" and "scientific blahty blah that," and our children would be exposed to a lifetime's worth of learning over the course of twelve months. Strong pitch, poor execution, as was evidenced over and over again as we visited sites of cultural and natural significance, where we found ourselves surrounded by families dressed as their favourite Precambrian spore with lesson plans and activity models in hand: "Okay, Billy, we were talking about this at breakfast; what layer of sediment would I be if I coughed up rounded gravel? Oooh, good guess, but Breccias is made up of angular rocks. I was looking for Conglomerates."

At home, our teaching always consisted less of the Socratic method and more of the traditional parental method of "Make it up. What do they know? They're only five and eight." And so it was on this trip as well. For instance, as we floated down a darkened subterranean river, engrossed in the endless expanse of glowworms more vast than the Milky Way in a light-free night sky, we told our kids the light radiating from the worms was simply the burning embers from their tiny cigarettes as they took a break from their eight-hour telemarketing shift. How this all parlays into future science fair projects may be of some concern, but we'll just pin it on our own underfunded education system. In those times when we did attempt to teach them something legitimate, usually due to either me or Daria overhearing some fact being conveyed between other parents, the kids would derail the whole process in a matter of seconds.

On one hike, my effort to get the kids interested in how strangler figs become the tentacled and cavernous sarcophagi that towered around us was absolutely pointless.

"Look at those trees. They're hollow!"

"Wow," Isla remarks, gazing skywards. "And Papa, those tentacles, they look like an alien."

"Yeah, or like the Terminator," adds Oskar, half-interested and without breaking stride.

"Uhhh, alien, yup, okay, I see that. Not so sure about the Terminator, though. Oskar, how do you even know about the Terminator?"

"I saw a picture on the airplane TV."

"Tell me you didn't watch that movie. Did you?"

"It looked really awesome."

"Did you watch it?"

"He's all shiny and metal-y. Like a robot."

"DID. YOU. WATCH. IT?"

"No, I don't think so. That's not where there's a guy cutting people up with a chainsaw, is it?"

"No, that's not... Wait a second, what were you watching on the plane?"

"Papa," Isla chimes in, now intrigued, "what's a Terminator?"

"What? Oh, it's a movie. And you're right, that tree does look like an alien of some kind—spooky, hey? Do you know how that happens?"

"What's the movie about?"

"It's complicated."

Both kids start chanting "Ter-mi-na-tor! Ter-mi-na-tor!" in unison for the next 300 metres until I finally give up on the whole strangler fig lesson.

By the end of this eight-kilometre hike, I'd given a thorough essay on the plots of the first two Terminator movies and a vague synopsis of the much weaker third and fourth movies. The kids came out of an extended hike through a tropical rainforest without

a shred of understanding about the natural history they had just walked through, but were now fully beguiled by, and versed in, the concept of a time-travelling cyborg that must visit the past twice in order to, in the first instance, kill the mother of her yet-unborn son, the future leader of the human uprising against the machines, and in the second instance, to protect that now-born son from another cyborg that was somewhat shinier and metal-y-er. To their credit, I'm surprised they understood the whole concept in only eight kilometres. A+ for both of them on that assignment!

Once this doorway was opened, future hike narratives revolved around similarly complex movie plot lines, and then, once those were all exhausted, moved into the realm of exploring the convoluted dating histories of Daria and myself. Hikes became filled with questions regarding present occupations (and incomes) of Daria's past boyfriends, with subsequent follow-up questions that revolved around why Daria would even think of choosing me over said future doctors (which elicited cash register "Cha-ching!" noises and giggles) and Captains of Industry (excessive cash register sound effects and wild laughter).

In the end, I think that even though we lacked identifiable goals, extensive education planning for our children, or proper preparation to understand the lands, peoples, and cultures we were going to visit, we all still managed to learn much in our travel year. Post-trip, I can now see how my kids took the experiences from that year and incorporated them into their schoolwork, playtime, and their everyday knowledge of the world. For myself, our travels brought about the realization that heading into the unknown for a year can actually be done without any loss of life. Every day was a bit of a challenge in some way, which in the end, was not something to be afraid of. The daily tasks I faced gradually heightened my senses and made each day uniquely distinguishable (for better or worse), differentiating them from the routines that are so easy to settle into at home. At times, it was stressful and difficult to plan, but it was also always exciting and gratifying.

Additionally, thanks to the continuous harping of my children as to why I'm not a doctor or a CEO, this past year also taught me that one truly can love and hate one's children at the same time.

BEWARE THE BEATEN PATH: IT'S FULL OF GERMANS

When you have the option to travel the world, it is actually quite difficult to decide where to go. One would assume that a full year (the equivalent to forty-seven "parent years"—calculated by determining how much one has aged over a specific period while spending "quality" time with one's children) would afford you enough time to do anything and go anywhere in the world. Well, it does ... and it doesn't.

When presented with an unlimited number of options, your brain will embrace every single one of these possibilities until you are left with an itinerary in which you spend no more than twelve minutes at any particular destination. For Niagara Falls, that's twelve minutes more than I need, but for the Louvre in Paris it's a tad tight on time, especially when our schedule requires us to be at Angkor Wat in Cambodia later that same evening.

After unfurling ourselves from the fetal positions we had

assumed while trying to digest the dizzying array of options, we began the process of narrowing it all down.

The problem is that we aren't the type of people who are obsessed with a particular item to the extent that it could be the theme of an entire trip. I presently do not have a spoon collection, and neither does Daria have a Hummel figurine fetish that must be placated by rare additions from exotic locales. There is also no need for us to taste a cheese made from the fermented earwax of Franciscan monks that can be sampled only at their secluded Spanish monastery. I'm not sure if this makes us uncultured, or simply boring, but it does complicate matters when planning a year of travel. To be honest, in the end, this trip had to pass the critical and complicated approval process of one slightly fastidious Isla Blue.

"Safari in Africa?"

"NO!"

"You'll see lots of animals, like zebras and lions."

"I can watch *Madagascar*."

"But these are real, not a movie."

"I like movies."

"Yes, I know. Wouldn't it be great, though, to see these animals in their real homes?"

"We can stay at their house?"

"Umm, not quite. They live out on the savannah—a big field that stretches forever."

"Uggghhh. I'll go if they come to the pool at our hotel."

"Hotel?"

"Okay, what about France?"

"NO! Too French-y."

"Machu Picchu?"

"NO WAY! Too Inca-y."

"How do you even know that?"

So, as a family, we had to think of what we enjoyed doing together and in which situations we might be able to actually

endure each other's company for an extended period of time. Camping had always been something that we all liked; thus, we thought that this would be a good way to start the trip. Now, when I say "we," I mean everyone except for, of course, Isla Blue. After rigorous negotiations, however, we were able to get her on board, but only once we promised her that we would travel and sleep in a luxurious camper van (lie), that she would be allowed to drive said camper van (also a lie), and that she would be allowed to gorge on glow-worms until her own stomach began radiating an iridescent blue (technically not a lie, since scientific research is still vague as to what exactly will happen upon the consumption of such large amounts of *Arachnocampa luminosa*). The beauty of young children is that, when they eventually discover that they've been duped, their fists are too small and their arms too short that the rain of fury that ensues will inflict only an insignificant amount of damage. This, I considered, was a small price to pay in order to construct the foundation of our year of family travel.

With our departure set for February, we chose to begin our itinerary with New Zealand, a country one could best describe as a compact, bonzai-version of Canada, where we could happily evade the Winnipeg winter chill. Any hesitancy the kids had about going to New Zealand vanished the moment we boarded our flight from Los Angeles to Auckland. Air travel is always exciting for kids, but throw in a media centre at each seat that puts the TV in our house to shame, and we were elevated to the status of gods in the eyes of our children. I hoisted my drink to commemorate our brief moment of glory, and subsequently doused myself in a fine New Zealand lager. Sitting in a puddle of beer for ten hours certainly dulls the shine of pan-Pacific air travel. At customs in Auckland, my passport was but a formality as the Immigration officers were able to identify my nationality from one hundred beer-soaked-metres away. I needed only a pet beaver and a suitcase filled with maple syrup to complete the stereotype.

Once Isla had calmed down and stopped trying to kill us

because of the camper van "misunderstanding," we were on our way in a very non-luxurious and un-camper-van-esque four-door hatchback. Our itinerary on the North Island of New Zealand was a hodgepodge of unorganized zigzagging between destinations that sounded incredible: Hot Water Beach, where you dig a hole in the sand and let the geothermal water bubble up to fill your home-made hot tub! Camping at the foot of Mount Doom! Hobbiton! Floating in an underground cave to watch glow-worms! It became even more chaotic once we discovered our new favourite fruit, the incredible omega plum. This fruit is summer epitomized, with a saccharine sweetness and soft-textured flesh that bursts bright crimson with every bite, driving us each to eat no less than ten in every sitting. Once satiated, our faces were stained a blazing red and dripping with juice, making us look as if we had just gorged ourselves on a fresh deer carcass. We became so obsessed with the plum that we began taking extended detours to find roadside fruit stands that peddled this Oxycontin of the Orchards. What's worse is that these stands were unattended, with an honour system drop box set up by the farmer, so there was never anyone to suggest that we might want to tone down our consumption. Eventually, after one stomach cramp too many, we reeled in our fruit-fuelled, car-nival driving style and focused on a more organized itinerary. On the South Island, this was easier to achieve anyway, as the South-ern Alps run along the spine of the island from north to south. The result is a driving loop that travels down the west side of the island and back up the east. Containing a number of hotspots—such as Franz Josef Glacier, the outdoor action-adventure centre that is Queenstown, and the towering cliffs that make up the fjord of Milford Sound—this loop is also crammed with what seemed like an excessive amount of German travellers. Excessive, that is, until I needed a pack of tight-shorted, Birkenstock-wearing, twen-ty-year-old Germans to lift (literally) our camper van (figuratively, for Isla's sake) out of a ditch and off the drainage pipe that I had backed onto. I take it back: there can never be enough Germans

around when you are travelling. This sentiment was further confirmed later in our travels on the island of Ko Pha-Ngan, Thailand,
when I was desperately trying to locate a German woman who had
collapsed in her hut and was faintly calling out for help. Lucky for
her, my German repertoire consisted of more than just bad Arnold
Schwarzenegger impersonations, and I was able to keep her talking
as I fumbled through the multitude of serpentine paths that con-
tinuously led me to the door of every hut on the densely forested
hillside other than hers. Intrigued by the strangulation of German
words that I was hurling into the jungle, a gentleman approached
me who not only knew the hut's location, but also turned out to be
a German doctor who was subsequently able to diagnose and assist
the woman in need. German High Five! *Deutsches Hohe Fünf!*

Throughout New Zealand, the state-run campsites, or DOCs,
were our principal place to overnight because they were cheap—
and made even cheaper by the fact that children under five stayed
for free. Now, how one interprets "under five" is subjective, of
course, and, subjectively speaking, we felt that a child who is
techincally five but regularly diminishes our joy of life falls directly
into the "under five" category. The fuzziness of this "under five"
delineation was something that we, as intelligent adults, were able
to grasp with ease. Oskar, however, without a fully developed cere-
bral cortex (poor child), had difficulty with the complicated set of
algorithms upon which this judgment was based. Oskar's confusion would be a reoccuring issue as the trip continued, as we introduced him to other, more complicated scientific concepts such as:
a) how four people become one person requiring two beds when
booking a hotel room online, and b) the fluid notions of "fault"
and "accident" when reporting said accident to car insurance and
rental companies.

Nevertheless, this definition of a "five-year-old" became a stick-
ing point with Oskar when he put himself in charge of submitting
the registration and pay forms at the camping self-serve kiosks.
My pride at his independence and responsibility was unfortunately

tempered by my irritation in having to conjure up more and more elaborate answers as to why he shouldn't declare his sister on the form. It got to the point where I found myself dependent on various non-related principles that I was able to dig out from the deep recesses of my education.

"So, why don't we pay for Isla?"

"Ever heard of Estoppel?"

"No."

"Famous legal rule. Something that you use as a shield cannot then be used as a sword."

"… ?"

"So, there you go. Hungry? I'm starved. Let's go make supper."

You would think that at some point during our nine weeks of camping in New Zealand, it just wasn't worth it to lie to Oskar about this in order to save a few dollars. Especially when it started to impact his own judgment and he began suggesting that we stop paying for gas.

"Well, that's not the same thing."

"Why?"

"Because gas is a commodity and a campsite is, well, it's recreational."

"But you still buy both."

"Hmm … true … but … well … gasoline doesn't fall under the rubric of Newton's Third Law, which essentially governs this sort of thing. Hey look, kiwi!"

But this is what being on a daily budget does to you. Saving a few dollars a night becomes important enough that you are willing to create phony legal and scientific loopholes to justify lying about your daughter's age. What's worse is that this became a life lesson that our children wholly absorbed, once they realized that the only thing Newton's Law of Thermodynamics proves is that their father is a complete ass. This was evidenced upon our return home, when one of Oskar's first assignments at school was to pick his favourite superpower and explain why. Telekinesis was his choice, and part

of his affection for this ability was because, as he put it, "You can also use it to secretly smuggle items out of the grocery store." Well done, parents. Well done indeed.

Looking back at this trip, I question the thought processes behind a lot of these decisions. Depending on the situation, Isla was told to act like a four-year-old ("free under five"), pretend to be a seven-year-old (minimum age for rides and diving boards), shrink or stretch to meet minimum height requirements, or pretend to be an orphan. Oh wait, that last one was just what we said when we were trying to pawn her off to other unsuspecting parents.

Naturally, forcing her to lie about every aspect of her existence has absolutely nothing to do with her development into the volatile sociopath that she is.

When we were unable to get into a DOC, or when our destination was too far from one, we would wind up at a chain of private campsites known as Top Ten. Generally, these featured a giant trampoline, playground, swimming pool, games room, and breakfast served by Belgian-bred red pandas that were quite charming and made a fantastic crêpe. After any length of time at these "campsites," our return to a DOC would result in a small rebellion expressed from the back seat of the car by a flurry of verbal assaults and projectiles extracted from bags of trail mix.

At one such campground on the North Island, in Hastings, our stay was constantly extended as Oskar and Isla refused to get out of the tent any time we tried to pack up and leave. It didn't help that a trio of Irishmen in their mid-twenties had befriended Oskar and came calling every day to take him to play tennis. After a few days, we began dropping hints to the gents that we needed to move on, and they would strike back with, "So soon? Have you had a chance to go the waterpark that's just down the road? It's grand." Or, "The go-kart racetrack was fantastic fun last night." Saboteurs. They had been there for a week already and it didn't look like they

were moving any time soon, as they had recently invested in a cornucopia of pool toys and floating lounge chairs. Any plans we had for the upcoming days were now doomed.

Along with the DOCs and Top Tens, there also existed independently run private campsites. These ranged from the backyards of people's houses, to an awkward night in Franz Josef Glacier on a narrow strip of litter-strewn space squeezed between a three-storey backpacker's hostel and the property's perimeter chain-link fence. Within this scenic vista, our tent was placed at arm's length from the dorm room window, out of which emanated a continuous loop of the *Lord of the Rings* theme song, whistled by various svelt Scandinavian men.

This hostel was also where we encountered one of the most memorable travellers from our trip: German Party Girl. You may have encountered German Party Girl at some point during your own travels. Found predominantly in hot-weather climes, German Party Girl can be identified by a diet that consists solely of other people's alcohol, and a loud, shrill call of, "Do you like to party? Yah, I *LOVE* to party!" Though once thought to be endangered, German Party Girl now seems to have made an astounding comeback, much to the dismay of everyone else on the planet.

In our year of travels, this hostel was the only place where I felt embarrassed to have brought my kids, and where the sideways glances from our fellow guests created an unwelcome atmosphere. The debauchery here seemed to have been amplified with the sole purpose to make us feel out of place. We stayed in many hostels on this trip that were filled with mid-twenties travellers, including hostels that were hosting Contiki tours (the Cadillac of short-term partying), but we were never made to feel like complete outsiders. We never expected anyone to embrace us and were always surprised when these young, childless travellers would go out of their way to engage our children in conversation or games. This, oddly enough, was the only place where we truly felt like no one wanted us there. Perhaps it was because Isla kept telling German Party

Girl and her entourage of hopeful male suitors that she, too, liked a party and she was excited to have some cake.

That night was spent in fearful anticipation that German Party Girl and Aragorn, son of Arathorn, would come crashing into our tent while engaged in an amorous embrace. I awoke early, brushed the used condoms and their wrappers out of sight, and began to take down the tent so that we could make our hasty exit. As we drove away, we could hear the faint trill of German Party Girl as she began foraging through the hostel's communal refrigerator for her next meal.

In truth, we should have known what we were getting ourselves into before we even arrived. This hostel, chosen by Daria, was the result of one of her "I'm-going-to-start-pulling-my-weight!" moments of clarity. Unfortunately, Daria's decision-making process relies heavily on problematic criteria, such as proximity to essential services (read: wine store), availability of important amenities (read: bottle opener), and design and layout (read: maximum separation between Daria and us while she is drinking her wine). The driving force behind the selection of this particular hostel was, however, the prospect of free soup at 6:00 p.m. To me, offers of free food generally denote something that no one else wants or something that no one should actually eat. I have been behind the scenes at one too many All-You-Can-Eat buffets to know that for five dollars, what is offered as "food" in unlimited quantities can only mean "Danger! Danger!" Daria, however, sold this highlight to the kids and the three of them joined a swarm of our cohabitants in a mad rush to inhale as much of this Gulag-style gruel as possible, appropriately served with the local bakery's month-old buns. Upon their return, the kids' sour faces were counterbalanced with Daria's upbeat account of mealtime. Her report seemed to have been buoyed by the mysterious disappearance of three-quarters of her freshly opened bottle of wine.

And so, our two months in New Zealand were spent driving through epic landscapes and experiencing amazing wildlife moments, such as our impromptu swimming sessions with the resident dolphins at Porpoise Bay, or our near-destruction of an entire generation of yellow-eyed penguins in Moeraki township, where our hike through their unmarked high-grass nesting grounds degenerated into a regrettable but aptly named game of "Murder Tag."

An unintended consequence of our route through New Zealand, however, was that we rarely spent any time with the local inhabitants. Overnighting at campgrounds tended to always put us next to fellow foreign travellers who were on some form of vacation as well. And although nine weeks seems like it would provide ample time to explore a small country, it turns out that we had stretched our itinerary so thin that we could never really stay in one particular place for an extended period of time. When we first arrived in New Zealand, we did decide to prolong our intended two-night stay at an Airbnb outside of Auckland, but only after Isla ran face-first into a closed glass patio door and we realized she needed a little more time to adjust to the jet lag. At a campsite in Marlborough Sounds, on the northern coast of the South Island, Oskar and Isla Blue were enjoying jellyfish fights with a group of local kids—literally picking up handfuls of oozing, pink, gelatinous-like flesh out of the ocean bay and throwing them at each other—so much so that we had to stay and enjoy this unique moment. This was, however, the most interaction that we had with any native New Zealanders because the country is so rife with unique natural beauty that you want to keep moving to see it all. You can go from one stunning area (e.g., geothermal hotpots) to another (e.g., dense tropical forests) in less than half a day, and travel through approximately 5,000 other microclimates along the way. Just as you become accustomed to one geographical region, it suddenly vanishes and you find yourself in a completely different, equally enthralling, environment. There is no six-hour drive through flattened prairies, just to get to the starting point for the

next six hours … of flattened prairies. And dotted throughout the country are hiking trails of every conceivable distance, guiding you through as much or as little of each of these unique settings as you would like.

The infrastructure for hiking in New Zealand is unparalleled, and it seems that hiking, or "tramping," as it's colloquially known as, is constitutionally entrenched into the makeup of the country. Tracks are maintained at an exceptional level, featuring overnight huts equipped with kitchens and bunks, whose distances from one another are perfectly situated to allow you to experience an enjoyable yet challenging day along the trails. They are often staffed by hut wardens, who, we discovered, were not shy in educating us and our children on hut etiquette and the importance of proper trail behaviour. We managed to do two overnight hikes on the South Island, each a section of the many "Great Walks" found throughout the country. The Routeburn Track allowed us to get deeper into the alpine mountainscape, while the Abel Tasman Coast Track had us walking along northern coast beaches, whose colour and texture made us feel like we were stepping on a lunar dreamscape of golden brown sugar. So why would anyone bother to stay in one place and get to know the people and the culture? We had mountains to hike, fjords to see, and natural breeding habitats to destroy.

As much of a positive learning opportunity as it was for our kids to be exposed to these incredible moments, by the end of our stay in New Zealand, they had become so spoiled by their encounters that any new experiences later on in our travels barely registered with them. We first noticed this trend while camping at the more remote Puriri Bay campsite near the northern tip of New Zealand during our final week in the country. On our first night, I took a late-night jaunt (fancy talk for a trip to the bathroom) and was amazed at the southern night sky, which was awash with the millions of stars that make up our Milky Way galaxy. In amongst those distinct pinpricks of light was what I can only describe as a white smudge or smear about the size of two thumbprints planted on

the sky above. I stared at it, rubbing my eyes to clear my vision, unsure if what I was seeing was a result of one too many before-bed IPAs. The next morning, I mentioned my observations to our Swedish neighbour, who happened to be an amateur astronomer (of course he was. See? Everyone else travelled with a purpose!), and was informed that what I saw was another galaxy, visible to the naked eye only in specific areas of New Zealand—the exact reason why the Swede was at this particular campground. The kids became so enraptured with the concept of seeing another galaxy and all the otherworldly possibilities that it conjured up—giant alien spaceships, Wookies—that I had to promise to wake them up that night. When I did, their response to the weird smear in the sky was understandably tepid. Not even the expanse of stars from our own Milky Way flooding the night above us tweaked any sort of response, and they were back to bed within ten seconds.

Really, who can blame them? Once you've kicked a few penguins to the curb, everything else just seems dull.

We did try to engage the kids in other ways during this portion of the trip, though with similarly poor results. We had read that one should include your children in the route planning and the activity organizing, which for periods of time, we did. However, there were only so many playgrounds and candy stores that we could endure. One task that we gave to Oskar was putting him in charge of tracking our daily expenses. He would take the receipts, punch them into his Expense Tracker app, and let us know what our daily costs were and what percentage of our budget was going where. He was overjoyed with his role in our trip, and we were very proud of him until he began to scrutinize our daily budget.

Now, anyone who has gone camping, or on any family vacation, for that matter, recognizes the importance of the post-bedtime drink. You have just spent an entire day—let me say that again—AN ENTIRE DAY—with your children. This is no easy feat, and so you have earned the right to have a drink or seven before bed. In New Zealand, as with most of the civilized world other than

Canada, you can buy alcohol at the grocery store, so our shopping list always included beer or wine. Under some delusion that alcohol was not a grocery item, Oskar began to separate our libations from what he deemed "real" groceries. Addled with rudimentary math skills, the poor lad kept coming up with what he thought was a proper accounting of our daily alcohol expenditures. Oddly enough, it was consistently one-seventh of our grocery budget. Oh, that does sound bad. But alcohol is not a cheap endeavour in New Zealand, and our children are not easy to live with.

Bless his little heart, though, for he suggested that our spending money on beer and wine is akin to his and Isla's spending money on ice cream and chocolate. As such, they should be able to spend an equal amount per day on their treats as well. Oh, to be a child and have such a wild imagination, where pink unicorns fly through the air and anything can happen! We, as sensible, intelligent adults, however, recognized his flawed analysis, which only compounded the sadness we were feeling after discovering his obviously weak mathematical skills. We recognized that he was no longer fit to continue the daily accounting. It is difficult to describe a parent's heartbreak at the realization that their child will never be a doctor or a lawyer, but is likely destined to become a carny, with a lifetime of grifting back and forth across North America looming large in their future.

The pain is that much more difficult to bear when you only have 14% of your daily budget to spend on alcohol to drink that sorrow away.

WARNING: EVERYTHING WANTS TO KILL YOU

art of travel preparation involves anticipating worst-case scenarios and proactively trying to mitigate those situations.
And in order to anticipate these worst-case scenarios, you need to
do a lot of research on diseases, thieving, hostage-taking, wild animal attacks, insect stings, group hugs, warm beer, loud Germans,
group hugs from loud Germans who smell like warm beer—the
list is endless. Unfortunately, so are the answers, or, at least, the
opinions. On each and every topic of concern, there are an infinite
number of Internet "experts" who espouse the best thing to do for
any given situation. The difficulty lies in cutting through it all to
separate those who are actually giving sound advice from those
who are hiding in their basement because the world freaks them
out. Even national health organizations from different countries
all have varying perspectives on the more grievous dangers related
to specific travel destinations. There is no clear-cut answer to any

situation—except on the subject of group hugs from loud Germans, where there is a broad consensus that they should generally be avoided.

Our personal journey through the world of death and disease began with a trip to our local travel health clinic. The meeting was filled with an expansive list of illnesses we should be fearful of, whose symptoms were detailed down to the most excruciating minutia, all of which invariably ended in "death."

"Your nervous system becomes compromised, inhibiting the proper regulation of the heartbeat, and you die."

"Your brain hemorrhages, which leads to bleeding from your eyes, nose, and ears in cascading streams reminiscent of a burst water pipe, and you die."

"Your lungs fill with fluid, you begin to call everyone 'Stan' while inappropriately high-fiving at non-celebratory moments, and you die."

This vivid montage of misery was followed by a review of a world map covered by Xs too numerous to count, scrawled into the confines of each of our prospective destinations' borders. Each individual X, we were told, represented one potential danger in that particular area. After listening to this list of terror, our two children now thought that the sole reason we were taking them out of school was to kill them. Turning to our travel nurse for some expert advice and calming reassurance, we asked what she would recommend. She looked at us, bemused, and replied, "I don't travel."

It felt like she was insinuating that it would be sheer lunacy to expose ourselves, let alone our young, innocent children, to such an evil world of pestilence and suffering. This, naturally, did not ease the tension between our children and us.

With this lack of guidance from the travel health clinic, we realized that we had to make our own educated guess—er, decision. We narrowed it down by eliminating all the diseases that weren't relevant to the geographic area or the century we were travelling

in (e.g., guinea worm, bubonic plague), balancing the risk versus our hesitancy to over-vaccinate, and the cost versus our own critical analysis. *Japanese encephalitis? Not going to Japan, no problem. Just saved $1,400. Polio? Hmm, an iron lung would take up a lot of space in our house and it's so hard to accessorize with the drapes; we should probably get that shot.*

For me, personally, the big one has always been malaria. Since you can't vaccinate against this disease, malaria has always instilled an unwavering fear in me and is the key reason why I have stayed away from a number of the world's more mosquito-infested regions. Ironic, really, since I live in one of the world's worst mosquito zones. Ours, though, are innocuous for the most part. They definitely don't host a disease whose symptoms are driven by the synchronized bursting of millions of your body's red blood cells, and whose parasites can hibernate in your liver for extended periods of time (years!) and return at any given moment—their reappearance undoubtedly coinciding perfectly with the day you finally pay off your credit card bill for the antimalarial tablets that you purchased but chose not to take because of some bad advice from an Australian of questionable hygiene.

What's interesting, though, is that in looking through all of the symptoms of malaria, I'm wondering if I haven't already had it for years, as a long-time sufferer of malaise, muscular fatigue, back pain, chills, and sweating. At the very least, I can now use it as an excuse in the future for not attending family gatherings, high school reunions, or doing laundry. "Sorry, I think I might have malaria. Feeling a little malaise-y."

Nothing spells "f-u-n" on a trip like spending your days defending yourself against a disease that is best battled by being swaddled in clothing from head to toe while travelling in regions where the temperature is a few degrees warmer than the surface of the sun. Of course, once you've cocooned most of your body, you still need to cover any and all patches of remaining skin (i.e., fingertips, the insides of your eyelids, the roof of your mouth) with a repellent.

In the interest of trying to keep our children away from unnecessary chemicals, we initially researched natural repellents and their effectiveness against malaria-carrying mosquitoes. However, it seems that these mosquitoes have started using citronella-infused products as a form of eau de toilette. So it was to DEET and its paint-peeling, plastic-melting abilities that we now had to turn. Though I'm not completely clear on how DEET works, I presume that it literally burns the layers of your epidermis into a patchwork of bubbly scabs. This, combined with the haze of poisonous fumes that result from your skin being chemically seared, creates an uneven and difficult landing surface for the bloodsuckers to latch onto. We tried to keep the DEET concentration in our repellent to a reasonable amount, somewhere between 10% and 30%. While travelling, we discovered that most Australians have given up on maintaining any layer of epidermis, and generally use 80% concentrations of DEET. We weren't quite ready to do that—yet.

Now, it's hard enough to protect yourself in such situations, but trying to explain to your kids that you are covering them in turpentine and sweaters in order to protect them, not to light them on fire, is an entirely different scenario. At the best of times, we can't get our children to put on parkas when it's minus twenty at home, so long pants in the summer were going to be a challenge.

Our final defense was a three-month supply of antimalarial tablets, for which we remortgaged our house. Unfortunately, this medication's side effects include hypersensitivity to the sun, nausea, diarrhea, heartburn, mouth sores, and upset stomach. Essentially, these pills protect you by actively making you so sick and fearful of the sun that you spend your entire trip lying on a darkened bathroom floor, cooling your face against the floor tiles—safely hidden from any malaria-ridden mosquito. Sadly, while lying in this comforting position, you will undoubtedly be punctured by some other multi-legged creature whose appearance you have not anticipated in your planning, leaving you now with a head that has ballooned to the size of a basketball.

It was against this backdrop of imminent death that we began our travels. Our first nine weeks were spent in virus/disease-free bliss, as the most dangerous thing in New Zealand is an unhealthy affinity for the sport of cricket. While we were travelling through New Zealand, though, one of the major news topics was the potential withdrawal of the national rugby team from a scheduled match set to occur in Samoa later in the summer. The concern was due to the recent outbreak of another mosquito-borne illness: chikungunya. Samoa was, unfortunately, our next destination, as it was relatively X free back at the travel health clinic. Oddly, no mention of this disease or the outbreak in Samoa—which, incidentally, was happening at the very moment that we were in the clinic—was ever made by the travel nurse.

The excessive fearmongering by the media, especially in New Zealand, where it was concluded that an infected national rugby team was the only way the Samoans could win the match between the two nations, made it difficult to determine what was really going on. So the moment we arrived in Samoa, we began trying to find any information about the disease. Our inability to pronounce the disease's name, along with the Samoan authorities' aversion to giving answers that actually made sense, made the process somewhat complicated. It also didn't help that we landed on Easter Sunday, the biggest holiday weekend in Samoa. For the first two days, the streets of the capital city of Apia were empty except for packs of dogs which, we naturally concluded, had to be the aftermath of the chimichurri epidemic. Without any information, we spent the first night holed up in a hotel room, windows and doors sealed with duct tape, and the air conditioning on full blast. Supposedly, mosquitoes hate air conditioning. And Meryl Streep, but that's a whole other issue. While we distracted the kids with bad TV, I hunted down any mosquitoes I could find, which seemed to be entering our room in a constant stream, thanks to what appeared to be a heavy reliance on Swiss cheese as a building material in Samoan construction.

The next day, still fearful of being cornered by a pack of ravenous dogs, Daria and Oskar finally made it to the government tourist office by slowly inching their way along sidewalks as they flattened themselves against the sides of buildings. Any questions they had were answered with a government-generated pamphlet on Ebola. It seemed to be a not-too-subtle way of saying, "Look, don't be difficult, it could be a lot worse. We could have this virus here. You're lucky you've only got to deal with something that sounds like it could be on a Taco Bell menu. Look at those pictures. They are bleeding from their eyes. Now that is a real disease."

What we did eventually find out was that nearly everyone we talked to had been infected at one time or another and over twenty-five percent of the population had incurred the disease in the six months since the outbreak. I'm not sure whether it's a cultural thing, but Samoans had a tendency to downplay the effects.

"Oh, it's not too bad. It's like a flu."

"So, just a fever?"

"That, and you can't move. Your legs and arms feel like they are on fire. Oh, and you can't eat anything. It's okay, though, nothing much."

"Uh, that sounds horrible. Does it last long?"

"Oh no, not at all. Couple of weeks, tops."

In the end, we finally met a pharmacist who gave us a level-headed assessment of the situation. Yes, the virus can be dangerous but this only happened in a few cases and usually involved people with weak immune systems. For the majority of people, though, the end result is actual flu-like symptoms, such as fever and chills, lasting three or four days in children and up to a couple of weeks for adults. She recommended the usual low-level precautions: be careful at dawn and dusk by either going inside or into a screened-in area, and use repellent. Seemed reasonable, except for the fact that the traditional Samoan house—called a fale—is a structure with posts and a roof but no walls. Or screens. Or beds. Your mattress is on the floor with netting to protect you while you

sleep, but offering no defence when you aren't in your 'bed.' Add to this that the one item most fales *do* have—and I suspect that they traded in their walls to get it—is a ninety-inch TV. This is also the fale's primary light source, which acts as a giant beacon and attracts every mosquito within one kilometre to our wall-less shelter and our now completely-stressed-out immune systems— perfect for maximizing the full effect of the disease.

We thought the one saving grace with both malaria and the chikungunya virus was that if you can act preventatively during the dusk and dawn periods, when the mosquitoes that transmit them are active, then you could at least enjoy the rest of the day in a somewhat-less-panicked state. It seems not. Mother Nature tuned into this little evolutionary loophole and decided to come up with something to fill the gap: our good friend, dengue fever. Not necessarily lethal, but it also has the ability to knock you out for an extended period. Everyone we encountered who had suffered through it was incapacitated for at least two weeks, only able to lift their left pinky finger during that time.

So let's review: we have three non-vaccine-treatable mosquito-borne diseases, whose symptoms range from bad to biblical-proportions bad, that occupy our surrounding airspace throughout the day in all of the countries we plan to visit AND we have two children who refuse to wear long sleeves or pants in weather above twelve degrees Celsius, whose intuitive response to the application of insect repellent is three quick jabs to the applier's eyeball with their index finger.

Now might be the time to actually have the family meeting that we should have had before we left: Do we feel comfortable exposing our children to such potential dangers? It's one thing to have Daria force me to face these threats, because I am theoretically sane and I can make my own, albeit poor, decisions. However, is it fair of us to risk the health of our children for a travelling adventure? I imagine myself standing in line at the grocery store, buying soft fruits to blend up into supper for my two bedridden children

who can no longer chew, being chided by the shoppers behind me for being the father who gave his children "the malaria." To be honest, coming from Canada, it's an enviable position for me to have the option to "decide" whether we want to risk our children's health to a disease that decimates the child population of entire countries. It is a problem of the privileged to even have this option, as opposed to the great swaths of the world's population who have no choice and suffer with these horrible diseases on a daily basis. That, however, is what makes these types of decisions so difficult. We have been given a great gift to live in a place where we don't have to spend an inordinate amount of time worrying if our children will even reach the age of three, and now here we are, in all of our developed-nation glory, debating whether we should expose them to this danger. What's worse is that to the locals, we must come across as a bunch of travelling idiots, with our antimalarials, mosquito netting, and high-priced repellents.

In the end, though, if you look at the odds of dying due to malaria, they are lower than a number of fatal everyday incidents that could happen to anyone, including slipping in your tub/shower, dying in a car accident, or by being stung by a wasp, bee, or hornet. It is, however, still more likely that you will die of malaria than from a hippo attack, chronic constipation, or by being murdered while at the Grand Canyon. Put that way, I suddenly love my chances of surviving this trip. As long as we don't come across any constipated hippos.

BEAR IN AISLE FOUR

Australia was never meant to be, as it was never once discussed during the planning phase of our South Pacific travels. I'm not sure why. Perhaps it was because we had visions of exotic locales in the South Pacific, where we would be exposed to unique indigenous cultures and swept away by turquoise blue waters. We found this in Samoa, and after a failed, albeit weak, attempt to get to the remote island that was home to the National Park of American Samoa, we found this in Fiji as well.

You would think that since we had gone to New Zealand, Australia would be the next logical destination—the Commonwealth, the Queen, and all that, pip pip. There was just something more intriguing about New Zealand, and I'm not sure if that was actually true or if it was just that we had fallen victim to the New Zealand propaganda that was being bandied about prior to our trip. Everyone who we talked to about our travel plans prior to leaving had amazing stories about New Zealand, yet not one person had

anything to say, at all, about Australia—which made it disappear from our planning strategy. If you can call it a "strategy," that is. We're still not sure what brought us to Samoa, other than a quick mention of the country in a mid-eighties Bloomsbury comic. And our plan after Samoa was to just slowly make our way to Southeast Asia, but after that, we had nothing.

Add to this, my understanding of Australia was condensed into overinflated parodies of its own characters. Crocodile Dundee. Steve Irwin. Dame Edna. This made it even less appealing, but I guess every country can be reduced to a parody of itself; Canada—Céline Dion, Doug Henning, Nickleback. Hmm, that was a little too easy. Our only other insight into Australia was from my mother, who was on a ten-day tour of the country while we were travelling in New Zealand. We would receive truncated updates from her at the time, itemizing how nice the accommodations were and how insanely dangerous the country was the moment she stepped outside of her hotel lobby. Her emails were akin to a field correspondent's harried reports from a war zone, barely managing to get out the details before the next round of shelling began and she had to bug out. Her final update, before she went dark, was: "Great Barrier Reef. Flushed out to Sea. Death imminent. Sandwiches at lunch excellent. Love, Mom."

While we were in Fiji, we kept looking for ways to get to Indonesia (exciting!), but every flight or itinerary always went through Australia (lame!), with a brief layover in either Brisbane or Sydney. It just seemed wrong to have travelled halfway around the world to be in the country only for a layover, because if anyone asked us after the trip if we had been to Australia, we would have to sheepishly reply, "Well, yes. For a few hours. We didn't much care for it. The airport washrooms were a tad unkempt." To avoid offending an entire nation/continent/island (Oh for God's sake, make up your mind!), we chose to stay for longer than an episode of *Miss Fisher's Murder Mysteries* (POW! How about that for an Australian reference?) and get an idea of what the country was all about.

If you are getting the sense that our planning procedure is slightly haphazard, much like the writing style in this book, you would be correct. It caused me no shortage of anxiety whenever I would meet other travellers who had their entire trip, or large parts thereof, planned and purchased far in advance. Our theory was that we would get more insight into countries or places once we were there and talking to people, and this would, in turn, guide our decision-making process as to where we should go. We kept repeating this, trying to reassure ourselves that our lack of any tangible research on destinations—other than, "I like Thai food, let's go there"—was going to carry us safely through an entire year of travel. Understandably, I would quickly enter a downward spiral of self-doubt the minute I began talking with any traveller who actually had any semblance of a plan. This was accentuated when they would start asking slightly pointed questions as to how our children were handling our "interesting" travel strategy.

And so, flights were booked to allow us to arrive in Brisbane and drive up the east coast of Australia (Queensland), and eventually fly out of Cairns. We found a cheap deal on the lowliest of camper vans with the intention of camping along the way, and travel visas were purchased online.

Our initial impression of Australia was that we were back in Canada. Everything about Brisbane, and most of the other places that we visited, were eerily reminiscent of our home country. Replace every Tim Hortons coffee shop on every corner of every street, alleyway, and sidewalk in Canada with a skin cancer clinic; swap endless snowdrifts and frozen lakes with sweeping crescents of sandy beaches on expanses of beautiful ocean; and replace an inferiority complex to the USA with a superiority complex to New Zealand, and voilà—Canstralia!

The one glaring difference between the two countries, though, is that Australians truly pride themselves on how nonchalant they are about how perilous their country is. As Canadians, we know a thing or two about backcountry danger: vast expanses of

land without cellular coverage and not a drive-thru coffee shop in sight—terrifying! And don't forget the wildlife, which can be daunting if you allow yourself to think about it. I know many people who are averse to camping in our provincial and national parks because of the presence of bears. In most of Canada, this would primarily be brown or black bears, which are generally near-sighted and just looking for a peanut butter fix. If you give a mother and her cubs a wide berth, you should be okay. I have had a number of encounters with bears and have managed to stay calm, keep my distance, and make a lot of noise. They seemed fine with this arrangement and went on their way. Things get a little dodgier when you start dealing with the likes of moose, cougars, and grizzly bears. All three of these animals seem to be a little bit, how shall we say, unstable.

This is relatively tame in comparison with what Australia has to offer. There is some serious shit happening on that continent. You are initially inclined to think that the madness is confined to the deeper reaches of the country, away from any urban setting. In Canada, for instance, you feel pretty confident that you're not going to be attacked by a grizzly in the checkout line of your local grocery store or mauled by a cougar at the bank. Though if these threats truly existed, it might actually help to expedite these monotonous routines; think of how much faster you would get through the grocery store if there was the imminent risk of being dismembered while trying to buy your weekly groceries. Shopping lists would be reduced to the bare essentials ("DO NOT buy honey!!") as you ran through the aisles at top speed, ever a watchful eye on the top of the shelves for the telltale signs of your would-be attacker, and an acute ear tuned into the store's PA system for the informative-yet-harried announcement of "Attention shoppers: Bear in Aisle Four! Bear in Aisle Four!"

In Australia, however, this is not far from the truth. Here, the big threat is saltwater crocodiles, which, in contradiction to their moniker, can inhabit any form of water, including freshwater lakes

and rivers, hot tubs, and coffee pots of a certain size. Because of their heavy weight and reptilian nature, they are usually found in areas around bodies of water, which, unfortunately, is nearly every rural and urban setting in Australia. The danger is so ubiquitous that you are on guard everywhere, especially when you are camping. Even in those campsites where there were no crocodile warnings, we sometimes all slept in the van because in a worst-case scenario, a thin layer of tent nylon was most definitely not enough to protect us from a mouth full of teeth.

At one municipal campsite in Airlie Beach (Population about 8,000), where there theoretically should not have been any crocodiles, I was engrossed in the nightly ritual of setting up the tent when Daria began yelling my name from the direction of the camp kitchen. Focused on the subtle intricacies of hammering tent pegs, I kept my head down and slipped into Husband Automatron mode. *Yes, dear. No, dear. Whatever you would like, dear.* Daria continued with her attempts to capture my attention until I finally lifted my head to look at her. With one arm laden with a stack of freshly cleaned dishes, she extended the other to shakily point at a spot just beyond where I was kneeling. Anticipating a cute koala moment or something similar, I followed her eyes to where she trained her gaze, and was unexpectedly greeted by a reptile that was about as long and as wide as a casket (at least, that's what immediately came to mind), ambling about two-and-a-half metres in front of where I was now fully immersed in the act of soiling myself.

There is a moment when, faced with imminent death, we as humans are divided into two camps: the courageous, who calmly assess the situation, reach for the nearest weapon, and casually stride forward to protect our family; and the other, slightly less heroic group, to which I belong. My response consisted of immediately springing up, landing off-balance, and then stumbling backwards like a drunken sailor on roller skates. Once I regained my equilibrium and was able to focus again, I determined that what

I was looking at was not a crocodile but some ungodly oversized lizard. Our Australian campsite neighbour, who had been casually watching the events unfold while frying eggs on his portable stove, gently informed me that it was a monitor lizard that was wandering a mere handbite away.

"Dangerous?" I asked.

"Naw. Only if they bite; their saliva is poisonous."

"Do they bite?"

"Why wouldn't they?" he replied, looking at me as if I was a total idiot.

"So, they are dangerous."

"Only if you get too close to them."

"How close is 'close'?"

"Depends. You're pretty close."

What. The. Grrrr …

It needs to be stated that there is a certain contingent of Australians who inhabit the campsites throughout the country, and our neighbour happened to be one of them. These individuals fit perfectly into the classic stereotype that we North Americans hold of Australians: a cross of Crocodile Dundee meets Mad Max. Outfitted with a leather vest, crocodile-tooth-studded hat, and matching utility belt that is filled with oversized hunting knives, they spend years driving around the country in a 4 x 4 that has been modified with a top exhaust and various other adaptations that will be quite helpful during the upcoming nuclear winter. They are not the least bit intimidated by the hazards Australia has to offer, and quite enjoy the humour of watching tourists adapt to the natural glory that is their country.

On a side note, the 4 x 4 trailers towed by these campers (if we can call them that—"survivalists" might be a more apt moniker) can best be described as a rolling, armoured apartment. I loved these things. In preparation for highway driving, the trailers are reduced to a squat, square sandwich, completely encased in galvanized steel plates, like a turtle retracted into its own shell.

DON'T TRY THIS AT HOME

In this configuration, they are utterly bombproof, ready for any off-roading adventure or missile attack that might happen in the Outback. Once parked, they spring to life, with every inch of space expanding into a bedroom, kitchen, bathroom, front deck patio, swimming pool, sauna, and a fifteen-seat movie theatre. Sadly, no robotic butler to serve you, but as I understand it, that modification will be available shortly.

Each time we were next to one of these portable bomb shelters, I had to engage the owner in conversation just so I could get a demonstration of this fantastic bit of camping prowess. And they would happily oblige. How could you not be proud of everything these trailers were capable of doing? Compartments were opened; walk-in closets were explored. I might have to move my mother into one of these things.

That was, fortunately, the closest we came to a crocodile during our trip, at least that we know of. Throughout Australia, though, I was on high alert whenever we were close to any body of water, especially since the typical surroundings of fallen logs and pebble-encrusted mud always looked exactly like a lurking croc. It was reminiscent of our time spent in northern Canada outside Churchill, Manitoba, when the van rental agency informed us that it would be unwise to get out of our vehicle at any time along the roadway, as the large white boulders strewn about the landscape tended not to be boulders at all, but resting polar bears. Which begged the question: "Why are you renting us a rolling coffin?"

Though the threat of crocs was diminished when we were away from water, this void was quickly filled by poisonous snakes (some one hundred snakes in Australia are poisonous but only twelve are likely to inflict a wound that could kill you— reassuring), venomous spiders, and non-venomous-but-insanely-large spiders that would fit perfectly over my entire face. Of these, huntsman spiders can grow to be about fifteen centimetres across and have a habit of attacking speeding cars by

throwing themselves onto the front windshield in order to gnaw into the glass while simultaneously reaching through the open side windows in order to gouge your eyes out. This latter part was based on information we received from a demure French couple who had obviously been scarred by their brief encounter with a huntsman, but whom we now held to be the foremost authorities on Australian arachnids. There's also the Australian tarantula and the golden orb spider, which makes webs strong enough to catch birds—I repeat, *to catch birds*—which they do then, in fact, eat.

Of course, what would be the point of such an outrageously dangerous country if it didn't also have insanely toxic plants to go along with the baseline of fear already created by the fauna? We tend to go by the rule that "if you don't eat it, you'll be fine," and if you do accidentally brush against an unfriendly plant, the worst that can happen is an annoying rash akin to poison ivy or poison oak. Thus, the warning notices for the gympie gympie plant at one trailhead weren't taken very seriously (especially given its name) until later in the hike when we came across a sign that explained how contact with the plant would cause an injection of neurotoxins into your system, with symptoms that could be recurring for months on end. Neurotoxins that are in the same family as sarin and its ilk of other deadly friends. After this, all I could think of on any hike was that the entire Australian rainforest was booby-trapped.

What compounds this incessant feeling of being hunted by anything and everything around you is that, at the end of the day, the onset of nightfall is both sudden and chaotic. Once the sun begins its final descent, giant flocks of birds take flight, covering wide swaths of the sky as they head for their roosting sites in a clamour of high-pitched shrieks and panicked cries. Against this setting, with nightfall dropping like a stage curtain at the end of an act, it felt like we were abruptly thrust into some horror movie where the oncoming darkness would unleash some unknown evil that would wrap itself around those who weren't smart enough to get to a safe

haven. With our senses now triggered and in full "fight-or-flight" mode, we assumed that everyone else around us must be experiencing the same state of dread as we raced against one another to get to safe sanctuaries. This bedlam was further intensified as some of the private campsites that we stayed at closed their gates at dusk and refused to admit any new registrants once the sun had disappeared. It was every person for themselves as I rammed seniors with my shopping cart to move them out of the way so I could get to our van and blindly throw the kids and groceries into the back. Once inside, the anarchy would escalate as we yelled at each other to hurry and buckle up, with Daria leaning out of the window, swatting the air with her hand, screaming at cars to move so that we could have a free path by which to careen out of the parking lot and down the highway—all so that we could make it to our destination in time to be let in. On those times that we didn't make it, we were left standing outside the gates, pleading to an uninterested voice on the other side of the intercom to please, *please* let us in as the darkness encroached. This feeling of isolation became further exacerbated by the sound of closing windows and shutters all around us, as local residents tried to block out the sound of four Canadians wailing, "PLEASE DON'T LET US DIE OUT HERE TONIGHT, YOU MERCHANTS OF DEATH!" It won't come as a surprise to anyone that I managed to amass $1,300 in speeding tickets during our short stay in Australia.

And so, against this panorama of death, we somehow became beguiled with the country. Moving up the coastline of Queensland, we were able to explore rainforests, climb peaks in national parks, and spend days on end living in picturesque beach towns. We stayed for an extended period in Mission Beach, where it felt like we became part of the community due to our frequent trips to the library and a local bar where Daria and I would alternate nights using the Wi-Fi to complete some work projects. We were excited by a boat tour to snorkel in the Great Barrier Reef but wound up being more enthralled by the side trip that took us to the stunning

Whitsunday Islands. Viewed from a hilltop vantage point to which we had hiked, the islands are encircled by crisp white beaches whose sand particles spread into the surrounding sapphire waters like the tendrils of a shot of cream in a cup of coffee. Once back at ocean level, we spent the afternoon plotting to one day return to the spartan campsites nestled at the forest's edge behind us—a plan that would afford us the luxury of enjoying the dazzling salt-like sand beach by ourselves at the end of the day. We stayed in Port Douglas, our access point to the Mossman Gorge and Daintree Rainforest, both World Heritage Sites, in which we hiked to waterfalls and ziplined from the forest canopy down to the ocean's edge.

Australia also supplied us with endless stretches of golden beaches. As Canadians, we have an inherent need to enter water whenever we see it unfrozen because we know it won't last long. What's frustrating in Australia, though, is that in order to be safe and to protect our family and all that good parenting stuff, we had to make sure that we swam only in areas where a lifeguard was on duty. On beaches that stretch for kilometres, such designated areas were only ten metres wide with one lifeguard monitoring the masses that jammed themselves into this narrow strip of water. To put this into context, imagine that you have just installed an aboveground pool that's four metres by four metres and all of your children's classmates have come over for a swim at the same time, with some of them bringing ironing boards into the pool just so they can swing them around. That's what swimming at the beach is like in Australia.

Even with a lifeguard on duty, you aren't really able to ever fully enjoy yourself, as it's recommended that you don't go into water any deeper than waist-height. So swimming with the children, if I wasn't holding on to them, meant I was only up to my shins in water. Even when I decided to venture out to my waist, I was so terrified about crocs, sharks, and jellyfish that I never took my eyes off the lifeguard standing on the beach, lest they frantically start waving their hands to inform me that a row of teeth had been

spotted just past my mouth-sized waist and my appetizer-sized children.

What I wasn't prepared for was the rip currents. I consider myself to be a strong swimmer and I have swum in many places that warned about dangerous waters (Hawaii, California, Noah's Ark Water Park at Wisconsin Dells—you do not want to get your head under that water), but what I experienced in Australia makes the current in all of those places seem like the gentle tug of water draining from the bathtub. In Agnes Water, a small town on the coast of central Queensland, I was playing with the kids in waist-high surf next to a mother and her two teenage children when I started to feel the pull. I tightened my grip on Oskar and Isla, bent my knees, lowering my centre of gravity, and dug in. Both of the kids were loving this feeling of being pulled out by the current, and they let their bodies rise up horizontally, pretending to fly while I clutched on to them, making my job even harder because they were acting like wings on a plane and creating a dangerous lift effect. When I turned to the mother and her family to share in a sarcastic "isn't-this-fun?!" moment, she was gone—swept out with her kids. I turned my head around and saw them about one hundred metres out, in hysterics, swimming frantically but getting nowhere. I dug in deeper and kept both feet planted for fear that if I even shifted an inch I would be funnelled out as well, undoubtedly sucked directly into the jaws of a great white shark waiting at the end of a giant straw. The rip eventually dissipated, the family was rescued, and I was able to make it back to shore, crawling up on to the beach like a survivor from a shipwreck. The kids seemed unfazed, jumping next to me in excitement about experiencing the riptide and hoping to go back in again. And, naturally, we did.

Unfortunately, the danger of the beaches wasn't just in the water. Since we did a lot of camping by the ocean, one of my favourite things was to wake up before everyone and go for a barefoot jog along the shoreline; sun rising, water glistening, beach perfectly smooth. Rainbow Beach, a state park campsite on the ocean,

afforded a beautiful backdrop to the early morning run. After a couple days of this, I bumped into another one of those hardcore Australian camper-types taking in the relative stillness that the morning had to offer. While we were chatting, he noted my lack of shoes.

"You may not want to do that," he said, motioning to my bare feet.

Here we go again.

"Oh?"

"Just might not want to step on something you don't want to step on."

Great, an Australian Yogi Berra. He gestured to the marble-shaped jelly globs that had washed up on the beach.

"I didn't think those were anything serious."

"They're probably just sea gooseberries. Then again, they could also be jellies. You might just want to be a little careful around them."

Advice heeded. Once we got back to a town with Internet, I did a quick check on marble-sized jellyfish, just to be safe in case I did get stung, thinking that there could be only so much damage that a washed-up, semi-dehydrated, thumb-sized jellyfish could impart.

Guess what?

It turns out Mr. Dundee had a point and that I might have been prancing around Irukandji jellyfish. Their stings can be so severe that they can cause fatal brain hemorrhages and, on average, they send fifty to one hundred people to hospital annually.

According to one article, "on a pain index of zero to ten, with zero being no pain at all and ten being the most excruciating pain imaginable, [a] Dr. Jamie Seymour ranked the pain of a sting from an Irukandji jellyfish a twelve."

A twelve. A twelve out of ten. And this is not some drummer from your high school buddy's band telling you how much it hurt after he accidentally dropped a bong on his foot. This is an

educated researcher giving an objective description of how intense the level of pain truly is.

That's it. I'm done. It's been great, Australia, but I have to leave now and go to a country whose wildlife has the common decency to stay within the boundaries of the one-to-ten pain threshold scale. Plus, I just found out that certain models of Australian refrigerators are poisonous.

THE HEART OF DARKNESS
AND THE INTERLOPER

Near the five-month mark of our trip, we had settled comfortably into our travelling routine. We had camped for over three of those months and were all still on speaking terms with one another. We had been faced with some minor setbacks such as seasickness, stomach ailments, and lice, and had dealt with all of them without much pain or suffering. In other words, we were getting the hang of travelling together for extended periods of time. Granted, the countries we had visited were fairly friendly when it came to inexperienced Western travellers. Indeed, all four were Commonwealth nations, which meant English was widely spoken, though in parts of New Zealand and Australia it was not necessarily readily understandable—"Ay, crikey mate," and whatnot. But now the plan was to move northward towards Indonesia, into what we presumed were some less-developed and more remote countries. My preconceived perception was that these were places

where we might be so deep in the backwoods (or is the politically correct term "backjungles"?) that we would be separated from what I knew as "civilization," both literally and figuratively, for extended periods of time.

As we moved closer to these areas, our unease was fed by a long list of horror stories that guidebooks and fellow travellers heaped upon us, involving the multitude of scams that existed throughout these regions. It seemed that each city or country had its own unique style of making things a little crazier for travellers. Bangkok was known for its motorcycle bandits, and we were told to just let go of our bags if someone grabbed them while zooming by—tourists had been dragged for kilometres as the bandits refused to stop. Other cities had moped rental companies whose owner would follow you and "steal" your bike using a duplicate key once you left it unattended, then charge you the full cost of a replacement. Money on the ground?—Don't touch it, it's a scam! Sprayed with mustard?—Refuse assistance, it's a scam! Fries with that or supersize your Coke? NO! It's a scam! "Oh, wait … sorry, I didn't mean to yell at you—I forgot I was ordering lunch."

To encapsulate my fear of the insanity we were about to encounter, I lovingly branded the entirety of Southeast Asia as the "Heart of Darkness." We were going up a proverbial river into a no-man's-land that was run by a lunatic. It was going to be a challenge to come out of this part of the trip alive, and I had already resigned myself to this fact.

Because tragedy loves company, we naturally agreed to endanger the life of our seventeen-year-old neighbour from back in Canada, who we invited on this portion of the trip. We had discussed the possibility of having him join us, but we never thought it would actually happen. Our email exchanges with his family in the weeks leading up to his arrival never felt concrete, as we were living so haphazardly at the time that actual plans seemed like a distant reality. Apparently, some people take the vacant ramblings of our family at face value, and we were told that we would be

receiving our adopted family member, Addie, ten days after we arrived in Indonesia.

Our journey into this country began in Ubud, where we were immediately hit with the realization that we had entered a completely different world altogether. Our surroundings had morphed both visually and aromatically overnight. Our home for the first week was a skeletal wooden building with a roofless bathroom and mosquito-net walls surrounding our bedrooms. We awoke each morning to a sun rising, whose vermillion colour and pudding-like texture was so rich and deep that it seemed to be hovering just beyond over the adjacent rice fields. This light was amplified by the haze that covered the ground, generated from the non-stop burning of incense and garbage that infused the air with its own unique fragrance (burnt-plastic patchouli, anyone?) as it mixed with the moist, earthy smells emanating from the lush plants and pastoral landscape surrounding us. Laced throughout this visual and olfactory overload was the constant, low drone of the Islamic call to prayer from some distance mosques, interspersed with the chanting of Hindu mantras. Ubud turned out to be an excellent introduction to Asia, as it was a smaller city that was heavy on culture, with museums, art galleries, and indigenous dance troupes, and light on craziness. Our days here consisted of exploring both the town and its surrounding countryside, while acclimatizing to our new surroundings.

The Interloper met us a few days later in the coastal town of Amed, and so began our descent into … *madness*! And there was no better place to start than on the island of Gili Air, just off the coast of Bali. A small island that could be circumnavigated in about thirty minutes, it had a sense of casual lawlessness, with no police presence on the island itself and magic mushrooms on every restaurant menu. Fireworks and other combustibles were readily available from roving bands of eight-year-olds at stands that were relocated daily, leaving darkened remnants of recent brush fires behind. Adding to this aura of recklessness was that our wallets had

ballooned to the size of bricks, as they were filled with 50,000 rupiah notes (essentially five-dollar bills), the only denomination we could get our hands on before coming to the island, whose ATMs, we were told, rarely worked. After one of the few times we did use our credit card, I promptly received an email notification that someone had just bought $7,000 worth of airline tickets with it.

Not one to be left out of the fun, our friend the Interloper had managed to get stung by a jellyfish, cut his foot on coral, and was bitten by a daytime mosquito that looked suspiciously similar to the dengue-fever-transmitting variety. So, in addition to vigilantly protecting our comically overstuffed wallets, I was now watching the Interloper for any signs of dengue fever or festering of his coral wound.

Oh, Heart of Darkness, you do not disappoint.

While Gili Air had its own sense of mania, it seemed like nothing compared to the Mad-Max-Thunderdome vibe given off by its sister island, Gili Trawangan. We stopped there only briefly on our way back to Bali to unload passengers from our 'boat' (loosely defined in Indonesia), but we were unable to see anything of the island itself due to the three-metre-high walls of empty beer bottle cases stacked all along its shore. With our view blocked, the yells and smashing sounds originating from the other side of the wall created the impression that a Wild-West-style barroom brawl was in full swing somewhere beyond Mount Heineken. As we watched the disembarking passengers disappear through a narrow slit in the beer case wall, we wished them luck in the upcoming MMA cage matches they would undoubtedly be partaking in during their stay on the island.

On the other end of the spectrum, Gunung Mulu National Park in Borneo, where we ventured later in our travels, exposed us to the remoteness of this literal "Heart of Darkness." Set deep in the wilderness of Borneo, this park seemed like a reasonable way to immerse ourselves in a jungle experience, as its strong infrastructure allowed us to explore the old-growth rainforests of

this UNESCO World Heritage Site. It earned this designation due to the wide array of geological, plant, and animal life that exists within its borders, including 170 different varieties of orchids and 109 species of palm trees, all of which create a deep carpet of green on the rolling hills and up to the limestone spires that flank the three mountains of the park. The park is home to some of the largest caves on the planet, and we were able to hike into the cathedral-sized chambers that housed millions of bats, and then watch as they streamed out into the sky at dusk, spiralling upwards as one giant corkscrew ribbon overhead. During the day, we hiked through and above the towering rainforest canopy, and at night a park guide introduced us to the vast insect populations that were hidden from our untrained eyes. While exploring the park, we stayed just outside its border in a family-run home that was one of the more interesting accommodations during our travels. We were lucky enough to get a room to ourselves, though our hosts had to jam our five beds into every available centimetre, forcing us to squeeze through a door that no longer swung open and to bounce from bed to bed in order to cross the room. Above this jumbled maze of mattresses, we attached a patchwork of mosquito nets to any available light fixture or nail to create a spider's lair of mesh webbing that enclosed us in a cocoon of safety during the night. Other travellers were scattered throughout the adjacent living room in makeshift beds that were shrouded by a fog of mosquito-coil smoke, a scene reminiscent of a late-night house party whose guests had overstayed their welcome. This was also the only place during our travels where we actually took our anti-malaria pills, though we all gave up on them within two days. An A for effort!

As deep as we thought we were in this isolated jungle environment, we were never really very far removed from civilization. There was always electricity (at least, during some parts of the day), we could always find clean drinking water, and there was always someone who spoke some form of English and knew some

weird cultural reference, like *The Big Bang Theory*. I am sure that there are still places on this earth where you can feel separated from the rest of the world, lost in place and time, but the reality is that you have to work exceptionally hard to get yourself into those situations. The world has opened itself to tourists, and in the past few decades, people are taking advantage of cheaper flights, more leisure time, and their higher incomes to invade all the places that were once rarely visited. Borneo is not as mysterious as it once may have been. My fear of the deeper recesses of Asia was alleviated here, as I came to realize that no path would take me so far off the grid that a can of Coke or a package of Oreos was unattainable.

On the other hand, the pure insanity (and subsequent hilarity) of the Heart of Darkness never diminished.

Now, it's not that I expect certain standards in life—one look at my own household, with its optional bi-monthly cleaning regime, will confirm that—but I do enjoy the fact that the part of the world where I live tends not to use a model of "outright, unadulterated chaos" as the cornerstone upon which its systems are built. At home, I know where shit is and I understand how things work. If I need groceries, I go to the store and pay the price that is listed on the package. If I need a bus, I look for a bus stop. So I'm not sure when and why some countries decided they would make travel within their borders more exciting by obscuring where to buy tickets, what the cost of said tickets are, or even where to catch the bus. "Bus stations" varied greatly, from a parking lot in the middle of a cemetery, to what seemed like someone's living room, brimming with knick-knacks, countertop burners simmering that night's dinner, and at least three to four dogs chasing each other around.

"Sorry, didn't mean to walk in on you while you were sitting on your couch, watching TV in your underwear. Oh, what? You're waiting for the minivan to Bangkok too? Oh, I see. You're the driver. Nice to, er, meet … you?"

In the early days of our travels, we'd often assume that we were being led to our demise, as instructions that we'd receive to get to

the bus took us through darkened, narrow alleyways, deep in the bowels of some strange city. This duress was naturally compounded by the nine bags that we had to lug along with us, of which I was usually responsible for six or seven. Why did we always need three bags of food for bus rides?

Our fears would be allayed once we arrived at said location and were immediately flocked upon by numerous excited vendors who let us know that, yes, in fact, we were their good friend and that they indeed were saving the best price for us. If the conversion price was any indicator, "Good" and "Best" turned out to be sub-jective terms, we realised, once we got away from the flurry of ges-ticulating hands and were able to convert the price into Canadian dollars. From guidebooks and fellow travellers, we would often have a rough idea of how much a ticket should cost, but those numbers would differ from the ones we received. A little gringo uptick here, a non-Spanish-speaking surtax there (cursed are the parents who teach their only child German!), and let's not forget the third-Tuesday-of the-month currency surcharge—if you're wearing a blue shirt.

In exchange, we'd sometimes get a scrap of paper that looked like something Isla had torn from a newspaper, but most of the time we just got a pat on the back and a turn in the direction of a group of buses or minivans, and then the "shoo shoo" wave towards them. We'd always be left with a sense of "what just happened?" as we walked towards the unsigned bus, minivan, or car that we thought was ours. And yet it always worked out and we managed to get to our destinations—perhaps not as cheaply or as elegantly as most, but arrive we did—and it almost always came down to a matter of trust. And maybe that's at the heart of what makes me feel so unsettled in these countries. I like to know what things cost and I don't want to have to ask every time I want to buy a bottle of water. I would always try to convert the price in my head under the antic-ipating glare of the seller, who would already be bagging things for me. I'd panic and just agree, and usually the price I calculated

seemed to make sense. I did, however, get screwed a few times. That's right, I'm talking to you, fruit boy on the first floor of the market in Ollantaytambo, in the stall next to the old lady selling North Face backpacks and Sony Walkmans—four bananas should not cost seventeen dollars. I'm on to you.

Our path from Indonesia took us up the Malay Peninsula towards Bangkok, through Singapore, Malaysia, and southern Thailand and the islands off its eastern coast. It was during this time that local families we'd meet started to ask if they could take pictures with Isla Blue, whose blonde hair and blue eyes were a stark contrast to their own features. She would be moved into position next to the family's own glowering child, and after a few pictures were taken, the other child would be goaded out of the frame and a few snaps would be taken of Isla Blue by herself. We didn't think much of this at first, as it seemed awfully flattering to Isla Blue. I, however, began to feel awkward about it when I actually thought about how I would feel if I were that age and my parents had done this to me. *Really? You need a photograph of a complete stranger's child without me 'tarnishing' the picture?* I imagined that this was the beginning of an emotional landslide for said offspring as he/she watched their own parents fawn over Isla Blue, propelling them into an emotional shell in which their resentment would fester during their formative years, only to end in a rampage of violence sometime in adulthood. Not keen to be the ones responsible for the next Pol Pot or Suharto, we began to reciprocate and take pictures of their children. This all seemed strange to us, but we had to do something in order to ensure future world peace. "Thank you very much, Rob and Daria," would be the correct thing to say at this juncture. You're welcome.

You would think that all of this attention might have actually helped to calm our own little dictator down. Unfortunately, not so much. The only thing that managed to soothe Isla Blue's temperament were prolonged showers of any temperature. At first, we would try to limit her shower time so that we could actually head out somewhere,

but once we realized that we were able to have normal conversations with one another when she was in there, we just let her go for as long as she wanted. We looked to the Interloper as the voice of reason in this situation—being a relative outsider to the family—and he seemed quite content with this "parenting strategy."

In terms of parenting, the Interloper himself was a joy to have along on this stretch of the trip. He was exceptionally responsible and aware for a seventeen-year-old, and seemed genuinely interested in being with our family. There were the occasional nights when he would hang out with some people closer to his age at the restaurant or bar attached to where we were staying, but he never stayed out too late or gave us any cause for concern. Additionally, we never really knew how much we should parent him, as he was a young adult and his parents were pretty liberal with their own parenting strategy. We should probably have delved into the issue of alcohol consumption a little more when he said his parents were indifferent to his having a beer or two—something that was not entirely true, as we found out once we were back home.

How much one can actually parent an older child who is not your own was unclear to us. It's difficult for so many reasons, but for us it was hard primarily because we had zero experience raising a teenager. Handling an eight-year-old whom you've watched develop, with whom you've created a relationship and layers of rules and standards that are expected of them, is quite different from suddenly being responsible for an almost-adult with whom there are no past parenting moments. Luckily, there was only one issue that caused things to become a bit tense between him and me: when he refused to listen to my advice about the stomach troubles he had developed. We knew that he was having issues every so often, but he never let on that it was no longer a sporadic thing and had become quite constant. When I kicked into hyper-substitute-dad mode (i.e., "You're not dying on my watch, kid!") and suggested that he should lay off the ice cream and dairy products for a bit and just eat bananas and rice while drinking

more Gatorade-like beverages, he countered by eating more ice cream and hiding the electrolytic fluids and bananas I kept foisting upon him. So, in other words, a classic parent–teenager standoff.

All of this feel-good parenting rah-rah was about to be put to the test as we brought the Interloper to Bangkok, his departure point to head back home. *Bangkok*. The name itself evokes images of opium dens and heroin smugglers. This was the home of lost souls, alcohol-fuelled, all-night parties, fraudsters, prostitutes, and ping-pong girls. We were entering ground zero of the Heart of Darkness. How was I going to protect the Interloper, let alone my family, from all this?

I had so sufficiently scared our travelling party on the way into Bangkooky that everyone was wary the second we disembarked the minivan in the heart of the city. Akin to Roman foot soldiers moving into enemy territory, we unintentionally closed ranks and formed a circle with our backs against each other while clutching our bags tightly in front of us. Even with such insane defensive positioning, no one around us seemed to take notice, as if this was just normal behaviour for first-time visitors.

Visually, downtown Bangkok lived up to all my frenetic expectations. Layers of buildings wrapped around each other, occupying every piece of vertical space, with multi-tiered pedestrian walkways and elevated monorail lines that snaked between it all. Brilliantly lit neon billboards seemed to hover in the night sky above us like floodlights at a football stadium, covering us with a continuous halogen glow that pulsed from red to blue to white, transforming the appearance of the buildings and people upon which this stark light fell. At street level, food vendors were wedged into the shadows of pie-shaped nooks between buildings, serving up dumplings and skewers to an audience not only looking for a quick bite, but also hoping for respite from the harsh glare of the street scene beyond. This city was obviously responsible for inspiring some of the set design in the original *Blade Runner* movie. This scene wouldn't be complete without some ludicrous traffic to go

along with it. In our traditional understanding, we look at the one-way street as, well, a one-way, where vehicles should be travelling in only one direction, and never against the flow of traffic. Not so in Bangkok. there always is. It's never straightforward either, like a truck barrelling directly into a stream of oncoming cars. Oh no, it's subtle and cagey, like the locals know that we might be looking for the obvious. No one had warned us about the old "Thai-Double-One-Way-Wrong-Way" maneuver.

To exacerbate this, we have a six-year-old and an eight-year-old who, for some reason, don't understand the reasoning behind such irrational driving. So when we are ready to cross, they are either a) paralyzed by fear and don't move, and we've lost the split second that we could have used; b) they think they should run as fast as possible out of the gate, thus throwing off the timing of what could have been a well-executed crossing; or c) they actually make it halfway across but then suddenly panic and freeze for a few seconds in the middle of the street, only to snap out of it and sprint back to where we started.

Amid this vehicular chaos, we huddled in our defensive position and shuffled off towards the hostel near the MBK Mall that was recommended to us by our friends, who had frequented Bangkok often.

We entered a restaurant squeezed behind the pillar of an elevated train and walked through its dining area into the kitchen, where uninterested cooks flipping noodles in their woks let us pass among them and exit out into a hybrid mechanic shop/lobby area, replete with a number of cannibalized vehicles scattered amongst sofas, and coffee tables. There, an older gentleman appeared from behind the motorcycle he was working on and greeted us while wiping his hands with an oily rag. Oddly enough, the directions supplied by our friends described these series of events exactly, right up to "watch for an old guy to pop up from behind a motorcycle."

Safe in our room and spent from the day of travel, Daria and I

turtled onto the plastic-covered mattresses in our spartan room and, in a moment of exhaustion, said, "Sure, sounds great," when the Interloper indicated he was going out to look for a bite to eat. After about thirty minutes, we naturally feared the worst. We switched back into concerned-parent mode and exited out into the cacophony that is the Bangkok streetscape, stopping ourselves at the entrance to our restaurant/autoshop/hostel. We couldn't just go out into this city looking for him. Where would we start? This was a city filled with every imaginable vice you could think of, and then some. The Interloper was gone and we probably weren't going to see him for days. We envisioned the dreaded call to his parents if he didn't show up later that night ("Oh, I'm sure he's fine. He's probably just hunkered down at some Candle Fire Blow Show somewhere; you know, getting a 'happy ending' massage and smoking opium."), and tried to think of what real parents would do in this situation. Stalling out at "they wouldn't have let their kid out in the first place!" and pointing fingers at each other, we were thankful to see the Interloper sauntering up the street towards us, gnawing on a barbequed chicken skewer. In this city, oozing with every conceivable temptation, the Interloper had spent the past hour watching an animated traffic officer doing his rush-hour, dance-inspired routine on a platform in the middle of Bangkok's early-evening traffic.

That night was spent walking around our neighbourhood, loosening our fears, and enjoying the weirdness that is Bangkok. I went to bed with the feeling that we would make it through this too; that as crazy and as intense as the urban part of Asia was, it was all just a matter of acclimatizing and adapting. We could handle anything that the Heart of Darkness threw at us. We had booked ourselves a bicycle tour through the back streets of Bangkok for the next day and had found cheap flights that would bring us to Cambodia two days later and expose us to yet another layer of Asian quirkiness.

The next morning, I found out my father had died of a heart attack.

WHO'S GOT DADDY ISSUES?

That morning, I woke to the persistent ring of my phone, alerting me that someone wanted to FaceTime. Although I was still half-asleep, I knew something was up, but I chose to stay in my semi-dream state, ignoring the real world. This is my classic response to most things I don't want to face. Unfortunately, it reached such a crescendo by 7:00 a.m. that I had to at least take a look at the phone. Buried among the missed FaceTime call notices was a text from my mother that read, "Please call me as soon as you can." So, naturally, I didn't. What I did do, however, was go through the news sites to see if there had been any attacks or bombings in Bangkok, hoping that she was just checking in to see if we were okay. A subsequent perusal of my hometown's local websites did nothing other than to reassure that Winnipeg continues to be Winnipeg. I recognize that hoping for some larger tragedy affecting a broader populace, rather than dealing with my mother directly, certainly does not shine a positive light on my

character, but avoidance is my key coping strategy when dealing with the possibility of personal loss.

At the next FaceTime chiming, I answered and got the news about my father. The good news was that it was a massive heart attack that killed him instantly while he was swimming in the pool at his rental property, which, incidentally, he never rented out. The bad news was, well, he was dead, and no matter how you spin that, it is never good.

Now, that's not to say that my father was the picture of health at age seventy-three, or that this was completely unexpected. In 2001, he had been admitted into hospital for congestive heart failure, although my father, with all of his years of medical training (read: none), vehemently disagreed with this assessment and continued his diet of chèvre cheese logs and alcohol.

His death, though, did come as a total surprise to me. Even with his bad dietary habits and previous physical ailments, I had assumed that he would outlive me. This is perhaps what all children believe of their parents. In a horrible way, though, I was always afraid of his resiliency. I feared that he would drift into his nineties with his physical condition slowly deteriorating and that I, as the only child, would be the one left responsible for taking care of him, either because he had outlived his wife or had driven her away. My stepmother, Ruth, and my mother have always said that my father was a "complex" and "difficult" man, but the truth is he could be a downright ass to those who were closest to him. He had a strong opinion about everything, and his opinion was always the correct one. Because he was intelligent, well-read, and had a wide breadth of knowledge about history, politics, science, and anything fact-based, he was able to defend his position on any topic. If you were a colleague, friend, or even a stranger, he was open for discussion and interested in your viewpoints. In fact, he was well-liked by most people he met because of his gregarious nature and endless cache of entertaining stories. But if you fell within the inner circle

of his life, you were not proffered such deference and your input could be chided or ridiculed.

The last thing I wanted was to become his primary caregiver. So in some ways, there was a sense of relief when I found out he had passed away. And I know that sounds horrible, but my relationship with my father was an odd one. This may have stemmed from the fact that my father never really wanted to have kids. When I was older, his mother explained to me that immediately after my parents' marriage, my father—the mathematician—was extremely proud of how he had worked out my mother's cycle, Venn diagrams and all, and went through his entire strategy of birth control with my grandmother. So precise were his calculations that I was born exactly nine months later, which, now that I think about it, must have haunted him as his greatest mathematical failure.

Throughout my childhood, I'm not sure that my father ever told me that he was proud of me or that he even loved me. It was just too hard for him to say or admit, for some reason. His method of parenting reflected this as well. During high school, my dating life was nonexistent, though I didn't think that my parents had even noticed. My mother broached the subject one day by stating that they knew I was gay. Not, "Is there anything you'd like to talk about?" or, "It's okay to be who you are; we'll love you no matter what." Just a declaration. When I asked what this conclusion was based on, she said that my father (who was visibly absent from this conversation) thought that this must be the case and that she should be the one to talk to me. Nice. And let's be clear, my parents are very liberal people and were not judgmental in any way about sex, race, or any of the other hot-button issues. They just leaned more towards the "cyborg" school of parenting when dealing with emotional issues. My father actually never talked to me about this at all, but I later found out that even before he could confirm any of his hypotheses, he had already informed my relatives living in Germany of my confirmed homosexuality. I'm sure that this time he had all the proper Venn diagrams to back up his research.

After high school, my mother moved out and my father began to cycle through a heavy depression because of her departure and suddenly being single after seventeen years of marriage. My focus was on university, music, and work, so our paths didn't cross very much. Additionally, he sought out opportunities that took him out of the country for extended periods of time, and I would spend large parts of my summer and Christmas holidays on my own. As such, our relationship began to move even further apart than the usual teenager-adult relationship.

I do know that my father cared for me, and he was kind in many other ways. When I was in my twenties and he saw that I needed a new guitar amp, he bought me one without hesitation. This kind of generosity continued when I had my family, as he treated Daria and the children very well. He felt more at ease buying presents than opening up to us emotionally.

In my late thirties, I began to make an effort to tell him that I loved him whenever we spoke. It was as much for me as it was for him, as I had to learn how to actually express how I felt to someone—I had never really done it throughout my upbringing. It obviously made him uncomfortable, but after a couple of years, he began to reciprocate with a nervous and quickly spoken "I love you" when we parted. As Oskar and Isla Blue grew, he would wistfully remark that he wished that he had been a better father to me. I reassured him that I had come out all right, and that if he really wanted to, he had a second chance with my kids. But as much as he might have tried, he could never really enjoy their presence. The old habits came out again, and he would distance himself from them when they were staying over, or he would become enraged with them when they were acting like children and jumping around and touching everything in sight. Watching him react to my children was difficult for me, as I was reminded of my childhood, enduring his sternness and living in fear that something insignificant could set him off on a tirade.

Still, in my adult life, I had carved out my relationship with him and knew what our boundaries were. My father was enjoyable to be around when he was in the environment that he chose and could control, and in those situations, I was able to interact with the sociable and likable person that he presented to others. He reintroduced me to hiking when I was in my late twenties and we did a number of trips together, the first of which was an eight-day trip to Waterton Lakes National Park, where we spent our days walking in the mountains, and our nights drinking beer and enjoying each other's company. Upon returning home, though, he would slide back into his old form of not-so-subtle verbal abuse.

Now, in Bangkok, I was faced with my feelings about my father. I wasn't even sure if I wanted to return home. Did I even need to? Would it make me a horrible person if I didn't? My father wished to be cremated and had asked that there be no service, so it was more an issue of dealing with the administration-end of things, and my stepmother seemed to have that under control. She might need my support, but it also sounded as though she had a strong group of people around her.

In the end, we decided to return. When we told Isla Blue that we were heading home, she burst into cheers and I had to gently remind her why we were going home. But she was homesick, missing her friends and family, and the concept of death didn't really resonate with her. She and my father had not become very close. For Oskar, who was almost nine at the time, it was more difficult because he understood what was going on and he did have a number of strong and fond memories of his Opa.

When we arrived home, Ruth and I met a number of times to talk about my father and try to understand him a little bit better; to attempt to pry away some of the layers that surrounded him and made it so difficult for him to show affection to those who were closest to him. Contemplating this, Ruth said, "That episode with the soldier had such a tragic effect on him."

"¿Cómo?"

It seems that postwar Germany in 1946 was not all bratwurst-eating contests and beer stein pong. There was some serious shit going down, most of which involved Russian soldiers who had arrived in the country and were not known for their postwar kindness towards Germans. At the time, my father was living in a rural area of the Harz Mountains with his mother and sister. While out in the forest one day, gathering wood with a family friend, he became separated from her for a few minutes as he wandered down a different pathway. When he caught up with her again, he found her being sexually assaulted by a Russian soldier. Confronted with this image of a stranger violently attacking his "auntie," my very young father took an axe to the man in order to save her. As they left the area together, she told him that he was not to tell anyone about what had just happened, and so he shoved it deep down inside.

Upon hearing this, I immediately realized two things: 1) that this had EVERYTHING to do with my father's failings, and 2) that I was, in fact, a Grade A Shitbag.

There is no proof that these events actually took place, but my father was not one to have made something like this up. This puts my entire relationship with him into a whole new light. Great. This chapter was supposed to be about poor old me and my emotional baggage and now he one-ups me by having killed someone and letting the episode fester inside him for years. Stupid dead dad. He even went to counselling later in life, but by the time he saw a specialist, his ways were already set and he was uninterested in trying to work through his past.

This is not to say that I have any regrets about the role I played in our relationship. I tried my best and I'm not sure that we could have become any closer; I think our friendship was as good as it could have been. My last conversation with him was about two weeks before his death and it was a fun one; he had enjoyed my stories of some of the ridiculousness that we had seen in Thailand so far.

Upon the completion of our year away from home, I was left to

contemplate how I should honour the portion of my father's ashes that were now in my possession. To me, no place better encapsulated my father, and my relationship with him, than Waterton Lakes National Park, where we became friends again after having drifted apart during my youth. And so, on our next camping trip out west, we stuffed my father alongside the tent, sleeping bags, marshmallows, and other essential fare for such a trip, and made the park one of the stops on an itinerary that was eerily dictated by the raging forest fires that were engulfing large swaths of the western states and provinces at the time. Waterton Park had suffered a devastating fire the year before, and three-quarters of it was now scorched and reduced to mountainsides of charred toothpicks that clung precariously to slopes that were once green and thick with aromatic pine forests. Though most of the park remained closed to the public, the hike that my father and I had enjoyed the most was one of the few that was still open, and my children were excited to tackle the eighteen-kilometre trail to Crypt Lake. That day took us upwards through a valley towards a narrow cliff-face path that eventually led to a naturally carved-out cave, whose constricted walls forced even the kids to crouch down and scuttle through, eventually exiting at the top like globs of toothpaste being squeezed out of a tube. Upon arriving at the shore of this brilliant blue alpine lake, we sat and enjoyed our lunch in the presence of the looming rock walls that surrounded us on all sides, and I shared stories of my previous visit to this lake twenty years ago with my father. As we prepared to leave, we each took our handfuls of ash, said our goodbyes, and released him.

I loved my father and I miss him—even if he was an axe murderer.

A QUICK WORD ON
TIPS FOR TRAVELLING
WITH KIDS

I understand that travel blogs and tourism outlets want to make you think that travelling with children is going to be a rich, rewarding experience, and that with just a little preparation, you and your family will have the journey of a lifetime. However, it turns out that this is all just, well, bold-faced lies. Do not be fooled like we were. Let me be clear: half-assed tips that lure you into believing that everything is going to be all right do not make *anything* all right. What they do, however, is make you feel as if you are not only a horrible parent, but also a horrible traveller.

TIP #1: GET THE KIDS INVOLVED IN PLANNING

In preparation for our trip, we bought a number of picture books and let the kids leaf through them to pick out places that they

wanted to see. Anywhere. In the world. Their research quickly degenerated, because naturally each child had to have the same book at the exact same time. Arguments ensued, which then escalated into full-blown battles with said travel books being used as weapons, either to deal direct blows to the head, or as projectiles hurled across the room at one another. Travel books were quickly destroyed and individual pages that became unglued from the spine of each book were stuffed into each other's underwear as a means of torture. The only page that survived this session of "planning" was the one that depicted a serene scene of a woman swimming in a freshwater lake with jellyfish in Papua New Guinea— and so that's what the kids fixated on, refusing to consider travel anywhere else.

TIPS #2 & #3: LET THEM CREATE THEIR OWN PACKING LIST *AND* PACK LIGHT

These two tidbits of advice are completely contradictory to one another. Allowing kids to pack their own bags will never result in a bag that is light. Initially, the thought was to let them fill their little day packs with things that would make the initial flight and any other long-distance travel more fun: their iPads, books, games, colouring items. We gave them free rein to bring whatever they wanted. The result: Oskar packed his rock collection (consisting of various stones collected from parking lots and hotel lobby plant pots—so, not a rock collection at all, but an insane hobo's building supply checklist), and Isla had packed a number of kitchen utensils and pieces of her bed frame that she managed to dismantle.

Over the course of the trip, this habit of packing what they felt were essentials did not diminish. At airports, while in a mad rush to get to a plane that we were invariably late for, we would watch as security staff went through Oskar's backpack and pulled out half-used bars of soap, a collection of semi-filled water bottles, and

74

curtain rods of various sizes. Isla's backpack slowly became filled with a collection of stuffed animals that made her pack so bulbous that after a certain point she refused to carry it anymore.

TIP #4: ARANGE TIME APART

Oh, excuse me? I thought I heard you say we should make sure that we have time away from our kids while we are travelling for a year? Oh, that *is* what you said. No problem. I'll just ask this nice bartender, who's been serving Daria and me drinks since 9:00 a.m., if he wouldn't mind taking our kids with him to his all-night poker game after work. That way, we can continue on a clubbing spree that will end with us watching the sunrise at a rooftop bar and retching our way back to pick up the kids. Then, we could ask that lovely couple who were lying peacefully in a semi-slumber next to us on the beach this afternoon, the ones who were entwined with one another (because they have no kids!), to watch our children the next day as we nurse our raging hangovers.

Do these family travel writers actually travel? Do they even *have* children? These pieces of travel advice strike me more as the wild rantings of a middle-aged hermit, emanating from a rarely vacated basement apartment. For shame, making us believe that we might actually have a moment of downtime where we could enjoy just being a couple again. For shame.

TIP #5: GET TO KNOW THE PLACE—LOOK AT FILMS AND BOOKS ABOUT THE PLACES WHERE YOU PLAN TO GO

"Does that mean we can watch *Scooby-Doo*?"

"No."

"*Big Bang Theory*?"

"No. Those are just TV shows that have nothing to do with where we are going. And why are you watching *Big Bang Theory*?"

"Gido and Baba let us. *Paranormal Activity*?"

"NO! How about *The Lord of the Rings*? It'll at least show you the landscape of New Zealand."

"Does it have a talking dog like *Scooby-Doo*?"

"Kind of. There's lots of cool creatures that talk."

"Do they solve mysteries?"

"In a way. They're looking for something."

"For what?"

"A ring that makes you invisible and the power that comes along with it."

"Uggggghhhhh, boring."

To be honest, Daria and I tried to do some video research ourselves, but we just ended up watching all the episodes of *Flight of the Conchords* (though that did help me develop my New Zealand accent, which became very useful when ordering food), and *Top of the Lake*, which just reaffirmed my dislike for Holly Hunter and made me think that Queenstown was a creepy place to visit.

TIP #6: LET THEM BE THE GUIDE WITHOUT AN APP, VIA MAPS

In Singapore, a city that is filled with endless entertainment opportunities for kids—night and day safaris at its giant zoo, Gardens by the Sea, Chinatown, Universal Studios, LEGOLAND, and on, and on, and on—we gave the kids control over where we were going. Granted, Singapore in June is oppressively hot, so this impacted the decision-making process. It started with them not wanting to leave the hostel. After we finally got them outside, the three-block walk to the subway station resulted in Isla's face turning the colour of a strawberry popsicle, and Oskar becoming completely drenched by his own sweat, looking like he had just come out of a swimming pool. Once inside the subway system, everyone's internal temperature balanced out and the kids were overjoyed to be out of the sauna that is the streetscape of Singapore. And so, we spent a day riding around the subway system, with the kids

picking destinations that were as far at the end of each subway line as possible. There, we'd surface and make a direct line for the nearest 7-Eleven for a Slurpee. Our path would then lead us to the next convenience store, just in time to replenish our Slurpee cups with another fill of sugary ice crystals. This continued until we finally lost our patience and snapped at the kids that we wanted to see something other than the inside of every convenience store in Singapore. So down we went to spend a few more hours in the subway, only to surface long enough to catch a quick bite in Chinatown, something not easily achieved or enjoyed, as Isla yelled at us the entire time that it wasn't fair that all these cities had a Chinatown and why wasn't there a Winnipegtown where she could get mac 'n' cheese and perogies? So down into the subway we went again.

Singapore, by the way, does have a lovely subway system.

TIP #7: TEACH THEM TO MANAGE MONEY ON THE TRIP
Wrong. This is how Oskar figured out that we spent 90% of our daily budget on alcohol and coffee.

TIP #8: TEACH THEM AN APPRECIATION OF FOOD
Isla's appreciation of food increased so much on this trip that she refused to eat anything but crackers, peanut butter, and Nutella for large stretches of time—not the most readily available items in Samoa, Indonesia, and Thailand.

The truth is that travelling with your kids is rewarding, but it never goes the way anyone tells you it is going to go. So plan all you want and get them involved as much as you can, but in the end, they run the show, like it or not. Just sit back and enjoy your Nutella sandwich and fourth Slurpee of the day.

AN ODE TO LA PAZ

La Paz, Bolivia, may be a beautiful city, but for us, it was just a way station and a transit hub. It never held any allure for us. We didn't go there to wander its city streets, admire the viewpoints, or immerse ourselves in its art and culture. We went there to catch a bus. And because of that, we never treated the city with much respect. It was just there; we went through it, but we made fun of its quirks and weirdness and were never wooed by it. The odd thing, though, is that it left such a lasting impression on us that it now regularly comes up in our conversations.

La Paz sits in a pothole-shaped bowl far up in the Andes, in the middle of a plain known as the Altiplano. In this city of two million, the houses that line the walls of this quasi-crater are so cramped and stick out at such a multitude of angles that, from above, it appears as if you are looking down into the over-toothed maw of some giant creature that has broken through the surface of the earth, gasping for air. The entire city looks as if it could come

toppling down at any moment, one listing house knocking over the next in a domino effect triggered by something as innocent as a child kicking a soccer ball against a wall.

In order to access this urban sinkhole, you must drive through the sprawling suburban neighbourhoods that ring La Paz and make up El Alto, Bolivia's fastest-growing city and now its second largest. Most of its buildings are ramshackle, half-finished brick structures with rebar poking skywards from incomplete walls, reminiscent of the antennae of an army of insects crawling along the dusty landscape. The majority of these buildings seem to be in a holding pattern, waiting for a second or third floor that may never come, or they have multiple storeys that are semi-completed but are empty, without fixtures or windows. We received various explanations for this state of incompletion. One reason is that property tax isn't charged until the dwelling is finished. So, make your house look like there is a second floor about to come, which never actually does, and you've got yourself an excellent tax-planning strategy. Others told us that it has to do with status and class: the larger the house, the better your standing. Thus, having a multi-storey house that is only half-finished still instils a level of respect, even without a toilet. Though I'm not sure how much respect you would get while you were defecating in the street in front of your incomplete mansion every morning. Then there is the drug trade; these houses may just be the result of needing someplace to hide the money.

These explanations are much like La Paz itself; you just never really get a sense of what is truly going on. For instance, La Paz was the only city where we were warned about bogus taxis. Not because of the possibility of being overcharged or duped, but because there are actual cars disguised to look like taxicabs that are not taxis at all. These impersonators will pick you up, only to take you to the nearest ATM, where the driver and an armed associate will aid in lightening your bank account. Since these entrepreneurs know a thing or two about deception, they anticipate that you would give them a fake PIN if they

just took your bankcard, so they wait patiently next to you while they force you to make the withdrawal yourself.

Accordingly, when we arrived at the bus station in La Paz, we thought it would be wise to get the police to direct us to where we could safely get a real taxi. However, where they sent us seemed to be the least safe place in the entire station. They may have been part of the scam, or perhaps they were just fake taxicab drivers dressed as fake police officers—who knows? It's La Paz! Cabs did, in fact, show up, and as we were attempting to distinguish between the real and fake ones, we were incessantly harassed to pick one or another by various individuals of uncertain character. Our only clue to finding a genuine taxi, we had read, was that the trustworthy ones had a radio and proudly advertised this fact. Unfortunately, that didn't help us much, as most of the cars had what *looked* like a radio, but closer inspection revealed them to be either a Walkman with a karaoke microphone attached or, even less sophisticated, a disconnected box with frayed wires poking out and leading to nowhere. Much like the houses in El Alto. In the end, who really knows? *Viva* La Paz!

After waving off a number of taxis, we began to feel the pressure to choose one quickly. The seemingly aggressive, coked-up, and self-anointed director of the taxi stand had moved himself to within half a metre of me, his vacant stare and incomprehensible rantings becoming more hostile with every car we chose not to take. Safety be damned. We looked for a taxi with the frailest, most elderly driver in the vicinity and quickly got in, with me strategically sitting behind the driver, ready to engage him in a chokehold the minute he tried anything. Or at least this is how I sold it to Daria, whom I made sit up front in the seat most likely to have a firearm aimed in its direction. This then also allowed me to fully enjoy the drive to the hostel, during which we passed numerous street merchants hustling car rooftop "Taxi" display bubbles and magnetic side-door panels advertising radio-equipped cabs.

The madness of the city is further accentuated by both the

altitude and the coca leaves that you chew and/or drink to combat altitude sickness. At nearly 4,000 metres, our family turned into more of a circus freak show than usual. We had first experienced high altitude when we flew directly from Lima, Peru, at sea level, up to Cusco, sitting at about 3,400 metres above sea level. For an extra twenty-five dollars a ticket, we had avoided twenty-four hours on a winding bus ride, but had lost the opportunity to gradually acclimatize to the change in altitude. The effects in Cusco were immediate, though not all of our symptoms were simply due to altitude sickness. Turns out that much of the nausea we experienced was the result of the fumes we were inhaling from the freshly varnished wood beams in our room—that, and having to constantly listen to the Extreme cover band playing every night in the bar below us. Once we got away from the hostel and the eternal loop of "More Than Words," we actually began to feel a little better.

Not so in La Paz. The entire time we were there, it felt as if someone was slowly squeezing my head to see if anything would start to seep out of my ears. The effect was comparable to being under water, combined with legs that felt forty-five kilograms heavier and mired in quicksand, and hands that kept falling asleep. This effect was instantly noticeable to everyone, but we each expressed it in our own way. Upon arriving at our hostel, the kids, who were obviously also feeling the increased pressure in their heads, immediately began to race around the common area, swinging brooms, bricks, patio table umbrellas, and anything that was heavy, dangerous, and not fastened to the ground. Oskar chased Isla into the courtyard's common bathroom, where she locked herself in while yelling at the top of her lungs for help. I ran up to Oskar, teeth clenched and eyes bugged out, fury radiating from every pore of my body. His look of terror indicated that I had gone too far, and I suddenly realized I had unconsciously brought my right hand and arm up into a threatening "I'm-going-to-slap-you-silly!" pose, made famous by dads across North America in the 1950s. I'm amazed the hostel still allowed us to check in.

During each short stretch that we were in La Paz, it felt as if we were laboratory subjects who had been secretly slipped LSD or undergone experimental brain surgery that tampered with the area controlling rational behaviour and were now being monitored to see who would disembowel whom first.

Against this new baseline of normality, we wandered through La Paz, buying supplies and waiting for our departure, all while taking in the city's eccentricities. Principal among these is that nearly every day there is a demonstration that winds through the streets of La Paz, closing down large sections of the city and creating a constant sense of bedlam. Accompanying these demonstrations is, naturally, a heightened police and military presence (or is it fake taxicab drivers dressed as police and military—who knows?) to ensure that the chaos is officially, and properly chaotic. Viva La Paz!

Bolivia has a strong "workers first" theme, and to this end, a cable car system was recently completed, linking the lower bowl of La Paz to the rim that is El Alto. In any other city, this would be a major tourist magnet, with its spanning views over the entire city and the Andean peaks that surround it. In La Paz, however, it was created purely as a utilitarian device to move workers efficiently between their jobs in La Paz and their homes on the plains surrounding the city. We should have realized the non-touristic nature of the funicular once we paid for our tickets. Something that would have had a hefty price tag anywhere else in the world charged only about fifty cents per ride. When we disembarked at the top, it was even more obvious that the ride was not meant for anything other than getting you from point A to point B as quickly as possible. At the top, we began to search for an unobstructed view that would allow us to take a look across the crazy city below us. After scrambling through courtyards and rusted gates, we eventually found a gap in a wall that was just wide enough for us to squeeze our faces through it. We were able to catch a short, contorted glance of the sprawl below us before we were chased away

by a pack of dogs that were undoubtedly hired by the local tourist office to ensure that visitors got the full La Paz experience.

On top of this, there were a number of odd, everyday occurrences that we stumbled across. For instance, in front of one building along the main pedestrian street, there was a table, behind which sat an impeccably dressed gentleman in a dark three-piece suit. On any day, at any given moment (morning or night), we would find him there, smiling, with his hands clasped on the table in front of him, while the Natalie Imbruglia song "Torn" emanated from the stereo next to him. Just that one song, over, and over, and over, twelve to fifteen hours a day. He wasn't selling anything or propositioning anyone. It seemed like he was just trying to make the world a better place by filling a void we didn't know we had in our hearts. Thank you, Gentleman of "Torn"; you have truly completed me.

Also populating this pedestrian corridor were shoeshiners, who are *everywhere* in La Paz, most of whom don balaclavas to mask their identity so as not to disgrace their families while doing a job that is considered to reflect low social standing. This creates an unsettling atmosphere, as you are constantly being propositioned by masked individuals who could either be robbing you or wanting to shine your flip-flops. It was always a little hard to tell, given our stunted understanding of Spanish. Perhaps they were just combining both skills to maximize their profits.

It made me wonder why this particular occupation had been singled out as socially unacceptable, when there are so many other jobs that I feel should require the "balaclava of shame": accountant, lawyer, real estate agent. I think I would actually respect these professions slightly more if my future dealings with them required them to be masked.

Another fun fact about La Paz is that the bus station that services all destinations east of La Paz, over the Andes, and down into the tropics below, is located next to the largest cemetery in the city. Thus, it is simply referred to as the "Graveyard." This becomes creepily ironic when you find out that, once upon a time, the

percentage of buses that careened over the side of the mountain after leaving this bus station was about one hundred percent. At least, that's how I interpreted it after listening to the glorious horror stories pressed upon us. This crash rate has since declined as the old road, fittingly named the "World's Most Dangerous Road" and "Road of Death," has been replaced with a more modern, better-engineered highway, subsequently titled the "Less-Dangerous-but-Still-Perilous-Enough-to-Keep-the-Bolivian-Nation-from-Positive-Population-Growth Highway." This new moniker is unfortunately a bit wordier and slightly more difficult to emblazon across the souvenir T-shirts that are available along its path. I'm sure the Union of Tourist T-Shirt Manufacturers will be protesting this fact in La Paz sometime next week. And in case you were afraid that they made the new highway less fun than the previous one, there still exists a pull-off spot at its apex, where foreign travellers can be seen retching by the side of their cars against the beautiful backdrop of the Andes and the jungle below.

This highway was also the starting point for Bolivian Bingo, the object of which was to spot and identify motorcyclists and their ever-increasing passenger manifest and luggage-handling capabilities. As we drove through the mountains and countryside towards the high-altitude jungle town of Coroico, this game kept the kids' attention focused away from their impending death by directing it instead to filling their scorecards as they watched for motorcycles laden with drivers' friends, family, and whatever else could be squeezed onto a two-wheeled motorized vehicle. Though we saw up to five people on one motorcycle, the eventual winner was spotted later in our travels in the town of Rurrenabaque, where we saw a motorcyclist holding a two-metre-long, one-metre-wide, solid wood dining table against his back with one hand while driving through the town. In the end, however, this sighting was unfortunately disqualified due to the fact that it appeared that his cat was operating the motorcycle. A clear violation of the rules of Bolivian Bingo.

On our final return to La Paz, we flew back directly from the

Amazon basin, where we had acclimated to low-level altitude once again, making the effects of the city even more pronounced. On this visit, our hostel owner now also warned us not to be on the streets after nine o'clock at night. Where was this warning the last time we stayed here? Or was this just a general rule about La Paz? Unfortunately, I had no choice but to go out after hours to buy bus tickets and pick up some of Isla's clothes that we had forgotten after our last visit. With my feet dragging like lead weights and my head full of oatmeal, the walk felt hallucinogenic, as buildings, streets, and Natalie Imbruglia's manager shifted in and out of focus. I also seemed to be discovering new neighbourhoods that I hadn't stumbled upon before: entire blocks that were just barbershops and hair salons, with row upon row of people trying to coax me into their shop for a trim. Then there was street after street of stores that seemed to sell only empty plastic yogurt containers and pool noodles. The next block was just combs and brushes.

When I finally returned to the hostel, I locked the door, slid down with my back against it, and looked up at Daria. "We need to leave—now."

So we did. And on our way out of our favourite-but-not-favourite city, we came up with some slogans that "capture" the essence of this fair burg that would allow it to promote itself in the future:

"Viva La Paz!
Come for the Madness, stay because your ability to think clearly enough to book your exit is diminished the moment you step into this thin-aired hell."

"Viva La Paz!
Nine out of ten supposed taxi drivers agree: don't trust the taxi drivers!"

"Viva La Paz!
What starts at the Graveyard, ends at the Graveyard!"

SCREW THE JOURNEY;
IT'S THE DESTINATION

In Arequipa,
All the fish say,
Won't you fly away with us?
Wish we could,
Then we would,
But we have to take a bus.

—Rob Krause

One affliction that our family suffers from is that we are prone to making rash decisions when we convince ourselves that we really, really want something, and that that something needs to happen RIGHT NOW. The Great Family Room Purge of 2014 was indicative of this. Three-quarters of all the toys in our house were unilaterally deemed "outgrown" because they, supposedly, had not been played with in years, at least according to Daria. These relics of bygone good times were hastily rounded up in the dead of night and deposited at the loading dock of an inner-city family help centre. It was a very covert action, akin to a WWII military maneuver. I protested, briefly, but was quickly informed it was for the best and that we should not discuss it. I chose to heed that advice.

The subsequent verbal abuse that was hurled at us over the following days by two, waist-high tyrants quickly motivated us to make another rash decision: to replace all of those used, second-hand, and gifted toys that we had disposed of with brand-new, full-priced items purchased posthaste from the nearest toy store. My constant interjections of, "I love this board game; we should buy it again like it's the very first time," did not manage to lighten the mood of the day.

In the first leg of our year of travel, we had managed to keep such rash decisions to a minimum. There were destinations that looked enticing, but we were kept at bay by the cost. We didn't hop on a plane to Bora Bora or the Seychelles even though we were tempted. We had a crude plan for our travel and budget, and we were actually trying to stick to it. When we did have a big expense, we tried to offset it in the following days by minimizing our activities or not letting one of the children eat for a day or so. They're resilient that way. Plus, it wouldn't be fair to reduce our budget for alcohol. That would just be inhumane.

This mindset seemed to have changed with the second half of the trip, partly due to my father's death. Losing him made me feel that my days were now also numbered—that I could die at any moment. Is this how everyone feels when they lose a parent? I was now missing a key component in my life (for better or worse), and the normal order of things had been completely rearranged, which made me feel vulnerable. Even though it had sometimes been tiring to listen to my father get worked up over insignificant details—like the order in which the dishes should be placed in the dishwasher—it was oddly comforting to have had that as part of my life. Without it, there is a void that now seems to be filled with uncertainty and a sense that anything could happen, including the possibility that I am now next in line for the "big sleep."

That particular mindset established the tone for this part of the trip. I suddenly cared less about money and more about making sure that we do what we can while we are here. When I went to

Utah with my dad a few years back, he made a passing comment that he was happy we were able to do the trip together because it would most likely be the last time that he would be able to enjoy this landscape. At the time, it struck me as an odd comment, but during my time in South America I had a vaguely similar feeling. This could be my last time here and I should make the most of it.

This sense of urgency was also heightened by the fact that we were now actually on a three-month timeline. At no point in the first half of our travels did we ever feel like the trip was coming to an end. Sure, there were definitely times that I may have been consciously willing it to end, but it never felt like we might run out of time. In this portion of the trip, though, we were travelling in a mild state of panic because we had only three months. *My god, only three months! That's barely one and a half summer vacations. How can anyone go anywhere or get anything done with so little time?* If you were lucky, you might, just *might*, have enough time to plan a trip with that amount time, but to actually go on one? Pure fantasy.

And so, the rash decisions began. It didn't help that South America seemed to have a stronger "Gotta-Do-It" feel than the previous part of our journey. And we were completely unprepared, so everything turned into a last-minute decision. Machu Picchu? *Martha Stewart says you have to see it. Plus, it's on the goddamn cover of the Lonely Planet guide to South America. We have to go. Book it!* The Amazon? *It's disappearing. I hear it's being paved over and turned into an Applebee's. Book it!* Lake Titicaca? *Those crazy Incas made floating islands out of reeds, and now they're building skyscrapers taller than the Empire State Building on them—at least that's what the Germans down the hall said. Book it!*

So, on the night that we returned to La Paz for the third time, after having spent five weeks bouncing between the stark land-scapes and high altitudes of the Andes and the oppressive heat of the Amazon, we decided we needed to be at a beach. In Ecuador. Today. Screw the journey; it's the destination. We weren't interested

in staying in La Paz for a minute longer. Not to take anything away from the city itself—it's spectacular in a weirdly ramshackle way. And the altitude made us crazy, while the cold nights and spring-like days were constantly reminding us that we would be returning to Winnipeg in February. We had to leave.

The decision was to make the journey by bus. I'm unsure why we chose this point in our South American travels to do an extensive bus ride, rather than take a plane. Perhaps we had some romantic notion that we needed to get our South American "street cred" by taking a fifty-two-hour bus trip. The problem with that approach is that the people with whom you would achieve such credibility by doing this journey are the same people you wouldn't want to spend time with because, well, they enjoy fifty-two-hour bus rides and generally smell like they've just been on one. We also reasoned that if we did take the bus, it should be done in one go, from La Paz, Bolivia, all the way to Guayquil, Ecuador. Treat it like ripping off a band-aid, one time, quickly, resulting in the least amount of pain. Except that the ride is not a band-aid; it's not quick, and you are travelling with two children who do not understand the concept of time or comprehend that this bus trip does, actually, have an end point.

One thing we certainly suffered from while in South America was the delusion that the travel distances weren't very vast. I'm not sure if it's because we had become accustomed to the shorter distances in Southeast Asia, or because the area of northwestern South America that we were focused on was only a teeny, tiny portion of the whole continent; therefore, the cities couldn't be that far apart. Unfortunately, as with most things that we believed we understood, we were utterly and completely wrong.

The distance that we were planning to travel was about 3,100 kilometres. This is equivalent to driving from San Diego to Seattle, turning around, and then doubling back to San Francisco to retrieve your tiny brain—something you obviously left behind if you actually believed that you could complete such a journey in

one shot. For most rational people, this is an insane distance. Add to this that there seems to be some sort of construction bylaw for highways in South America that ensures that every metre of roadway contains a curve (preferably hairpin, with at least a twelve percent grade) and that all guardrails and safety features be removed to maximize each vehicle's flight potential at any given high-altitude turn. In retrospect, we should have taken a plane. But "hindsight is 20/20," is what clever parents say to impress and confuse their children who were unwittingly birthed into such a carnival of idiots.

The first leg of this epic journey was a light, twelve-hour jaunt that would take us from La Paz to Arequipa, Peru, where we would have another twelve hours to do nothing but enjoy the sunshine, maybe bake some cakes, or take in a "How to Build an Incan Temple" course before boarding the next set of buses that would swallow the following forty-one hours until we finally reached our destination. This initial Arequipa leg allowed us to gently ease into the busing culture of South America. The interesting part of travelling by bus is experiencing the ridiculousness of land border crossings. Our previous experiences ranged from the precise science of the Singapore border—a vast, multilevel building reminiscent of a hamster city, where travellers are herded through tubes crisscrossing between the multiple check stops and processing points—to the mild confusion of the Thai/Malaysian border. There, after having already crossed into Thailand, I found myself mistakenly and illegally back in Malaysia after exiting the bathroom. This posed a dilemma: Do I take the proper route and return to Thailand through customs without a passport and try to explain what happened? I imagined a back-and-forth between myself and border security, trying to explain where I had gone by acting out the process of taking a pee—leaning back unnaturally while gesturing to a fictional and overemphasized arc of urine coming from my groin—wide-eyed and smiling ludicrously at the official while emphatically shouting, "See? See? Pee-pee." Realizing that there

was no way that discussion could end well, I opted to sneak back into Thailand via the bathroom path I had used in the first place.

The Peru/Bolivia border at Desaguadero made the Thai/Malaysian crossing look like a fine-tuned piece of Swiss engineering. The area surrounding the Peru/Boliva border is inhabited by a giant flea market/kitschy carnival, teeming with hawkers and market stalls in a labyrinth of narrow streets that struck us as complete chaos. Everyone else who was there, however, seemed to know exactly what to do and where they were going. When the bus could no longer push through the throngs of people trying to sell its passengers everything from toothpicks to new generators, we were dismissed with a flurry of arm waves and a caution in broken English to watch out for bandits and pickpockets—which came across as, "Señor, these people do not like you and will kill you for the lint in your bellybutton. Now, go. Enjoy! See you in Peru!"

After walking down a few narrow streets in search of this elusive border—for all we knew, we could have been in a city in central Bolivia—we came to a building that had a long line of individuals snaking around it, indicating that this was either an important government building, a bank about to go under, or the ticket line for Bolivia's best Pink Floyd cover band. After waiting two hours, we discovered that it was, in fact, Bolivian Immigration, and we were finally able to see the one official working that day. Once stamped out of Bolivia, we were again waved off into a vague direction that we thought was towards Peru. There were no signs, no border per se, and we passed only one individual who could be considered a border guard, and he was more engrossed in haggling over the price of his lunch with a local vendor, than paying attention to the masses around him. We asked a few people for directions in our comical version of Spanish, and I realize now that we must have seemed like complete fools, standing less than one hundred metres from the border and pointing in all directions, shouting, "Peru? Peru?" It's akin to standing in downtown Buffalo, NY, pointing wildly while asking, "Canada? Canada?"

We followed a throng of people across a bridge and then latched on to a couple whom we profiled as tourists, letting them guide us into a nondescript building that we thought might be the Peruvian Immigration building. It could also have been the Department of Water and Utilities for all we knew, but either way, somebody stamped our passports. Upon resurfacing into the chaos, we saw our bus right in front of us. How the bus managed to get across that narrow bridge jammed with pedestrians, without crushing hundreds of people in its wake, was, like Machu Picchu, one of the great mysteries of South America.

The next day, our plans for an action-packed excursion into Arequipa were dashed as Isla informed us that she was woozy with a tummy-ache. We tried to convince her that she should come outside with us, and that the fresh air would help to relieve her nausea. Her rebuttal consisted of several trips to the bathroom, where she unleashed an endless stream of what might colloquially be called a "shit storm." By the time we got on the bus that night, she was feeling better and had inhaled the complimentary dinner faster than you can say, "Are you sure that your stomach is ready for room-temperature chicken with congealed slime sauce?"

The answer to that question came in the dead of night when I was awoken by Isla's confusion as to why her clothes were uncomfortably damp. At that point, I knew there are only two reasons why a six-year-old with an unsettled stomach could be wet, and neither one proffered enough incentive for me to actually turn on a light and investigate. I sat in the dark and waited, hoping that this would somehow just resolve itself on its own.

Alas, it did not, and so the clean-up in seat 7B began. Both Isla and her seat were drenched—and I'm not using hyperbole here for a comedic effect; this is a literal description of the pool of vomit that I was faced with, which must have cascaded from her mouth in great streams (now, that last bit, with the cascading part, that was hyperbole). Granted, given the two options as to why she was

sopping wet, this was obviously the clear winner, but not by much of a margin.

Where does one begin in such a situation? The initial impulse is to look for the reset button, somewhere, *anywhere*! It should be there on the armrest, right next to the button for the overhead reading light. WHERE IS IT ?!?! Oh God, please let this be a dream and I'm actually sleeping on a plane, on our way to Ecuador because we realized what a stupid idea it was to take a fifty-two-hour bus ride through high-altitude, mountainous terrain with two children.

Failing that strategy you look at what supplies you have on hand to deal with these circumstances and begin methodically attacking it, one step at a time. In my bag of tricks I had three napkins, seemingly made out of rice paper, a paper clip, and two bottles of hand sanitizer. That should be enough … to … not be of any use at all!

Meanwhile, Daria had sidled up beside me, wide-eyed and frozen with fear. She does not do well with vomit and, faced now with the copious amounts that had spewed forth from her daughter, she was rife with panic. I actually thought she was in a state of shock, as she refused to acknowledge my requests to get a change of clothes for Isla out of the backpack stowed above us. I began talking to her very slowly, hoping that she'd snap out of it. I gingerly lifted Isla out of her seat, doing my best not to disturb any of the pools of vomit that had formed around her, or to create new rivulets that might run over onto the bags of food that we had intelligently placed at the foot of her seat. After giving her a shake to get the loose bits off, I turned to Daria, who had now been joined by a bus attendant who looked at the scene in silent horror. As Daria's gag reflex kicked into high gear, I handed Isla over to her so that she could deal with cleaning her up. As they left for the bathroom, the attendant disappeared as well, under the guise of looking for cleaning supplies, but was never seen again for the rest of the bus ride. Clever woman.

This moment, stuck on a moving bus, faced with a puke-filled seat accessible only by maneuvering around the fully reclined

backrests of the passengers in front of us, was exactly what I dreaded most about going on a year-long trip with my children. I had feared that our travels would be filled with a non-stop barrage of similarly horrific situations. But now, confronted with this reality, I realized that it was actually not that bad. Much like anything as a parent, you just deal with it. It sucks, but you work your way through it. Though this was, by far, the most catastrophic incident we had encountered on the trip to date, it was just one of the many challenges we were inundated with over the course of the year. Without realizing it, we had managed to navigate our way through all of them; from lice in Australia, to just figuring out how to make our daily meals in unfamiliar kitchens. We had walked through shifty city neigbourhoods and visited questionable washrooms at roadside pull-offs, and we had survived it all. Armed now with the knowledge that we could prevail over most situations, it seemed that the rest of our travels did not inspire the same anxiety that I had experienced before embarking on the trip. We had gotten into the rhythm of travel, and nothing seemed insurmountable anymore.

I focused my attention back to Daria, who had returned with Isla, and used Jedi mind power to get her to move again.

"You *WILL* get me some toilet paper from the washroom ..."

"I think I should go get you some toilet paper."

Using that and the hand sanitizer, I was able to get Isla's seat back to about seventy-five percent of its normal condition. Unfortunately, for Isla, seventy-five percent was nowhere near good enough for her to return to that particular spot. After she settled herself into my seat, I hovered around her for the next little while, springing into action any time I heard or saw her making any kind of movement. At one point, Isla began to throw up again, but I was there immediately with the only version of a receptacle that I had: a thin cellophane bag used to wrap some food we had brought on board with us. As I was trying to figure out what to do with my clear bag of vomit, Daria informed me that it was leaking all over

my shoes. At least I had chosen not to wear flip-flops on this particular bus ride.

An hour later, I heard Isla rustling again.

"Do you have to throw up?"

"No."

"You sure?"

"Yes."

"You look like someone who has to throw up."

"I DON'T! But I really have to go pee."

FANTASTIC! That I could deal with. I picked her up and ran her to the bathroom, pulled down her pants, and sat her on the toilet. While I was basking in the glow of my accomplishment, Isla leaned forward and threw up all over the floor.

Naturally, not one to be left out, Oskar began feeling nauseous as day broke, and I spent an hour holding his head over the open toilet, inhaling the sweet smell of a tank full of urine, while keeping him from slipping into it as the bus navigated through the winding roads of what was probably quite a beautiful Peruvian countryside.

We made it to Lima, Peru, without further incident and, after two hours there, boarded the next bus bound for Ecuador. With everyone cautiously back to normal, and a bus that had unlimited movies in English to watch, we gave the kids free rein to do whatever they wanted for the next twenty-seven hours. Admittedly, not one of our finer parenting moments, but in light of what had just transpired, I couldn't give a shit. And I didn't want to clean one up, either.

My behavior at the Peru/Ecuador border acted as a fine bookend for this pinnacle of good parenting. Unfortunately, our strategy of unlimited movies on the bus ride backfired, and Isla decided that she did not want to go through customs because it meant getting off the bus. I lured her out with the promise of a washroom that was both stationary and had been cleaned in the past twenty-four hours, allowing her the opportunity to use the toilet without peeing all over her own leg. Our debate about why

she had to go through Immigration, however, stalled on the sidewalk immediately outside the bus. Isla refused to be convinced, even after I ramped up my parental superpower of embellishment and told her that if she didn't cooperate, she would be left in this barren no-man's-land, never to see her grandparents or friends again, only to toil away the rest of her days trying to hustle tourists to buy paperclips in this horrible excuse of a border town. As I scanned the faces of the locals in the immediate vicinity to see if they understood my tirade and slight against their home, Isla kicked into full freak-out mode. In response, I employed Parenting Strategy 66(b) of the *World's #1 Worst Dad* handbook and picked Isla up, flipped her upside down, and swung her back and forth like a pendulum while holding her ankles. Oddly, this only served to increase her anger. I now had to employ a new strategy, so I sat her on my lap, wrapped my arms around her so she couldn't move, and began singing old punk rock songs to her—which she hates— while rocking back and forth. After a few minutes, she lulled me into trusting that she had calmed down, so I released her. She got up, punched me in the chest, and got in line. Who knows how to parent? That's right, World's #1 Worst Dad does.

When we arrived at our hostel in Guayaquil, Ecquador, the journey and its horrific moments had already become a hilarious memory. That is, until I found the bag of vomit-drenched clothes that Daria had stuffed into my bag without rinsing them first. Forty-eight hours was just the right amount of time to perfectly ferment Isla's clothes into a semi-liquid mass, with a smell that quickly reminded me that the words "vomit" and "hilarious" can never co-exist when you are the one left holding the proverbial bag after everyone else has gone to bed.

TRAGEDY MAKES GOOD READING

How do you prepare for a trip of this magnitude? What will you encounter over twelve months and multiple continents? On our past vacations, we have always packed a first aid kit, but the one required for this trip would have needed to be the size of a small Baltic nation, based on the frequency of accidents in our family.

The first concern is that a haggard, middle-aged man like myself already has a certain amount of health-related baggage. I have a notoriously bad back that started over twenty years ago while I was moving a billiards table with my co-workers at an Asian restaurant. Everyone around the table was communicating with one another in their native dialect, and I was just following along, until it seemed that the direction to "let the table go and see if we can snap Rob's spine" was given, and I was left holding the very heavy table.

Since then, something in my back pops out every few years and makes me completely immobile for a day and Neanderthal-esque in stature for a week. The worst of these incidents happened while I was walking across our campsite in South Dakota. Seizing up mid-stride, I dropped into a heap on the ground. I was quickly surrounded by my family and fellow campers, and once I managed to crawl up someone's leg, I was offered a multitude of medications to deal with the pain. I chose a labour-pain inhibitor (who brings these camping?) and waited for the pain to subside, while hoping not to begin dilating.

Background ailments aside, we knew that a world trip could involve a host of hazardous situations. To some extent, we could predict what we might face, as we knew that travelling in different countries would indubitably result in stomach issues of some kind. This is impossible to avoid, unless you have had your intestines replaced with copper piping. I do know of one person who has travelled the world without ever being incapacitated by any sort of stomach bug. During our own trip, his stories of indulging in undercooked street skewers, washed down with water scooped from a gutter, were all the more annoying, as I was forced to eat chewing gum for dinner for a third night in a row.

The only way I felt I could prepare myself for this reality was to assume that I was not going to have a normal bowel movement for an entire year. Once I wrapped my head around that idea, having a bout of traveller's tummy every other week would be a blessing. But, as with most of our preparations and travel planning, we were primarily concerned about our children. When you are travelling on your own, you tend to be able to roll with the situation, no matter how bad it gets. Not so when your kids are along for the ride. Not only are you more concerned for their welfare than you would ever be for your own, but you also need to anticipate how they deal with being sick and react accordingly. Oskar will lie down and go into full system shutdown while the sickness runs its course. Isla Blue, however, in her wonderfully defiant way of

dealing with everything, will not admit she is sick. If you even hint that she might not be feeling 100%, she will shower you with such a barrage of vitriol that you begin to wish that her symptoms were actually worse so that she would be unable to open her mouth and would stop yelling at you. She will not lie down, she will not take medicine, and she will not interrupt her busy schedule of being a kid. However, the reality is that she *is* sick, and because it interferes with her having fun, she naturally becomes angry at her parents until the sickness passes.

Since we were cooking most of our own meals in New Zealand, our first true brush with potential stomach issues came in Samoa. It took only a day for the kids to tire of me constantly hounding them to practice good hygiene; "wash your hands," "stop picking your nose," "don't touch that dog," "don't pick that dog's nose," and so on. However, it was Daria and I who were the first to come down with stomach troubles. I can pinpoint the exact moment that the microscopic bug got into my system: after all the warnings I gave my kids about watching what we ate, I was lured by the sweet smell of a coconut pastry that was offered through the window of our bus during a stop in the midday heat. As I chewed the first bite of what turned out to be quite a delicious Samoan dainty, my brain began processing the warmth of the pastry, recognizing that it had less of a "fresh-out-of-the-oven" kind of vibe, and more of a "sitting-in-a-cooler-all-day-being-heated-by-the-hot-Samoan-sun" quality. A perfect environment for … ugghh. Too late. I swear I could feel the marauding hordes of bacteria swarming through my stomach and into my intestines, where they were now hastily building a shanty-town rivalling the favelas of Rio. They were in it for the long haul.

Of course, everyone has their own remedy for gastric distress, and since we wanted to believe that everyone knew what they were talking about, we tried them all. *Eat only bananas.* Didn't help. *Drink only beer.* Fantastic, but only made us more dehydrated. *Eat only rice.* I'll go back to beer, thank you very much. We eventually latched onto eating a tablespoon of papaya seeds every couple of

hours because it was proposed by a Samoan who looked elderly and wise, and it seemed like a local remedy—very tropical and fruity. However, it made things exponentially worse. We stuck with the treatment for about five days because she was Samoan and old, so she undoubtedly had to have known what she was talking about. Once we stopped eating the papaya seeds, though, our systems went back to normal. The seeds probably acted like a hail of bowling balls aimed at the ramshackle village of bacteria, destroying everything in their path. Systems were stable just in time for another long bus ride through the Samoan country-side, with stops at roadside vendors with enticing coconut pas-tries that tasted so delightful and were wonderfully lukewarm … dammit. Not again.

The kids, luckily, never really suffered from many stomach issues over the year, which was great, because in the end, there really isn't much you can do to combat it. Just let it run its course, stay hydrated, and hope that you don't crap your pants. Isla did catch a bug upon our initial arrival in South America, causing her to throw up for the first time in her life. Because she had lived through her first six years without being violently ill, she couldn't grasp what was happening, making her even more agitated. How-ever, once we quelled her fears by explaining that she was not having a baby, because I guess at some point we had mentioned that giving birth is one of the most painful experiences in life, she relaxed and began to interrogate us about how exactly one becomes pregnant. Little did she know this was just the first stop on her "Spew Across Peru" Tour.

Most of the other health situations we faced along the way were easily treatable, as they required only an antiseptic of some sort. I became rather adept at putting iodine on every lit-tle scrape and cut, and it became a wonderful game between me and the kids, as whoever wasn't wounded would start chanting, "I-O-DINE! I-O-DINE!" much to the chagrin of the child who was about to be drenched by my number one sterilizing technique.

Generally, the scrapes and cuts were kept to a minimum and were usually obtained by engaging in fun-filled activities like:

a) falling down a cliff face into the ocean;

On the eastern side of the island of Ko Pha-Ngan in Thailand, we stayed in a hut nestled into the rocky cliffs that overlooked a bay and its golden sand beach. While the cliffs that the hut was built on were a jumbled maze of pathways that coiled up and around the stone faces to each individual dwelling, the formations on the opposite side of the bay were smooth mounds of rounded, apartment-sized rock that were separated from one another by one-metre-wide crevices that plunged into the ocean below.

Oskar tried to jump across two of these rocks, but misjudged the distance between them and slid about seven metres down a barnacle-encrusted wall before dropping into the ocean. As we were nowhere to be found (it was cocktail hour and we THOUGHT that the Interloper was with him), the high-pitched screams he emitted while flailing in the beautiful azure waters that surrounded him attracted a couple of sea kayakers, who deftly plucked him out and brought him back to shore. When Daria's motherly instincts kicked in and she realized that the sound was not just a dog being tortured, but actually our son yelling for his life, I reluctantly headed down to the beach to the spot where he had been deposited. His stomach was heavily scratched, but luckily, that was it. All he needed was—I-o-dine! I-o-dine! And a new set of parents who paid more attention to their children.

Or, b) falling into sewers.

On the island of Bali, the municipal infrastructure is a little dodgy, so if you choose to walk on the sidewalks in a town such as Ubud, you should make sure there is actually a piece of solid concrete below your step. If you don't, there's a good chance that you will drop into the one-metre-deep sewage trench that runs directly underneath most sidewalks. We had a moment of panic when Isla's whole body disappeared into the sidewalk. After the initial shock, it became difficult to withhold our laughter, which did not help

the situation. We tried to save face by complimenting Isla on the fact that she kept her head above the waterline. Way to go! Once we got her cleaned up (I-o-dine! I-o-dine!), it seemed that she was actually quite pleased with herself, as her journal entry later that week was, "Bali, I fell into a sewer," with an accompanying picture. We're so proud of our little girl.

My second most important medical skill was that of administering anti-nausea tablets. Our family is not prone to taking medication to begin with, so we didn't use these during the early part of the trip at all. Though we felt a little woozy on some of the car rides in New Zealand, the drives were short enough, and the air-conditioning strong enough, that the nausea would quickly disappear once we got out of the car and walked around a bit. This anti-medication mentality changed once we arrived in the curvier countries where the mode of transport became crowded, hot, and sticky. I gave the kids a little Gravol when we were on a bus ride in Bali and it suddenly made things so much easier. Everyone fell asleep, only to wake up refreshed at our final destination. From then on, I was pushing those pills at every opportunity.

"You sure you don't want a pill? It's a long ride and you're looking a little pale."

"Papa, the bus ride isn't until tomorrow."

During our travels, we also gleaned that ours is truly not a seafaring family. Any boat ride we took resulted in three-quarters of the team breaking into a cold sweat and gravitating towards a horizontal position on the floor. This was understandable, considering some of the questionable conditions on the boat rides we took, including a car ferry crossing at Lake Titicaca in Bolivia. You would think that crossing the bay of a lake by car ferry wouldn't be such a bad experience. The boats, however, were no larger than the buses they carried, and the decks strained to stay above the waterline while accommodating the weight of the vehicles they were meant to transport. With a single, underpowered outboard motor, the scene that played out resembled a flotilla of top-heavy,

unbalanced rubber ducks floating in a bathtub, except the ducks were half a dozen bus-boats slowly bobbing their way back and forth across the bay on half-metre-high waves. Passengers on our bus were visibly miffed when we were asked to get off the bus and take a separate passenger boat in order to cross. Their displeasure at the situation quickly evaporated upon seeing the panic-stricken faces of passengers who chose not to disembark a neighbouring bus, and were now floating aimlessly between docks as their "captain" attempted to restart the stalled boat motor. As this lamed ferry narrowly missed our own boat and listed out into the larger lake, it became apparent that getting off the boat for the crossing was not a wholly unreasonable request. It seems these boats, akin to floating soda crackers, do not do well in choppier waters if the "captain" can't properly position his vessel to break the waves that crash against it. With about forty passengers leaning over to one side of the bus to see what was going on, the disabled ferry came dangerously close to flopping over completely. Gravol, anyone?

Unfortunately, what we couldn't prepare for, even medically, was our own stupidity. One thing we've always tried not to do is push our kids too far—which sounds like total garbage now that I read this—with the belief that "less is more." Naturally, this personal directive was thrown out during the trip. One such example was our first legitimate snorkelling opportunity, just off the weird, cult-infested island of Caqalai in Fiji. We weren't quite sure what was going on at this supposed Methodist-run research facility and scuba certification school, but it was cheap and it was beautiful. We should have, however, been wary from the moment we were deposited at the unmarked bus stop the owners had directed us to. With the only visible structure being a derelict building that would not have been out of place in a ghost town in the American West, we sat at the side of the road surrounded by grassy marshes, waiting for someone to come and take us to the island. After being asked by a passing police car if we were okay, and refusing their offer to take us back to the main city about forty-five minutes away,

we were finally approached by two men carrying supplies who took us to their boat and out onto the open ocean.

Our accommodations, set in the centre of a small island no larger than two football fields, consisted of a spartan, garage-like structure stuffed with bunk beds and surrounded by towering palm trees that swayed in the constant trade winds that blew off the ocean. The island was ringed by one continuous beach that extended to shallow sand shoals during low tide, doubling its land area and affording us the opportunity to walk and wade to neighbouring islands some kilometres away. Our hosts were eerily friendly, tactile, and accommodating, with a strict policy of no alcohol that seemed pointless, especially considering the amount of kava (fermented root alcohol) that they inhaled every day— which may have explained their unnerving nature.

From this island, we were told, a ten-minute walk at low tide would bring us to some spectacular snorkelling around the regrettably named Snake Island. After alleviating our children's fears that the island's moniker came from the innocuous water snakes that sometimes inhabit its mangrove roots, and not from cobras, we set forth—just before lunch, in the heat of the day, without snacks. By the time we got to Snake Island, which of course turned into a forty-five-minute walk as we explored the freshly exposed sand bars and mushroom-shaped coral outcroppings that loomed large just under the water's surface, the kids didn't want to be there. Being the nurturing parents that we are, we ignored their pleas to return and forced them to enjoy themselves. Oddly, this strategy did not work. Between their howls of pain due to hunger and dehydration, and the frustration that water kept leaking into their adult-sized snorkelling masks (stupid, tiny, childlike faces), I was able to dip my head under the water for seconds at a time and marvel at the explosion of colour. Spiked corals of iridescent blue, giant brain-like mounds of dark green, and round, terraced shelves of magenta surrounded me on all sides.

By the time I finally convinced Isla to just take a look, we had

drifted slightly away from the shallows of the coral area and were now over open water, looking back at a coral wall so immense that it filled our entire scope of vision horizontally, and plummeted deep out of sight in front of us. As I followed the wall down with my eyes, I saw that the coral was replaced by some sinister-looking shadows waaaaaay down below. That put an end to our snorkelling expedition.

The swim back in the rising tide waters solidified the trauma of our excursion, as both kids refused to go into the deep, shadow-infested channel where the gentle current would have pushed us back to our home island. As we watched our two fellow snorkellers drift leisurely back to the safety of our beach, I had to return by swimming through a maze of coral blooms with Isla latched onto one leg. Since this slowed me down considerably, Isla became ever more irate, condemning the whole concept of snorkelling the entire way back.

From that day forward, Snake Island became a part of our lexicon to indicate the nadir of suffering that one could endure—the new benchmark for an all-time low. All other experiences were now measured against this demarcation point, as in, "Well, at least we're not snorkelling at Snake Island."

Apart from the emotional scars, we managed to avoid any medical catastrophes during this ill-fated expedition, and we made a concerted effort from then on to minimize the kids' exposure to any more of our own poor judgment. For the rest of the trip, we were fairly successful at upholding this new directive, although I did have a hiccup on Ko Pha-Ngan when Isla took her solo night walk and, fortunately, came out unscathed. Other than that, all other events were purely accidental and should not be considered our fault.

It was not our fault that the kids made a game of chasing hulking cane toads in courtyards throughout Fiji. We warned them that they were poisonous. Did it stop them? Nope. Nothing says "I love you" like scrubbing your kids' hands for hours on end, but— and this is the important part—not our fault!

It was also not our fault when the matted and ratty-looking

monkeys in Ubud jumped our kids and stole their ice cream, leaving them in shock and never wanting to read *Curious George* ever again. We told them not to taunt the monkeys. Did they listen? Nope. Not our fault!

I'm not sure that we need to point fingers when we talk about who is responsible for Isla getting her foot caught in the front tire spokes while we were biking in the Galápagos. She was sitting on what was considered to be a child seat, at least for Isabela Island, though I guess we could have questioned a design that simply entailed a small plank of wood bungeed to the top of the bike frame. Really, if anyone is to blame, it's that gigantic tortoise's fault. If he and his friends hadn't distracted us, none of this would have happened.

We did let our guard down and allow our stupidity to surface once again near the very end of the trip, which could have ended badly for all of us. With only ten days left before we were to fly home, we began our journey through Colombia towards Bogotá and our airport of departure. The border crossing between Ecuador and Colombia was one of the more organized setups that we encountered while in South America, with permanent buildings on either side of the boundary that were actually labelled as "Immigration." However, in the spirit of South America, there were still no barricades on the road that forced you to stop, and they incorporated a "pay-as-you-go" system that rivalled a neighbourhood lemonade stand. At customs in Ecuador, we were informed that there would be a hefty visa charge once we checked in at the Colombian Immigration office. Unexpected as this was, we were able to cobble together the fee in US currency by scrounging through our backpacks/pants/wallets, with the final ten dollars reluctantly being supplied by Isla. With exit visas and US cash in hand, we were directed by the Ecuadorian officials to cross a narrow bridge spanning a deep gorge over the Río Chiquito that would deposit us into Colombia. For a brief moment, we looked at each other, harbouring the same idea to just walk past

Immigration, a nondescript building set off the road, and enter the country without paying the onerous entry tax. There were no guards or security measures of any sort in sight.

It should be noted here that our extended travels created a new mindset regarding money and our personal possessions. Everything became very dear to us, and spending $250 USD on visas that may or may not have been official (it was hard to tell once we were handed the clearly photocopied, hand-cut piece of paper after we paid) was a difficult decision to make. The value of everything we purchased was quantified based on its effect on our finances as a whole, and this payment would affect how we would budget the next few days. Our frugality had also made us overly protective of everything that we carried on our backs, partially due to the extra cost of replacing anything we lost, but more so because finding a replacement would mean an excruciating investment of time to determine where to find said replacement, and then to actually go and procure it. In Thailand, when we forgot our sad excuse for a clothesline (a frayed nylon rope with nine worn clothespins) at a hostel on another part of the island, the owners couldn't understand our determination in hounding them to get it back. But we knew that the effort invested in tracking them down would be far less than trying to find a new piece of rope and clothespins somewhere else. It was only when we finally coordinated a meeting with the hostel owner that we realized how insane we were acting. This tatty piece of rope became our quest, and when we finally had it back in our hands, with the realization that we wouldn't have to try to figure out where to get a new one, we were overcome with a joy that rivalled parents being handed their newborn child. Our ex-hosts kept asking if there was something special about the rope. Nope, just a means to hang up some worn-out underwear at the end of the day. This might give some context to what $250 USD meant to us and why we even considered skipping out on paying it.

In the end, we did show some common sense and paid the visa fee, but not without showing our dissatisfaction by directing stern

looks at the Immigration agent processing our paperwork. After exiting Immigration on the Colombian side, we needed to get to the nearest town to catch a bus to Popayán, the safest and reportedly most interesting city near the Ecuadorian/Colombian border. At the time of our travels, there was a dearth of information about southern Colombia, as it was still caught in a decades-old civil war among the Colombian government, paramilitary groups, and guerillas, making much of the area a no-go for travellers. Popayán was one of the few places even mentioned as a potential travel destination in this part of Colombia.

Perhaps because we were so close to going home and had made it through other tough situations unscathed, we were lulled into believing that nothing nefarious could happen on this final stretch. For that reason, once out of Immigration, we simply walked up to a gentleman who was leaning against his very used car at the side of the road and asked if he would take us to the bus depot about five kilometres away. After all our fearmongering in La Paz about fake taxicabs and masked gunmen, we got in a car with an individual who was just hanging around at the border that afternoon (which, in itself, seemed odd, because I know I can count on one hand the number of times that I've driven down to the US/Canadian border and waited for families to walk across with their backpacks so that I could drive them to the nearest town).

Though this may not have been the wisest decision, it turned out to be our introduction to some of the friendliest people we would encounter on the entire trip. In every country, we met wonderful individuals who treated us with extreme kindness, but in Colombia, their openness was unparalleled. People would cross streets purely to welcome me to their country and wish me happy travels. The first few times, I instinctively checked to see if I still had my wallet after they walked away. It was off-putting to meet such genuinely welcoming folk. Their friendliness could be the result of fifty years of civil war and the relief that, with its near completion, there were still people who wanted to visit their country. The

conflict in the southern region of Colombia was, however, still a danger when we were there, so much so that we were warned not to travel at night. When we started out earlier that day in Quito, Ecuador, we were scheduled to get into Popayán by about 10:00 p.m. Early enough, I assumed, that the bandits would just be waking up and having breakfast, allowing us to arrive safely. As with most bus travel in South America, this timetable was not accurate. Our route through the mountains of southern Colombia was a slow one because, for the first time on this continent, our bus driver actually travelled at a speed that suited the contours of the highway. Though the snow-covered peaks of the high Andes in Ecuador and Peru soften and taper off in Colombia, creating an undulating countryside of lush jungle that stretches from the valley floors to the tops of the now-rounded summits, the roads are still sprinkled with harrowing turns, designed exclusively to tip our bus onto two wheels.

Further delays, missed connections, followed by a flat tire and engine trouble, had us still on the road at midnight. What was unsettling was that once darkness hit, our bus had merged with a convoy of ten other buses that, together, snaked their way along the winding highways carved through the valleys and along the mountain walls. Every twenty minutes, the buses would pause, huddled together in a cluster like a litter of kittens looking for warmth. I'm not sure why this was done, but I think it was to wait for an "all clear" from one of the multiple military barracks that were stationed along the highway. With a presumable thumb's up from a heavily armed soldier manning the garrison, the convoy would begin rolling again. Moving at this stutter-stop pace, we eventually arrived in Popayán at 3:30 a.m.—prime time for bandits! However, instead of being greeted by a collection of rubes and suspect individuals, we were met at the brightly lit and bustling bus station by a friendly taxicab driver who then brought us as close to our accommodations as he could. Our hostel that night was located in the middle of an enormous city square in the old town, an area

about the size of four city blocks, closed to all vehicular traffic. As such, our driver was forced to drop us off on a side street next to the deserted and darkened square. We exited the vehicle holding our sleeping children, thinking that this is where the trip would take a nasty turn. To our surprise, the cab driver stood by his car and watched us like a nervous parent sending his young child off to school for the first time, guiding us as we crossed the three hundred metres to the front door of our hostel, ensuring that we were able to get in before he drove away.

In other words, this night went perfectly according to plan. There would be no new low of, "At least we're not on a bus going to Popayán."

THE OTHER, OTHER
HEART OF DARKNESS

From the onset of our arrival in South America, we were plagued by the question of whether we should go into the Amazon. It's the Amazon, for God's sake! That mythical place we've all seen on TV—the lungs of the planet, home to one-fifth of Earth's freshwater, clearing house for every consumer good you can imagine—oh wait, wrong Amazon ... that one's in Seattle. But experiencing THE Amazon, or some part of it, would be a learning experience for our children that I assume they would never forget. This is the place of movies and grade school discussions. How amazing would it be for them to one day stand up in their classroom during a lesson and say, "When I was in the Amazon ..." Their teacher and cohorts would turn to look at them admiringly, mouths agape, breathlessly waiting for our children to shower them with tales from the deepest recesses of our planet Earth. Though, in reality, it would probably play out more along the lines of Oskar's classmates

asking, "Did they serve knuckle sandwiches in the Amazon, Count Dorkenstein?" and Isla Blue's teacher questioning, "What does the Amazon have to do with you pouring glue down Lucas's pants?" Still, though, they could at least feel proud and worldly in that brief moment before they were sent, respectively, to the nurse's room and the principal's office.

Yet, here we were in our first few weeks in South America, not really taking THE Amazon very seriously as a destination. This might be because we associated the Amazon with Brazil, and we were in no way going to support that country after having been denied entry due to their stringent visa requirements (and, to perhaps a lesser extent, our lax attention to the details of said visa requirements). Fancy Brazil and its dubious entry regulations. The fact that the Amazon was part of Brazil made us skeptical of the whole thing, anyway. Does it even exist?

As we met more travellers, however, we became acutely aware that 1) the Amazon did in fact exist, and 2) we were the only ones who weren't making plans to visit it in some capacity. A pleasant discovery on this front, though, was that none of the people we met were venturing to Brazil to access the Amazon. We were delighted to find out that the Amazon was such a popular destination that franchises have opened in a number of South America's other countries, including Peru, Bolivia, Colombia, and Ecuador—all nations that we would be visiting. After extensive investigation by Daria, she proposed that Peru would be the logical entrance point through which to experience the majesty of the Amazon. When asked why Peru, her reasoning seemed vague and without much substance. When pressed, however, it was revealed that the weight of her decision was based primarily on the opportunity to partake in a traditional Ayahuasca ceremony, where one could consume an indigenous psychoactive brewed from native plants that would make the individual violently ill upon ingestion, and whose hallucinogenic effects would enlighten and guide said individual to find their true path in life. Now, it may be that I'm not the most

supportive spouse, but my immediate reaction was to explain that I thought her true path in life at this particular moment was to not become a bag of shit for forty-eight hours while I was left to take care of our two children in the middle of the Amazon. Unfortunately, this opinion only shifted the discussion in a direction that I didn't need it to go, as Daria then suggested that I should be the one to do the ceremony instead, since it was really me who needed to find myself.

Is this a regular thing in marriages? I ask because, to me, when your spouse essentially says, "You have no direction," it strikes me as a bit of an underhanded jab, no? Like saying, "Hey, you look great for someone who has no style." Plus, how am I supposed to have any direction when I've been whisked away on a world trip that has me waking up in new places every day? Feeling slighted, I shared my view that perhaps the ceremony would enlighten me and thus guide me to throw off the marital and parental shackles that had been burdening me for so many years, allowing me to find my true path in life as a DJ at a foam bar in Ibiza. Evidently, there are limits to what you can and cannot say in a marriage.

Thankfully, our decision-making process, and our marriage, was saved by the input of our two friends who had spent a number of years in Bolivia and had travelled around South America. Their recommendation for an Amazon experience was the Chalalan Ecolodge, located in the Madidi National Park in Bolivia. Created in the early 90s by the community of San José de Uchupiamonas, the Ecolodge, and the push to preserve the region as a national park, was their response to the lack of development, employment, and investment in the region, which was contributing to the slow death of the culture of the area. Set deep in the jungle on the shores of a small lake, Chalalan Ecolodge wouldn't be considered in the same breath as African safari lodges frequented by A-list celebrities, but with its rustic cabins and flush toilets (!), it was an ideal location to experience one of the most biodiverse regions of the world.

The journey to Chalalan was the perfect balance for us as a family to get to a remote destination in the Amazon. The six-hour ride from the outpost town of Rurrenabaque, up two rivers by means of a narrow, outboard-powered motorboat in the hot Bolivian sun, made for a long day, but getting any deeper into the jungle would have required a multi-day hike with overnight camping along its path—something that would involve sleeping in shifts so as to watch out for various jungle threats, such as fire ants and large, undomesticated felines. Our decision to take the less adventurous, riparian pathway was reaffirmed during our break for lunch on shore, where we were made aware of fresh jaguar tracks along the riverbank. Even though our guides were a bit nonchalant about it, it did remind me that we were not necessarily the apex species anymore, a position that we don't often find ourselves in during our day-to-day lives, other than at the local coffee shop, where the servers constantly remind me of my status as a lower species.

On the boat ride, we and another couple were escorted by two guides, one of whom was a gregarious wealth of knowledge, constantly spewing out factual tidbits relating to the surrounding landscape and its history, while the other, perhaps newer, less experienced, and less comfortable conversing in English, nodded politely and proffered single-word answers to questions we directed towards him. We were naturally attracted to the more flamboyant guide and were disappointed when we were assigned the less conversational Mario for the rest of our stay.

After a two-kilometre hike through a narrow jungle pathway that took us from the landing dock on the riverbank to the lodge, our first order of business was to investigate the lake that lay adjacent to our accommodations. Though Mario nodded affirmatively when we asked if it was safe to swim in it, we also asked the other guide and two other individuals just to make sure that we were all on the same page. At this time, Mario had not yet instilled a level of trust we felt comfortable with and was considered "silent but deadly." Surrounded by a thick curtain of hanging foliage that

flowed down to every inch of its rounded shoreline, the lake was a small, dimple-like depression in the middle of the verdant jungle. Its surface layer was warm from the heat of the day, so we dove into its depths to find an icy coldness that immediately refreshed us from the long journey. We and our children are happiest when we are playing in lakes, rivers, and oceans, and we stayed in the water until we were called for dinner. As we exited this jungle oasis, two men guided their canoe to the dock after an unsuccessful after-noon of fishing for piranha. We were quickly told that we were not in any danger and that it was perfectly safe to swim in the lake, a reassurance undoubtedly prompted by the looks on our faces and the immediate "Extremities Inventory Game" we initiated with Oskar and Isla Blue (*Ten fingers? Check! You've won two high fives!*). We played another round of Extremities Inventory after hearing that the day before, they caught one piranha that weighed about a kilogram.

"Oh, but don't worry; that's as big as they'll get," they informed us.

Reassuring.

Early the next morning, I was awoken by a low, guttural moan that seemed to be exuding from every corner of the wall of veg-etation that surrounded us. The sound had no discernable point of origin, and was a cross between the whooshing made by my father's old Coleman stove as it sputtered to life and a horror movie soundtrack featuring wayward souls from another dimension swarming around me and pleading for my attention. So chilling was this groaning wail that I truly believed that the local spirits were awakening in anger due to the presence of foreigners on their sacred land. It took my rational brain a few minutes to catch up with my irrational brain—which was already back at the river try-ing to start the boat— and explain to it that this must be the call of the howler monkey that our fellow travellers had discussed at the previous night's dinner. Howler monkeys were just one of about a hundred things that the three other groups that night had on their

"MUST SEE IN THE AMAZON!" list—a quest that had them travelling to various regions of the continent to ensure that they would be able to check off every species on their inventory. Dinner became a time to compare notes about what each had already recorded and what still needed to be observed in order to make the trip worthwhile. The gregarious guide engaged equally in this ritual of bragging and fuelled the fire by listing species that weren't even known to our fellow travellers, causing them to develop a number of unhealthy twitches. Trying to ignore the fact that, once again, we had underprepared and had no list of any sort, the dinner discussion at our table revolved around the Fruit Loops toucan and whether we might see him serving breakfast one morning.

Understanding now that I was listening to the early-morning yowls of a howler monkey, I spent the rest of that dawn enjoying this cacophony of grunts and groans, absorbing a richness of sonic texture I had never before experienced. When we arrived at breakfast a few hours later, our fellow lodge patrons were proudly exchanging stories of how they managed to track down the howler monkeys and get a glimpse of them high in the canopy above. It struck me that they may have missed the opportunity to appreciate the actual symphony of sounds since they were so focused on finding its source. The trees through the forest, I guess. A point not lost on Mario, who took me aside later that morning as we were preparing for our hike and handed me the binoculars to look at the top of a towering tree nearby.

"Toucan," he whispered. "Very rare to see." He smirked at me and looked over his shoulder to check that he hadn't been overheard by our fellow guests, possibly hoping that "toucan" would remain unticked on their checklists.

This was the beginning of a beautiful relationship between us and Mario. For the next few days, he would lead us on a maze of trails that crisscrossed through this area of the national park, not looking for anything specific, but just allowing us to absorb the experience of being in such an incredible jungle landscape.

Giant leaves and vines surrounded us on all sides and completely blocked out the sun's direct rays, while also creating such a muggy environment that our shirts were soaked through with sweat the minute we began walking. On a night hike, he introduced us to tarantulas and other gigantic spiders whose bodies and web sizes seemed to be horrifically exaggerated in the dark. Although, once we knew what to look for, we found equally large insects and webs during the day, which made us walk faster while keeping our heads up to look out for webs.

"Not too fast, though," we were warned. "You might step on a snake."

"But not too slow, either," Mario would correct, and explained that we would always have to be vigilant for army ants and bullet ants, the latter whose name is derived from the fact that their bite is akin to being shot.

"Do you have rheumatism?" Mario asked.

"No."

"That is too bad. It would make the pain less when you get bitten by the bullet." Giggle.

As we got to know Mario, and he became more comfortable with us, his giggles became a recurring form of expression when he was addressing safety concerns. When I asked why he was gingerly climbing over a log, he said it was to ensure that he did not disturb any anaconda. When I reminded him that he had previously said that anaconda were not a threat, he replied with his trademark giggle and that was the end of that conversation.

At one point along a trail, he nonchalantly said, "Time to run," and jogged ahead with another giggle. Daria and I were left looking at each other in wonderment until she suddenly started yelping in pain. Her open-toe-sandalled feet were covered in army ants, and their stinging bites caused her to do a series of swats, brushes, and stomps that looked oddly like the Ukrainian dancing moves she had learned at Veselka camp many years ago. Once we got the ants cleared off, we sprinted the one-hundred-or-so metres

to catch up to Mario. It was then that I noticed he was wearing long pants tucked into his socks.

"I understand," I said while motioning to his fashion choice.

He giggled as he pointed to my bare legs and shorts.

Mario was also very thoughtful in his approach to our jungle experience. On our last afternoon at Chalalan, he walked us the two kilometres back to the boats that had brought us up the river, and we travelled a few more kilometres upstream to an abandoned village whose structures still remained on the shores of a larger lake system. There was no sign of anyone around. We launched a canoe into the water and Mario handed Oskar and Isla Blue simple fishing rods made of a stick, a line, and a hook, which he had baited with a larger piece of fish. Now it was our kids who were fishing for piranha and they couldn't have been happier. Over the course of the afternoon, Oskar pulled in a number of these menacing teeth-repositories on his own, and they were later served to us at dinner, where we shared them with our fellow travellers, who were now upset with themselves that "Fishing for Piranha" was not on their to-do lists.

In a weird stroke of luck, or a premeditated attempt to get us to spend more money in the area, we were told on our last day that our flight back to La Paz from Rurrenabaque was cancelled, and that while we waited for a new flight, we would be able to go to the Pampas, the uglier stepsister of the Bolivian jungle. The Pampas are the wetlands that surround this portion of the Amazon, and it offered an experience that was the exact opposite of everything we had just encountered at Chalalan. Though you are granted a greater opportunity to see more wildlife, this is only because the animals have all been squeezed into a narrow strip of land that lies on either side of a well-traversed river. Due to the continuous encroachment of ranching and farming, the only protected land runs parallel to the waterway, so what you see as you travel the three hours down the river is a dense population of birds that now have nowhere else to breed or live, including storks, egrets,

kingfishers, herons ... oh my! Undaunted by the constant parade of small outboard boats cruising by, and perhaps exasperated by the circumstances that led to their waterfront location, this rich assortment of waterfowl show no signs of skittishness as we drift up close to their feeding holes and nests. We point in silent awe as we pass one long-legged, majestic bird after another, whose heads and necks look as if they have been delicately painted with bright blues and reds. We stop our gawking only to look skywards from this incredible parade and see a nest the size of an inflatable kiddie pool, thatched together in a jumbled weave of arm's-length sticks which are wedged precisely into the high crook of a long-dead tree. To confirm that this is not my imagination gone wild, the bodies of three storks elegantly rise from this avian inner tube, stretching their wings to their full length before settling down again to ready themselves for the next passing boat. The entire scene was so unbelievably vibrant with wildlife and their rich, garish hues, that it felt like an attraction at Disney World, and we were half expecting the onset of a simulated neon sunset.

Sadly, because of the neighbouring humans' disregard for these surroundings and its wildlife, an air of exploitation seemed to permeate all other aspects of this region.

Our accommodations were definitely more low-key and dubious, in that it catered to a low-budget, backpacker mentality, with negligible emphasis placed on conservation or ethical practices. The building we stayed in was definitely not a lodge or a hostel, with "dilapidated" being the best way to describe it. A series of raised platforms and rickety walkways, connected to one another on the riverbank, housed an open-air kitchen, dining area, and a dorm area enclosed in wire meshing that was full of holes and, in most places, no longer attached to the wooden frame that surrounded it. We spent one day in giant rubber boots, marauding through grasslands with ten or twenty other groups, trying to flush out anacondas. No concern was given to the consequences of disturbing or aggravating the fauna and the habitat in which they existed, and

when a cobra (pardon?) was found, a number of guides ran to corral it, rodeo-style, eventually pinning it down with a forked branch so everyone could get their picture taken with it. The entire region had a sideshow/amusement park feel to it. One of the outing activities was having a drink at the "sunset bar," another beaten-down, wooden establishment with a front porch and volleyball net in front of it. Joined by the guests from most of the other camps in the area, we watched the sun set below the cattle fields in the distance, which have now completely replaced the natural grasslands.

Though the Pampas smacks of hucksterism and commercialism to the nth degree, it was also the place where our kids gained one of their fondest memories: swimming with the blind pink dolphins that inhabit the river. Having been annoyed immensely by the cobra rodeo the day before, I chose to stay in the boat as our kids and Daria played with a pod of dolphins that swam around them for the better part of an hour. Though it seemed staged, and was undoubtedly played up every day with a new set of visitors, our kids couldn't get enough of it.

Now, after experiencing both the best and the worst versions of Amazonian excursions, I can only hope that my children will one day recognize the value in experiencing these environments in a more respectful manner, as was demonstrated in Chalalan, versus the exploitative tourism of the Pampas. I hope they can distinguish between each establishment's efforts (or lack thereof) to protect and sustain the environments in which they were situated. Where Chalalan created their own monitored sewage lagoon, ensuring that all waste was properly treated before anything was released back into the environments, our Pampas camp had us walk along rickety gangplanks to outhouses that had pails underneath. How these full pails were dealt with every night is best left to the imagination ... or not. With a daily onslaught of human interaction, it would not surprise me if the river dolphins and snakes out in the marshlands are stressed into non-existence within the next few years. I can only hope that Chalalan, and the guides and workers

who both created it and sustain it, will continue to flourish in their symbiotic relationship with the jungle around them.

THE 'HOLY SHIT!' MOMENT OF TRAVELLING

When we were planning this trip, we anticipated that the entire journey was going to be an explosion of life, comprised of one "holy shit!" experience after another; an expectation probably fueled by too many movies where some incredible event drives the protagonist to have a revelation about their own life course, allowing them to understand their place in the world. And so, I kept waiting for some Brazilian billionaire to unleash my spiritual awakening. Alas, this was not to be. The closest I came to that was a solo Danish woman whom we kept bumping into along the Australian coast, as she had a similar taste in spartan campsites. My attraction to her did not stem from a desire to be with her physically; rather, I was attracted to her world and its accompanying lifestyle. As I was cleaning the dishes after yet another chaotic breakfast, she would unfurl from her camper van at a leisurely pace and start the day with some yoga stretches, followed by a

relaxing coffee, which would lead into an afternoon of reading and general loafing. I would watch her and enter a dream world, where I imagined myself as the one rolling out of the camper van every morning, ready to enjoy another peaceful day of self-awareness. I would usually recover from this fugue state after a few minutes, with my hands still soaking in the bucket of dishes and the Danish woman now standing at the camp host's site, lodging a complaint about the creep on the other side of the campsite who had been staring at her vacantly for the past half-hour.

A trip of this scope is not a cavalcade of non-stop adventure. It is, however, comprised of a number of little things that do happen, mixed with an extensive amount of time waiting for *other* things to happen. This is rounded off with the daily mundane chores that you would also do at home over the course of a year, like laundry. I've washed our underwear in some of the most beautiful settings in the world—the Amazon, Milford Sound in New Zealand, various islands in the South Pacific, the jungles of Borneo, the Galápagos, along the Inca trail to Machu Picchu—but, in the end, it is still just scrubbing underwear, no matter what your view. That's the real essence of a trip like ours: doing tedious chores in new places every day, under circumstances that test your abilities. I should note that it isn't easy doing laundry in a sink the size of your fist, using a wad of chewed-up bubble gum as a drain plug.

In contrast to this, though, when I was asked to identify the worst thing that happened, I had to say that there was never truly a moment that ruined the trip, with the exception of my father's death. There were some hardships, but one is challenged by those on a daily basis at home as well. Though it is sometimes more difficult to handle these tribulations when you are on the road, it is also so much easier to enjoy life when you get to wake up to new environments, people, and cultures every day. The routine that we all follow at home has the ability to dull our enjoyment of life itself. It is so easy to become accustomed to your surroundings and your schedule that you forget to appreciate them, only because they

become a continuous repetition. I'm not sure what it is about being on the road, but when I travel, I exit that cocoon of regular custom and find that even the most annoying chores have a vibrancy to them. We all feel it when we go on vacation. It's not just that you get a break from work; the new environment you find yourself in tends to motivate you and heightens your awareness. Things taste better, mornings are fresher, and I become more handsome. What I was astonished by was that this feeling didn't diminish over the course of a year of travel. I had that "vacation buzz" the entire time that we were away from home. This must be the result of being exposed to something new every day, whether it was the challenge of figuring out what something costs in a grocery store or sitting on a beach to watch the sun set over the island of Bali for the first time. Or it may be that being challenged on a daily basis, even in the smallest way, causes you to actively participate in the day, rather than just coasting through it to make it to bedtime. Life engages you.

There were still moments that felt excruciatingly horrific when we were experiencing them, but, in the end, their sting was diminished and overshadowed by everything else that was a part of the year. One of my most enduring memories from this year of travel is something that was so simple, yet which left such a lasting impression on me—I hope it had the same effect on my family as well. We began the Harry Potter series just before we left on the trip, reading a chapter or two before bed each night. The kids were so enthralled by the first few chapters that we took the first three books of the series with us and acquired the rest of them during our travels. Reading these books to Oskar and Isla Blue over the course of the first four months of our journey encapsulated what this trip was truly about: spending what felt like an unlimited amount of time with my family. In the Yasawa Island group in Fiji, our days were filled with hours spent cuddled together in a hammock, reading until my voice went hoarse, the adventures at Hogwarts interrupted only by chicken fights between members of our family in the cerulean waters that surrounded us.

That's not to say that there weren't also many specific highlights over the course of the trip. We got to swim with sea lions and penguins in the Galápagos, we played on some of the world's most spectacular beaches, we fished for piranha in the Amazon, and we camped in what was, effectively, a grassy parking lot in a pint-sized town in Australia—our tent squeezed between rows of hulking Winnebagos filled with Australian seniors who embraced us with friendship while demoralizing us with their endless loop of "Little Bitty" by Alan Jackson. We had jellyfish fights in Queen Charlotte Sound in New Zealand, snorkelled in the Great Barrier Reef, and experienced life on a working coffee plantation in Colombia. Daria got to spend her birthday being shuttled from winery to winery in Martinborough, New Zealand, and Isla Blue hang-glided over Lima, Peru. I hiked to the top of Mount Agung in Indonesia, where, from my vantage point 3,000 metres above sea level, I watched as the rising sun cast this volcanos' perfectly cone-shaped shadow across Bali, engulfing the island in a triangle of darkness, as if a giant spaceship were hovering above, readying itself to unleash a ray-gun blast upon the unsuspecting Balinese below.

Uhhh … wait a second—HOLY SHIT!

In the end, what lessons did we actually learn from this trip? Did we grow as a family? Did we get a better understanding of each other or the world around us? Debatable. But what our adventures most certainly *did* do was to allow us to just spend time together—something that is at a premium during the course of our everyday lives. Between racing to get kids to school, yourself to work, preparing meals, and all of the scheduled activities that kids are enrolled in, the simple act of being with, and focusing on, one another is often lost.

Daria and I still had to manage the big decisions on our trip, but other than figuring out where we would go next and finding

a half-decent place to stay, we were just focused on, well, nothing really. This freedom of time allowed us to actually be a family and just concentrate on one another, giving Daria and me the chance to become incredibly close with our children. Developing this bond was a pleasant and unplanned outcome of the trip. I see this now, being back home, as I watch Daria chase Oskar around the house, trying to smother his face under her raised arm while yelling, "Smell my pits!" to prove to him that her new deodorant is working. A year of living in tight proximity certainly helped to create an air of casualness between us and to drop a number of boundaries—one too many, one might argue.

In the long run, I hope that this year together laid the groundwork for a strong relationship with our children that we can build on as they become older and more involved with unsavoury middle-school characters of the neck tattoo variety. I have no doubt that our children will be faced with some tough decisions as they grow, but I hope that this trip cemented a bit of a moral compass in them, as well as the knowledge that when faced with difficult decisions, we can get through them as a family. My wish is also that this trip granted them the confidence to feel good about their own choices and to not be so reliant on what those around them might be thinking or doing. Whether any of this theorizing actually pans out has yet to be seen. I suppose we'll find out in a few years when we discover that both our kids are profiteering off the opium den they are running in the basement.

However, I do recognize that at home, after a day of work, I have to make a concerted effort to get outside and play with my kids. My de facto move is to enter the supine position in front of a TV because it's hard to stay motivated and find the energy to play. But on our trip, this was never an issue. All we did was play and explore, and on some days we'd be in the ocean or lake all day long. What was so extraordinary is that this became our new normal, for months on end, which is something most vacationing families don't truly get to experience. First, vacations tend to be short; thus,

getting into a true "we-don't-have-to-do-anything-except-hang-out" mode is difficult. Second, parents on vacation often want a short break from their kids and the everyday world of work and chores as a chance to re-energize and alleviate stress. And finally, on short family vacations, there is often a lot of planning involved to make the most out of the time off, which leaves fewer opportunities for unscheduled play. Case in point, the hardest I've ever worked in my life was the week I spent in Orlando at Disney World and Universal Studios, which either gives you a little insight into my employability (i.e., nil) or the relative enjoyment that Disney supplies to parents. Between desperately scrolling through the parks' apps to search for ride time availability and running across each park to line up at the designated time, I'm not sure that we stopped once to see if everyone was actually enjoying themselves.

What I also recognized, once we were home, is the discernable feeling of actually returning to the metaphorical rat race. While we were travelling, we didn't think about what we had or didn't have, or what other people owned. We had a finite amount of space and what we brought with us was all that we could transport. Additionally, both our awareness of advertisements and our exposure to neighbours with new gadgets dropped to zero, so we never had a sense of missing out on something or subliminal pressure to purchase anything. Without noticing it, consumer tendencies were removed from our day-to-day activities, giving us a sense of commercial liberation that we did not tune into. Upon our return, though, I immediately felt it all come creeping back—the unconscious needs and wants that are linked to middle-class life in North America. This was not due to any amount of one-upmanship or tech-gloating from our neighbours or friends, but was just a result of the structure of our world at home and its dependency on the continual upgrading and purchasing of goods. It definitely puts a gentle pressure on one to earn more money in order feed this beast, rather than to just go without. Simply being aware of this subliminal tugging has made it easier to cope with these outside

pressures and to just enjoy the opportunities that are afforded to me. I am more cognizant of why I am buying certain items, and whether a purchase is something that is truly needed.

At the outset of this trip, one thing we did have in mind was that it would be a great way to informally teach our children about the culture we live in and to help them develop an appreciation of the world around us. We certainly don't belong to the One Percent, but we are pretty fortunate—inherently so because of where we were born, who we were born to, the opportunities that came with these first two points, and some hard work on our own part along the way. Had one of these factors been slightly altered—the geographic region of my birth, or the class, race, or lineage of my family—I might not have had an opportunity to travel at all, even though my abilities and skills would be the same. I hope that our kids now have sense of just how fortunate they are after living amongst and playing with people who, just by geography, don't have the same opportunities that they themselves will have.

Spending time in a number of these communities also exposed our children to the true effects human pollution has on the earth. An unfortunate consequence of the efficient waste and recycling programs we have in our hometown is that our kids don't get a sense of the true cost that packaging, bags, and other forms of pollution have on our world. On occasion, they have come with me to the landfill on the outskirts of the city, but the context is entirely lost on them, because in their eyes it's an amazing treasure trove of free items set in a confined landscape that isn't meant to be anything but an area of refuse. However, seeing the consequences of a more laid-back approach to waste disposal in other communities, such as creeks full of plastic bags in Indonesia or our decision to not swim at a beach because the smell of raw sewage seemed a bit too strong that day, spontaneously opened up a dialogue between us that was genuinely driven by probing questions from our children.

Our year of travel also helped us to debunk our preconceived

notions of the world and the dangers that lurk within it. The deepest jungles and the craziest cities were just places and environments no different from our own home, each just having its own unique and varying challenges. I'm sure that there are travellers who view Canada with much the same trepidation because of their intrinsic fear of Loverboy, Justin Trudeau, and flannel button-downs.

Now at home, reflecting on the memories of that year, I am the one asking those questions that were asked of me before I left: What did this year mean to me in the grander scheme of things? In my life, I rarely take a moment to reflect on what I've done or what I hold as truly important—Daria and I can go for weeks on end without ever really talking to one another, other than discussing the essentials of the day, like why there is no clean underwear. Prior to this trip, I would never have said that there was anything wrong with my life or how I spent it. This year off, however, made me aware that perhaps the path I have chosen is not the best. Sleepless nights are a regular occurrence for me, as I'm either kept awake by an overactive brain or awoken by anxious thoughts in anticipation of the upcoming day. This, however, was never an issue during the entire year of travel—a year that was filled with anxious unknowns and questionable domiciles, where I should have been kept awake by the sound of small rodent feet skittering across the floor.

What I realize about this year of travel is that it was so crammed with fun and wonderment that these things became the focus, which in turn allowed me to be joyful every day—something that I had forgotten how to do. My life has not been without happy moments, but it is rare to go through extended periods where every day exposes me to new experiences and challenges while allowing me to enjoy the day for all that it is. It wasn't until I got home from the trip that I recognized how happy I was during the course of that year.

I was given perspective on what it is that I truly love to do and experience—both with my family and within the environment surrounding me. When I am caught in the routine of life, it is

132

hard to identify those things because my responsibilities take priority. Though it may be a while before we can take time off for another world trip, I do regularly reflect on our year abroad and am reminded of what brought me joy and peace of mind; this, in turn, allows me to approach my days at home with a mindset to create more of those moments with my family.

So take a year off to travel, what have you got to lose—other than your children (but once again, NOT MY FAULT). It may not seem like the easiest thing to do but it's not that hard. Though we deferred some salary, the income we made by working from the road, renting out our home was enough to keep us travelling. And from the moment we boarded our first plane out of Winnipeg, we never once worried that we had made a mistake.

Take that, Deepak Chopra.

Rob and Daria would like to thank their children, Oskar and Isla Blue, for going along with this ~~debacle~~adventure, as well as their parents for continued support and free babysitting services. Daria would like to thank her UBC CNF classmates, and instructors Kevin Chong and Wayne Grady. Thank you to Andrew Davidson for thoughtful feedback, Geoff Ripat for Spanish translation services, and agent Samantha Haywood for insight and support. And, of course, this book would not have been possible without the efforts of editor Patricia Sanders and vision of Turnstone Press.

Lastly, we'd like to thank and acknowledge the kindness and inspiration of the many people we met on our year abroad.

I pet a koala

Twett Somewhere

Today I went swimming with turtles. We fed
them palya and they like papaya. they are
cold blooded.
reptiles lay eggs and turtles are cold blooded.
Best their change tempature hot hot the reptile is cold
It the pH tomorrow is the pH tomorrow weir it
would be hot. If the turtles is cold, the turtles weir it
the reptile is cold and theirs hous were hard there
Pretty big and theirs house were hard there
were about six or seven turtles.

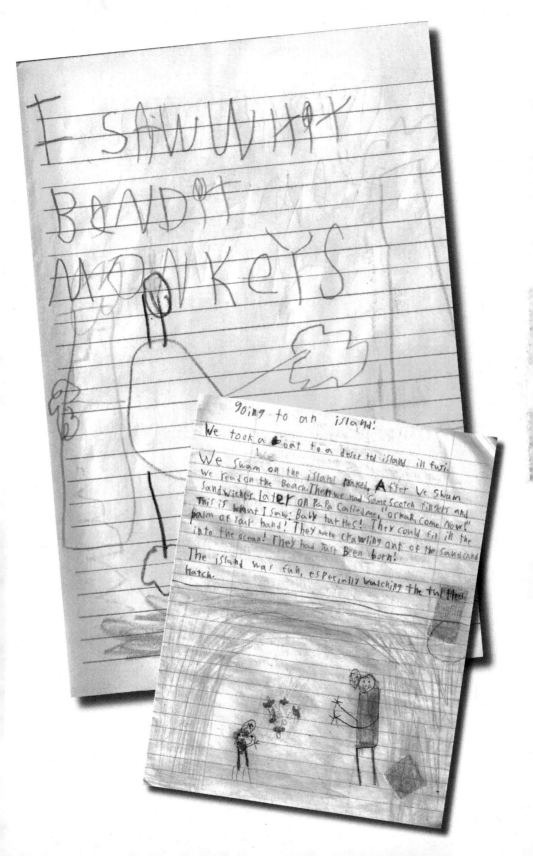

I SAW WHAT BANDIT MONKEYS

going to an island:

We took a boat to a deserted island in fiji.

We swam on the island naked. After we swam we read on the Beach. Then we had some scotch fingers and sandwiches. Later on papa called me, "oskar, come now!" This is what I saw: Baby turtles! They could fit in the palm of your hand! They were crawling out of the sand and into the ocean! They had just been born!

The island was fun, especially watching the turtles hatch.

I went somewhere

glowworm caves

Today I went to the glowworm caves. They are so cool! They make a light that doesn't use heat. their light is deadly. lots of bugs are born in water and come out of their eggs in larve witch glowworms love that kind of bug. even though they live on the ce... the bugs don't want to brake their w... so they fly up towards the stars... night. But they are not going towa... the sky, are they? glowworms are insects. they act like spiders. They make strin... that have sicky stuff on it that the bu... get caught in the webs.

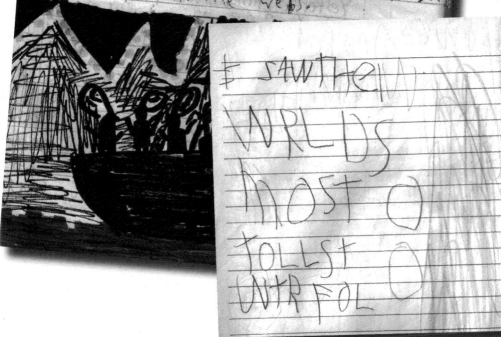

I SAW THE WRLDS MOST TOLLST WTRFOL

Rob and Daria would like to thank their children, Oskar and Isla Blue, for going along with this ~~debacle~~adventure, as well as their parents for continued support and free babysitting services. Daria would like to thank her UBC CNF classmates, and instructors Kevin Chong and Wayne Grady. Thank you to Andrew Davidson for thoughtful feedback, Geoff Ripat for Spanish translation services, and agent Samantha Haywood for insight and support. And, of course, this book would not have been possible without the efforts of editor Patricia Sanders and vision of Turnstone Press.

Lastly, we'd like to thank and acknowledge the kindness and inspiration of the many people we met on our year abroad.